The Philosophical Foundations of Hinduism

Contemporary Researches in
Hindu Philosophy & Religion

(ISSN 0971-9628)

1. Idealistic Thought in Indian Philosophy; by Shuchita C. Divatia (ISBN 81-246-0021-X)
2. Karma and Reincarnation: The Vedāntic Perspective; by Muni Narayana Prasad (ISBN 81-246-0022-8)
3. Stonemill and Bhakti: From the Devotion of Peasant Women to the Philosophy of Swamies; by Guy Poitevin and Hema Rairkar (ISBN 81-246-0059-7)
4. Śaivism: Some Glimpses; by G.V. Tagare (ISBN 81-246-0076-7)
5. Advaita: A Conceptual Analysis; by A. Ramamurty (ISBN 81-246-0067-8)
6. Mind-Body Dualism: A Philosophic Investigation; by Alpana Chakraborty (ISBN 81-246-0071-6)
7. Hinduism and Scientific Quest; by T.R.R. Iyengar (ISBN 81-246-0077-5)
8. Indra and Other Vedic Deities — A Euhemeristic Study; by Uma Chakravarty (ISBN 81-246-0080-5)
9. Brahma-Vāda: Doctrine of Śrī Vallabhācārya; by G.V. Tagare (ISBN 81-246-0112-7)
10. The Science of Enlightenment: Enlightenment, Liberation and God — A Scientific Explanation; by Nitin Trasi (ISBN 81-246-0130-5)
11. Retrieval of Sāṁkhya History: an Ascent from Dawn to Meridian; by Lallanji Gopal (ISBN 81-246-0143-7)
12. The Philosophical Foundations of Hinduism, by A. Ramamurty (ISBN 81-246-0163-1)

Contemporary Researches in Hindu Philosophy & Religion, no. 12

The Philosophical Foundations of Hinduism

by

A. Ramamurty

D.K. Printworld (P) Ltd.
New Delhi

Cataloging in Publication Data — DK

Ramamurty, A. (Aryasomayajula), 1935 –

The philosophical foundations of Hinduism.
(Contemporary researches in Hindu
philosophy & religion; no. 12).
Includes bibliographical refersnces (p.).
Includes index.

1. Hinduism. 2. Philosophy, Hindu.
I. Title. II. Series: Contemporary researches
in Hindu philosophy & religion; no. 12.

ISBN 81-246-0163-1

First published in India in 2000

Published and printed by:
D.K. Printworld (P) Ltd.
Regd. office: *'Sri Kunj'*, F-52, Bali Nagar
New Delhi - 110015
Phone: (011) 545-3975, 546-6019; *Fax*: (011) 546-5926
E-Mail: dkprint@4mis.com

Preface

ALTHOUGH much work has been done on Hinduism dealing with its various aspects very little is done to understand comprehensively the nature and meaning of Hinduism. And most of the work on Hinduism is based rather exclusively on either the Śruti or Smṛti tradition of Hinduism. Most of the modern Hindu thinkers have tried to identify Hinduism with its Śruti tradition though Hinduism as believed in and practised by most of the Hindus is largely based on and developed by the Smṛti tradition. Most of the modern Indian interpreters of Hinduism have paid little or no attention to Smṛti tradition of Hinduism, and some are even averse to it, and consider that the Smṛti form of Hinduism is not real Hinduism. What does Śruti tradition stand for is a matter of interpretation, and every interpretation is influenced by various factors, individual, social and historical. The Smṛti tradition of Hinduism, which accepts the authority of Śruti, and adopts its world-view, is also a sort of interpretation of Śruti tradition. Besides being an interpretation of Śruti, Smṛti tradition has an identity of its own which is due to its independent origin.

Every interpretation of Śruti, in so far as it is influenced by various factors, either individual or social or historical, will not have the same authority as that of Śruti. At the same time, every interpretation is helpful in understanding the meaning of Śruti, and by making explicit or by fully developing the ideas and insights of Śruti it helps in enriching the Śruti tradition. In this sense Smṛti tradition is an interpretation of Śruti, and as an interpretation of Śruti the Smṛti tradition is integral to Hinduism. Every interpretation of Śruti in so far as it accepts the world-view of Śruti is significant in the life and development of Hinduism, though no interpretation may prove itself to be universally meaningful and valid.

While Śruti represents that aspect of Hinduism which is stable and whose validity is not bound by time, space and other circumstances, the Smṛti tradition represents Hinduism in its dynamic aspect. While Śruti gives Hinduism its identity and character, the Smṛti tradition represents Hinduism in its growth and development. We may say that while Śruti represents the soul of Hinduism, the Smṛti tradition forms the body of Hinduism. The development of Hinduism, its richness and integral character are due to constant interaction between the two traditions in which each tried to influence the other. We find in the history of Hinduism a subtle form of tension between Śruti and Smṛti, and the development of Hinduism, and its integral character are due to significant efforts made by various creative thinkers and saints in reconciling and harmonising the two traditions. Hinduism is what it is due to such efforts. This process continues as long as Hinduism remains alive. The Smṛti is not a closed tradition; it is ever growing. And its object is to interpret Śruti or to make its world-view intelligible and meaningful to all keeping in view the changing circumstances and the religious needs of the people.

Our understanding of the nature and meaning of Hinduism will not be comprehensive if we do not pay sufficient attention to both the traditions. Hinduism cannot be identified either with the Śruti or with the Smṛti tradition. Both of them are integral to Hinduism, and help in comprehending its nature and meaning. As an attempt to interpret and adapt the Śruti tradition to changing circumstances and religious needs of people every interpretation of Śruti will have only derived authority, and depends for its justification ultimately on Śruti.

An attempt is made in this work to understand the nature and meaning of Hinduism which is more than all its sects and their sectarian theologies. It transcends all the sectarian concerns and identities. The sectarian traditions of Hinduism lose their sectarian character to the extent they accept and adopt the Śruti world-view. The world-view of Hinduism, which is based on and shaped primarily by the Śruti tradition, is what is common to all the sectarian traditions of Hinduism.

I express my sincere thanks to Shri Susheel K. Mittal, Director, D.K. Printworld (P) Ltd., New Delhi, who has taken keen interest in publishing this work.

Hyderabad,
10th May, 2000 **A. Ramamurty**

Contents

1
Introduction

SEVERAL attempts are made in modern times to comprehend the nature and meaning of Hinduism, and in all of them certain beliefs and doctrines are projected as being fundamental or central to Hinduism. In so representing Hinduism each thinker is guided by what he regards as fundamental to Hinduism as a religion. As most of the scholars and thinkers, at least during the beginning of this century, who worked on Hinduism, and tried to comprehend its nature and meaning happened to be non-Hindu, they tried to understand and present Hinduism in the light of a concept of religion which is developed and formulated mainly on the basis of Semitic religious traditions, more specifically Christianity. Most of them, therefore, tried to find in Hinduism clear answers to certain questions or problems which are considered to be typically religious, and tried to pattern their understanding of Hinduism on the lines of Christianity which has a clear doctrinal focus and theological coherence and unity that can be clearly formulated and expressed. In other words, they tried to comprehend and represent the nature and meaning of Hinduism within the theological framework of Semitic religious traditions in general, and Christianity in particular.

The basic problem one faces in trying to comprehend the nature and meaning of Hinduism is to clearly identify and define the sources which are basic to Hinduism, and whose authority is accepted as final by all the Hindus. Moreover, traditionally the Hindus have made no systematic attempt to define their religion, or at least to indicate what they regard as the essence of their faith. All the attempts at understanding and defining Hinduism are modern. However, there are several traditional works dealing with what is essential to various sects of Hinduism, like Vaiṣṇavism and Śaivism, the major forms of Hindu religious life and worship. But Hinduism cannot be defined or characterised in terms of anyone or all of them, even though they are basically Hindu. They are the major or significant forms of expression of Hinduism. Even though an understanding of them is essential to understanding Hinduism, yet it is not sufficient to comprehend the nature and meaning of Hinduism. Understanding of Hinduism though requires an understanding of the various sects that form and express Hinduism, Hinduism cannot be equated or identified with its various sects. Hinduism has an identity which cannot be reduced to or equated with that of its sects, and, therefore, the nature and meaning of Hinduism cannot be comprehended and determined in terms of anyone or all of its sects. The various sects of Hinduism express or manifest Hinduism without determining its nature and meaning.

Even if we try to define Hinduism as that which is based on or inspired by the Veda it will not help us in comprehending the nature and meaning of Hinduism. It can only be a formal definition of Hinduism, which is primarily intended to distinguish those who accept the authority of the Veda, and follow the form of religious life that is based on or inspired by the Veda from those who do not accept the authority of the Veda, and hence follow the form of religious life based on it. It is also meant to exclude all those forms of religious life and worship that go against the spirit of the Veda, or are not compatible with the Veda, even though some of them are based on Smṛti tradition which is a major source of Hinduism.

Now, we may for the purpose of understanding Hinduism define it as the religion based on or inspired primarily by the traditions of Śruti and Smṛti. It is proper to identify Śruti and Smṛti as two traditions because they do not represent the teaching or wisdom of any one person or book. The Veda or the Śruti refers to a genre of literature, which includes within itself the Vedic *Saṁhitās*, *Brāhmaṇas*, *Āraṇyakas* and the Upaniṣads, and Smṛti, in a general sense, refers to the literature which is not included within Śruti but is nevertheless revered and regarded as an authority in religious matters by the Hindus. And in practical religious matters of Hinduism the authority of Smṛti is deemed final, because it is the only available source and authority in such matters. It includes the sacred texts and traditions of various sects of Hinduism, and for all practical purposes its authority is regarded as equivalent to that of Śruti by the followers of different sects of Hinduism. The term Hindu is a generic term which all the sects of Hinduism, despite their differences, which are significant, share in common.

The revelatory character of Śruti, and, therefore, its ultimate authority in religious or spiritual matters is accepted by all the Hindus. But conceptually revelation involves a belief in the existence of a personal divine being or God who chooses to disclose or reveal Himself to someone of His choice, as the person who is literally responsible for its existence considers himself as only an instrument or representative of God. Revelation, therefore, does not represent his wisdom but that of God, its real source, and hence its uniqueness, supreme authority and infallibility. In this sense the one who is historically associated with the text of a revelation is regarded only as an instrument of God. All else is a matter of theological debate. The Veda, especially the *Saṁhitā* part of it, is a revelation though revealed to a class of people known as seers (*ṛṣi*) and seer-poets (*kavi*) over a period of time. These seers and seer-poets do not claim to themselves the source and authority of the truth or wisdom expressed through the hymns of the Veda. The knowledge or wisdom of the Veda is divinely inspired, but not acquired by the seers and seer-poets in terms of their own effort and understanding. Therefore, the Veda does not represent the wisdom of the seers. It represents the divine wisdom as revealed to the seers of the Veda in the state of divine inspiration. In this sense the Veda is impersonal (*apauruṣeya*), and its wisdom or truth has no agent or author though its literary expression in the form of Vedic hymns is associated with the names of various seers.

While the Vedic *Saṁhitās* are a poetic expression of the divinely inspired truth or wisdom in its purest and simplest form, the other Vedic literature, particularly the *Brāhmaṇa* literature, involves human agency and understanding. The *Brāhmaṇas* are an attempt to understand, and even to interpret, the divinely inspired wisdom of the Veda (*Saṁhitās*), mainly with the object of employing it to serve the practical religious needs of man. They are the earliest interpretation of the Vedic revelation or the Vedic *Saṁhitās*, and are also the first to evolve methods of Vedic interpretation. We find in the *Brāhmaṇa* texts attempts to interpret the hymns of the Veda, and the purpose of the *Brāhmaṇas* in interpreting the Vedic *Saṁhitās* is to develop, on the basis of Vedic revelation, a form of religious life and worship.

The Upaniṣads are mostly a philosophic restatement or representation of the Vedic vision or wisdom poetically expressed in the *Saṁhitās*. They criticise and even reject much of Vedic theology and cosmology, mostly developed in the *Brāhmaṇas*, and try to articulate the basic ontological vision of the Veda (*Saṁhitās*). The approach and attitude of the Upaniṣads to the basic problems concerning the nature of human reality, the nature and meaning of the divine, etc., are philosophical. In other words, they represent the philosophy of the Veda (*Saṁhitās*) in which the divinely inspired truth or wisdom of the Veda is philosophically interpreted. Thus, while the *Brāhmaṇas* represent one type of interpretation of the Vedic *Saṁhitās*, which is religious, the Upaniṣads represent another type of interpretation of the Vedic *Saṁhitās* which is philosophical. It is undeniable that the Upaniṣadic thought or wisdom presupposes or is based on the Vedic revelation of the *Saṁhitās*. They reflect or represent the essence of the Veda (*Saṁhitās*), as the word Upaniṣad can mean also essence, and is so used in the Śruti literature.[1] The Upaniṣadic knowledge is not speculative as it is based on the divinely inspired and directly experienced wisdom of the Vedic seers as expressed in the hymns of the Veda. We do not find in the Upaniṣads any description of the direct and immediate experience of the divine or *Brahman* though the Upaniṣads talk of Brahma that is directly and immediately experienced. The Vedic *Saṁhitās* describe the divine as directly experienced or divinely inspired. The Upaniṣads can, therefore, be regarded as representing the philosophy of the Veda or a philosophic restatement of the Vedic wisdom. Hinduism, as a religion, is not simply a metaphysic or theology but is founded on the truth revealed or divinely inspired to the seers of the Veda which the hymns of the Veda express. The Veda is, therefore, the supreme authority for Hinduism, and is regarded as sacred and infallible.

The mutual antagonism between the Pūrva Mīmāṁsā and Uttara Mīmāṁsā or Vedānta, both of which are based on the Veda, is due to the importance and value they attach either to the *Brāhmaṇas* or the Upaniṣads in understanding the real import or meaning of the Vedic *Saṁhitās*. While the *Brāhmaṇas* are an attempt to develop a form of religious life and worship on the basis of Vedic revelation, the Upaniṣads are an attempt to understand and present the Vedic vision of truth philosophically. Thus, the Vedic *Saṁhitās* gave rise to *Brāhmaṇa* form of religious life and worship, and to the Upaniṣadic or Vedāntic form of philosophy. The fact that the Upaniṣads have not given rise to any form of religious life , but are intended to be studied, reflected upon and meditated by those who are not satisfied or dis-enchanted with the ordinary or ritual form of religious life

---

1. *Śatapatha Brāhmaṇa*, 10.3.5.12; see also introduction to the Upaniṣads by F. Max Muller; *Sacred Books of the East* series Vol. I pp. ixxix to ixxxiv. Truth is the essence (Upaniṣad) of the Veda, restraint is the essence of truth, charity is the essence of restraint and austerity is the essence of charity (*vedasya upaniṣad satyam satyasya upaniṣad dama damasya upaniṣad dānam dānasya upaniṣad tapaḥ tapasya upaniṣad tyāgam*). *Mahābhārata*, Śānti-parva, 251.11-12; 299.13.

and worship, shows that the Upaniṣads are not the source of Hinduism as a religion. The Upaniṣadic thought or wisdom cannot be adapted to the popular religious needs and aspirations. It cannot also be used to support or justify the beliefs and doctrines of popular form of Hinduism.

While the form of Hindu life and worship as developed in the *Brāhmaṇa*s is strictly restricted, both in theory and in practice, to the twice-born of Hindu society or in real practice to the rich patrons of *yajña* form of religious worship, because the performance of various kinds of ritual-*yajña* as elaborately dealt with in the *Brāhmaṇa* literature involves considerable amount of wealth and direct employment and participation of several brāhmaṇas. And both of them are not possible and open to all the sections of Hindu society. The majority of Indian population, therefore, must have had their religion which is not strictly speaking Vedic, either in inspiration or in content. The religious life of the common people of India or the popular form of Hinduism is represented by the Smṛti tradition of Hinduism. The Smṛti literature fully reflects and represents the religion of the people of India. Smṛti includes the various Dharma-śāstras, the epics of *Rāmāyaṇa* and *Mahābhārata*, the Purāṇas and Āgamas, and other Hindu religious traditions and literature. The Dharma-śāstras and the epics have not much to do directly with Hinduism as a religion. They also do not contain much that is not to be found in the Purāṇic literature. They are not, strictly speaking, religious texts of Hinduism though they can shed much light on the beliefs and practices of Hinduism. It is the Purāṇas and Āgamas which represent Hinduism as believed in and practised by almost all the Hindus. There are no Hindus who are born *Vedāntin*s as there are born Vaiṣṇavas, Śaivas and Śāktas. Vedānta does not represent any sectarian form of Hinduism as the Vaiṣṇavism and Śaivism do. Vedānta is not sectarian in character as there is no Vedāntic form of religious life and worship. They do not represent any sect of Hinduism. But all the sects of Hinduism accept the authority of the Vedānta, and try to adapt its ontological vision to suit their theological needs and demands. Generally speaking, the Hindus aspire to realise the Vedāntic truth which is regarded as the consummation of Hindu religious or spiritual life. In this sense the Upaniṣads are the common source of inspiration to all the Hindus. They belong to all the Hindus, irrespective of their sectarian differences, which is not, however, the case with the sectarian literature of Hinduism. The Upaniṣads are the common source of inspiration to all the Hindus, and almost all the sects seek the authority and justification of the Upaniṣads to their theological beliefs and doctrines. With the exception of certain extreme and exclusive forms of religious life and worship most of the Hindus have the freedom to choose the deity of their worship.

The Smr̥ti tradition in its literary form is much later to Śruti tradition. And almost all the Purāṇas are compilations or collections (*Saṁhitā*), compiled by Vyāsa. But as a religious tradition, representing the non-Vedic form of religious life and worship, Smr̥ti tradition must have been as ancient as Śruti. We find in the earliest Śruti literature the mention of Viṣṇu and Śiva, major or prominent deities of Smr̥ti or Purāṇic form of Hinduism, and the conception of the divine in feminine terms, the basis for the development of Śākta form of religious worship. *Devī Bhāgavata* claims that the worship of the divine in feminine form (*devī*) is as ancient as the *R̥gveda* because it regards Devī as a form of Vedic Gāyatrī.[2] However, the deities of Viṣṇu and Śiva are not central to the Vedic form of religious life and worship. They have no place in the Vedic form of religious worship (*yajña*) as developed in the Brāhmaṇas. Now, the fact that the Smr̥ti tradition is as ancient as Śruti, and is more pervasive in its influence in the development of Hinduism may mean one or two things. As maintained traditionally the main object or purpose of Smr̥ti tradition is to adapt the Vedic wisdom or revelation to the changing religious needs and demands of the people keeping in view the heterogeneous character of Hindu society. The Smr̥ti tradition which is represented primarily by the Purāṇas and Āgamas addresses itself to the task of adapting

2. *Devī Bhāgavata*, 8.8. 84-93.

the Vedic wisdom or revelation to meet the religious needs of all the sections of Indian society, especially the religious needs of those who are denied direct access to the Veda. It is developed by the enlightened people of Hindu tradition who are fully informed by the Vedic wisdom, and are at the same time aware of and sympathetic to the religious or spiritual needs of those who are denied direct access to the Veda, and are, therefore, prohibited from participating in the *Brāhmaṇa* form of religious life and worship. Just as the various codes and manuals on *dharma* are formulated keeping in view the changing social reality or circumstances, the Purāṇas are an attempt to interpret and adapt the Vedic wisdom to the religious needs of all the sections of Indian society, including the tribes like Niṣādas and Kirātas, who are outside the fold of Hindu social organisation or caste system. Purāṇas are also an attempt to bring all the sections of Indian society, including the various tribes, into the Hindu or Vedic fold though indirectly, and to spread or make available the Vedic wisdom to all the sections of society by presenting it in a form which is intelligible and meaningful to popular understanding. And more importantly the object of Purāṇic literature is to reconcile and harmonise the popular or Smṛti form of Hinduism with the Śruti tradition, and to provide Vedic authority and sanctity to various sects of Hinduism. In this process most of the popular forms of religious worship, and most of the popular religious beliefs and doctrines remained unaffected; only the sectarian theologies or sectarian theological ideas and beliefs are sought to be reconciled and harmonised with the world-view of Śruti.

It is not easy to determine whether a particular interpretation of the Veda gave rise to a particular sectarian form of Hinduism or is it the other way round, that is, the Veda is interpreted to lend its authority and justification to already existing sectarian religious traditions. The Purāṇas and the *Mahābhārata* often assert that they are only representing the truth or wisdom of the Veda or Vedānta in a manner which is intelligible and meaningful to popular understanding. Nevertheless, it is more meaningful to think, keeping in view the tension and conflict between Śruti and Smṛti, that Śruti is not interpreted and re-interpreted to establish new sects within Hinduism but to support and justify the theological claims of already existing religious sects. Moreover, as the Smṛti texts very often make the claim that their teaching is in conformity with the wisdom of the Veda or Vedānta we have to suspect their claim. The Śruti and Smṛti traditions are not completely compatible with each other, as most of the basic religious ideas and doctrines of Smṛti tradition are not consistent with Śruti, and its world-view. They even go against the spirit and wisdom of Śruti. We do not find any basis or justification in Śruti for most of the religious ideas and doctrines of Smṛti tradition. The various theological ideas, beliefs and doctrines of the Smṛti tradition do not find any kind of support or basis and justification in the Veda, nor do they follow logically from the Vedic thought. And most of the religious beliefs, ideas and doctrines that go by the name of Hinduism, and are believed in by almost all the Hindus have their source and development only in the Smṛti tradition. And to meet the criticism that there is no authority of Śruti for most of the religious beliefs and doctrines of Smṛti it is asserted that those Śruti texts which could corroborate or justify certain beliefs and doctrines of the Smṛti tradition might have been lost. This claim is difficult to justify. It may be true that some of the Śruti texts or rather certain recessions of them might have been lost, but that does not, however, mean much. If we compare the available Śruti literature with the Smṛti literature that is available in respect of certain basic ideas, beliefs and doctrines we do not find any agreement between them. They differ very significantly or even basically in their approaches and attitudes to the nature and meaning of religion. There is no compatibility between them in respect of certain fundamental religious beliefs and ideas which cannot be wished away or justified in terms of lost Śruti texts. Thus, there is a basic difference between Śruti and Smṛti with regard to fundamental problems of religion which we cannot explain without accepting their independent origin and development. Nevertheless, the

Smṛti tradition, which is recognised by most of the modern scholars as the real or major source of Hinduism, is in basic agreement with Śruti in so far as the world-view of Hinduism is concerned. The Hindu world-view is based on or shaped by the Śruti tradition, and the Smṛti tradition adopts it. The Smṛti tradition accepts the world-view of Śruti, and tries to integrate itself with the Śruti tradition in terms of the world-view. And the world-view of Śruti has been the common source of inspiration for all the Smṛti sects and thinkers.

The saints and thinkers of Smṛti tradition often claim that the object of Smṛti tradition is mainly to make available the wisdom of the Veda, by which they really mean the wisdom of the Upaniṣads, to common people who are denied direct access to the Veda. This traditional explanation for the emergence of Smṛti tradition though seems plausible, and is accepted by most of the traditional thinkers and scholars, does not, however, stand the scrutiny of textual evidence. We cannot also say that Smṛti is a sort of interpretation of Śruti because what Smṛti says about Śruti or the various religious beliefs and doctrines it attributes to Śruti have no basis in the Śruti texts, or we do not find any Śruti authority for them. More often the Smṛti texts claim the authority of the Veda for their theological views and doctrines, but we do not find in the Śruti texts any evidence in support or justification of the claim. For many of the religious beliefs and views of Smṛti there is no corroborative or confirmative evidence in the Śruti literature. At the same time we do not have any clear textual evidence, either in the Śruti or in Smṛti, to show that the two traditions are alien to each other. In other words, there is no clear and unambiguous textual evidence to show or prove that the Veda or Śruti is Āryan in its origin, while Smṛti represents the native religious and cultural traditions of India, particularly the Draviḍian tradition of south India. Whatever may be the historical justification for the Āryan-Draviḍian divide, if we confine our attention to the textual evidence we find a spirit of accommodation and respect for each other because of which efforts are constantly made to reconcile and harmonise both the traditions. We cannot, therefore, say that they represent two radically different traditions of religious life and thought belonging to two ethnic groups, antagonistic, and even hostile to each other. The fact that the Smṛti tradition constantly invokes the authority of Śruti for its theological beliefs and ideas, and wants to be recognised as an extension of Śruti or as truly representing the vision and wisdom of Śruti does not betray any sense of antagonism or opposition between itself and Śruti. Furthermore, the fact that the Smṛti tradition adopts the world-view of Śruti on its own shows the harmony between the two traditions. The Hindu world-view is common to both the traditions. The Smṛti tradition not only adopts the world-view of Śruti but also tries to reconcile and harmonise itself with the Śruti tradition. Though Smṛti criticises and even rejects some of the religious ideas and doctrines of Śruti it has not criticised its world-view. On the other hand, in an effort to reconcile and integrate itself with the Śruti tradition, Smṛti tradition tries to adjust its theological position so as to make it consistent with the world-view of Śruti. Thus, while Śruti represents one stream of thought which has no immediate practical or religious application in view, the Smṛti tradition represents the religion of the people or the popular form of Hinduism. We do not find either in the *Saṁhitā*s or in the Upaniṣads any significant discussion or description of the religion of the common people of India. And this does not mean that they had no religion of their own. While the *Atharvaveda* describes some aspects of popular religious life and beliefs, without showing any disrespect or contempt for them, they are not discussed in any other Śruti text.

The fact that the Purāṇic tradition was known to the Upaniṣads even though the Purāṇic texts were composed or compiled much later shows that a religious tradition represented by the Purāṇic tradition must have been as ancient as the Vedic tradition. In any case the religious beliefs, doctrines and even sectarian theologies must have been in existence long before they find their literary representation in the Smṛti literature.

The over-emphasis in the Smṛti texts that what they enunciate or their teaching is compatible with Śruti may mean that the Smṛti tradition seeks to claim for itself the sanctity and authority of the Śruti.

The *Mahābhārata* and the Purāṇas clearly state that the Smṛti tradition or the Smṛti form of Hinduism is open to all the sections of society, which is not, however, the case with the Śruti form of Hinduism. In understanding the relationship between Śruti and Smṛti, and their importance in the development of Hinduism, we have to admit that though theoretically Śruti enjoys supreme authority in Hinduism, in real terms Hinduism is largely based on and shaped by the Smṛti tradition. The Smṛti tradition is the real source as well as the authority and justification for most of the Hindu religious beliefs and practices. In other words, Hinduism as it is popularly known and practised is mostly based on and developed by the Smṛti tradition.

What is then the place and value of Śruti in the religious life of a Hindu? Or what is its importance in the development of Hinduism? As it has been traditionally maintained, which is also philosophically valid and significant, the Upaniṣads have no application or use, either religious or secular. They do not have direct religious significance and value, or as traditionally maintained they have no application or use (*viniyoga*) in any religious ritual. They are not meant to serve and fulfil the religious needs of people. They are to be studied, reflected upon and meditated to have direct experience or realisation of the divine, and that is purely the concern of an individual as a human being. The Upaniṣads are intended for those who are not satisfied or dis-enchanted with the ordinary form of religious life. They reveal or express truth; and truth has no application or use. Truth can only liberate one from untruth and falsehood. This is also true with the Vedic *Saṁhitā*s as they are not in the first place composed by a person or group of persons keeping in view a religious purpose or goal in attaining which the truth or the wisdom of the Veda could be meaningful and useful. If the Śruti texts, like those of Smṛti, are composed by someone with a purpose or end in view, like material prosperity or heavenly bliss, then they will not have the character and authority of Śruti. However, we are not here concerned with what different schools of Vedic thought and interpretation, like the Pūrva Mīmāṁsā, say about the meaning, validity and object of the Veda as no interpretation of the Veda is final, and enjoys the authority and sanctity of the Veda. They are subject to modification and improvement, and can even be rejected. Even the modern interpretations of the Veda stand to Veda as Pūrva Mīmāṁsā to Veda. Unfortunately, most of the modern Hindus go by what the schools of interpretation of the Veda, like Pūrva Mīmāṁsā, say about the Veda, and often accord the same authority to such views or interpretations as that is due to the Veda. They accept what the schools of Vedic interpretation say about Veda than what the Veda says about itself. The *Brāhmaṇa*s, which are traditionally regarded as forming part of the Śruti tradition, are in fact an interpretation of the *Saṁhitā*s or certain hymns of the Veda with the purpose of employing them in the performance of various rituals developed in the *Brāhmaṇa*s. Of course, what the Veda stands for is a matter of interpretation, but the most important thing about interpretations is that no interpretation is final and enjoys the authority of the Veda. Therefore, they do not have the same status and validity as of the Veda. This is also the case with the views of Smṛti about the meaning of the Veda. As interpretations all the schools of Vedic thought will have the same validity and authority as any human wisdom or understanding can have.

It is Pūrva Mīmāṁsā, a school of Vedic interpretation, which thinks that the primary object of Veda is *dharma* or religious action effective in securing heavenly bliss to its practitioners. It denies ontological validity and meaning to the Veda, and regards that the ontological claims of the Veda and Vedānta are intended to justify *dharma*, the real object of the Veda. Accordingly, they interpret the hymns of the Veda in terms of their ritual application and relevance. Such an understanding must have been the basis for developing elaborate and most complex rituals in the *Brāhmaṇa*s. *Brāhmaṇa*s describe in minute detail the performance of various rituals as well as the possible results of their performance. Somehow, in course of time, the *Brāhmaṇa*s are regarded as forming part of the Śruti tradition. Interestingly all the criticisms, attacks and even protests against the Veda, and the Vedic form of religious life and worship, are in fact directed against the *Brāhmaṇa* form of Hinduism, and its ritualistic form of religious life. Criticism of the Veda, either from without or from within, is really criticism of the *Brāhmaṇa* form of religion, in which the dominance of the twice-born, especially the brāhmaṇa priests, is well pronounced or established. The ritual form of religious worship developed by the *Brāhmaṇa*s is not divinely inspired but humanly devised. It is a collective form of worship involving elaborate rituals and considerable wealth, and is exclusive, both in theory and in practice, to the twice-born of Hindu society. It is not open to all, as the śūdras who constitute the majority of Indian society, and women are excluded from the *Brāhmaṇa* form of religious life and worship.

The Upaniṣads, as pointed out earlier, have no religious application and value. They have no ritualistic value and significance. Theoretically they are intended, and are also meaningful to those who enter the fourth *āśrama* or final stage of life (*saṁnyāsa*) in which one is expected to be free from the attachment to the ordinary or ritualistic form of religious life and worship, or the religion of means and ends. And *saṁnyāsa* is not open to all the sections of Hindu society. *Varṇa* (caste) system, whatever may be the source of its inspiration, did not remain a social system. It influenced the religious life of the Hindus. And if Hinduism were to be identified with the *Brāhmaṇa* form of religious life and worship then majority of Indians should not be regarded as Hindus as śūdras and others who form the majority of Indian society are excluded from participation in the *Brāhmaṇa* form of religious life and worship. Not only the śūdras but also women of all castes were excluded from direct participation in the *Brāhmaṇa* form of religious life as they are not entitled to the sacrament whereby one is twice-born. However, at a later stage in the development of Hinduism the meaning of *yajña* is not confined to ritual performance of various *Brāhmaṇa* sacrifices but is extended to comprehend every sphere of human life. In the *Mahābhārata*, service (*sevā*), the ordained duty of a śūdra, is regarded as a form of *yajña* (*sevā-yajña*). The *Bhagavad Gītā* interprets *yajña* to comprehend the whole of human life. Thus, by extending the meaning of *yajña* to comprehend all the spheres of human life the brāhmaṇa concept of *yājña* is given up or rejected. And the Smṛti form of Hinduism developed several forms of religious life and worship which are open to all the sections of Hindu society, including those who are not included within the Hindu social order (*pañcama*).

Does this mean that all those we are denied the sacrament of *upanayana* are not Hindu, and have no religious life of their own? Is it the case that after the rise and spread of Buddhism attempts were made to bring under the fold of Vedic religion all those who were excluded from the Vedic form of religious life and worship by developing a form of Hinduism which is not strictly speaking Vedic, but is nevertheless developed on the basis of the Veda to suit the religious needs of the common people? Can we say that the Smṛti form of Hinduism has come into existence as a result of such attempts? This seems to be a plausible explanation, as many consider that Hinduism which is open to all the sections of Indian society, including those who are outside the caste system, like the various tribes of India, was developed due to the impact or influence of Buddhism. Buddhism which does not consider one's social or cultural status as having anything to do with his religious or spiritual life must have provided a challenge as well as positive inspiration to *Brāhmaṇa* form of Hinduism. Although the Upaniṣadic thought is universal, for we do not find in it any kind of discrimination among human beings as all are regarded as the manifestation of the divine or *Brahman*, in practice the caste division of the Indian society influenced the religious life of the Hindus, and the caste system was given religious significance and value. Though the Smṛti tradition is more universal in the sense that it is open to all the Hindus, irrespective of their social and cultural status, yet it accepts at least in principle the supremacy of the *Brāhmaṇa* form of religious life and values.

The non-Vedic religious tradition must have been in existence long before the Smṛti tradition was crystallised. The religious tradition or traditions that find their literary representation in the Purāṇas must have been in existence long before the Purāṇic texts were compiled. The Smṛti as a tradition is as ancient as the Vedic tradition though the Purāṇic texts which represent it are composed or compiled much latter. The various Purāṇas, and to an extent the epics, represent the religious life and values of the Smṛti tradition. The śūdras, unlike others or tribes like Niṣādas, Kirāṭas, etc., who are known as fifth group of people, are not outside the Hindu social system. They form part of *varṇa* system, and are spread throughout India. The Smṛti tradition mostly represents their religious beliefs and practices. Although historically the Smṛti tradition is as ancient as the Śruti tradition the literary tradition of Smṛti is not ancient. The earliest recorded Smṛti form of religion is *Pañcarātra* which is well represented in the *Mahābhārata*. In the *Ṛgveda* we find mention of Viṣṇu and Śiva (Rudra), the principal deities of the Smṛti tradition, though they are not regarded as ontologically independent. They also do not find any place of importance in the Vedic form of religious worship.

The Smṛti tradition though developed independently of the Vedic tradition has made significant attempts to reconcile and harmonise itself with the Vedic tradition. There has been continuous interaction between both the traditions in which each has influenced the other. Though we find tension between the two traditions, which is more pronounced during the modern times, a harmonious relationship prevails between them. The thinkers and saints of the Smṛti tradition have adopted the ontology of Śruti, especially that of the Upaniṣads, so as to provide philosophical basis and justification for the religious beliefs and values of Smṛti. In other words, attempts are constantly made to reconcile the theology of Smṛti with the ontology of the Upaniṣads. Over the centuries the ontology of the Upaniṣads proved itself spiritually inspiring to all the Hindus irrespective of their sectarian differences. It has been the common source of inspiration, and the principle of unity for all the sects and sub-sects of Hinduism. The Śruti world-view which is adopted by all the sects of Hinduism helped them to live in harmony; it also gave them their Hindu identity. All the sects and sub-sects of Hinduism are Hindu because of their acceptance of the world-view of Śruti. It also helped their development and enrichment. Almost all the sects of Hinduism are drawn to the Vedāntic world-view or ontology, and are positively influenced by it. Every sect of Hinduism in its own characteristic way has tried to reconcile and harmonise its theology with the ontology of the Upaniṣads. This has been the dominant concern of most of the Smṛti thinkers. The attempts at reconciling the theological tradition of Smṛti with the world-view of Śruti also helped in removing or reducing the tension and conflict among the different sects and sub-sects of Hinduism, which are otherwise antagonistic to each other. The process of reconciliation and harmonisation between the traditions of Śruti and Smṛti has significantly contributed to the growth and development of Hinduism. And Hinduism is a harmonious blend or integration of the traditions of Śruti and Smṛti. While the Śruti tradition provided the basic vision or world-view and ontological stability to Hinduism, Smṛti gave Hinduism its dynamic character. Therefore, to comprehend the nature and meaning Hinduism it is not sufficient to understand either of them. However, in modern times efforts are made to over-emphasise the importance of one or the other in understanding the nature and meaning of Hinduism. Most of the modern Hindu thinkers lay more emphasis on the importance of the Upaniṣads in understanding the nature and meaning of Hinduism. But Hinduism as believed in and practised by almost all the Hindus is based on and inspired by both Śruti and Smṛti. As a matter of fact Hinduism is based largely on the Smṛti tradition. Beyond providing a world-view and ontological stability and justification to Hinduism, the Vedānta is indifferent to the practical religious needs and problems of man. It rather transcends religion or the religious concerns of man. However, it is of foundational value or importance to religion without itself being a source of religion directly. In other words, the Hindu world-view is Upaniṣadic, while Hinduism as a religion with all its beliefs and practices is mostly based on and shaped by the Smṛti tradition. We may say that while Śruti is the soul of Hinduism, the Smṛti forms its body.

Therefore, instead of trying to understand and determine what is central or fundamental to Hinduism it would be meaningful to understand what is central to each tradition. It may not be so much meaningful to understand what is central to both Śruti and Smṛti as they are two distinct and independent traditions with more or less distinct identities of their own. However, due to continuous interaction and mutual influence they have developed something in common even though they differ basically in their approaches and attitudes to religion. But we cannot say that their differences are radical. Therefore, instead of trying to understand what is basically common to both the traditions we should try to understand what is basic or fundamental to each tradition. Each is a major tradition with its insights, beliefs and doctrines, and in certain important aspects their differences are basic.

The Śruti is distinguished from Smṛti not in terms of its teaching but in terms of the nature or kind of knowledge it represents. The authority of Śruti is not in terms of its teaching or wisdom, but in terms of the nature of knowledge it represents. The Śruti knowledge is revealed or divinely inspired, but is not due to any kind of human effort. Its validity is not, therefore, conditioned by the limitations of the knower. It is divinely inspired knowledge, and the Vedic seers regard divine inspiration as a divine gift. It is not due to their endeavour they have known the divine, but because of divine inspiration. The seers are passive in knowing the divine, and, therefore, what is revealed to them is not conditioned by the spatio-temporal, and other limitations of the seers. As maintained by Svāmī

Dayānanda Sarasvatī, Śruti texts start and end with *OṀ*.[3] They do not speak about the efficiency or usefulness of their wisdom or knowledge in achieving certain human ends. Śruti does not speak of rewards and punishments; it is not a motivated literature. The wisdom or truth which Śruti represents transcends the realm of means and ends. On the contrary, Smṛti literature is motivated. Its object is to influence or induce people to follow a particular form of religious life and worship. Even though the Smṛti texts are attributed to various authors, the beginning of Smṛti as a tradition cannot be definitely ascertained. Smṛti literature is full of polemics and controversies, and is composed or compiled by several authors with a definite purpose in view. It fully reflects the preferences and prejudices, and various other human limitations of its authors. And as the Smṛti texts are intended to motivate and influence people to follow a particular form of religious life they take into consideration the religious needs of the people. It accordingly plans and adjusts its religious instruction.

Although the *Brāhmaṇas* are traditionally classified under Śruti they really do not have revealed character. They too speak of rewards either in this world or in the world which one is supposed to attain by following the *Brāhmaṇa* form of religious life. Is there then anything that can be regarded as being central or fundamental to Śruti? Those who have tried to understand Hinduism, especially in terms of its essence, tried to find support and justification in Śruti for almost all the Hindu beliefs and doctrines, including those which have their origin and justification only in Smṛti. As we shall discuss this problem independently we are here interested only in hinting at or indicating what is central to Śruti. Most of the Hindus think that the Veda contains or is the source of all the religious ideas and insights, just as most of the Hindus think that almost all the religious or theological ideas and beliefs are present within Hinduism. Since many religious ideas and beliefs find their

3. Light of Truth (*satyārtha prakāśa*), Dayānanda Sarasvatī, pp. 198-9; see also his introduction to the commentary on the *Ṛgveda*.

expression in Śruti, it is very difficult to judge which of them form the essence of Śruti or are central to Śruti tradition. It is difficult to identify an idea or a belief or a doctrine as being central or fundamental to Śruti, as all the ideas of Śruti enjoy the same sanctity and authority of Śruti. Nevertheless, underlying all the myths, ideas, beliefs and doctrines of Śruti tradition there is a vision or world-view which is clearly reflected in all the Śruti literature. However, all the ideas, beliefs and doctrines are not shared commonly by all the texts of Śruti. On the other hand, it is the world-view which is commonly reflected in all the Śruti literature, and, therefore, what is central to Śruti is its world-view. And all the myths, ideas, and beliefs of the Śruti tradition reflect and express the same world-view. The Smṛti tradition adopts the world view of Śruti, and, therefore, all the sects of Hinduism share the common world-view. The world view is common to Hinduism whether it is represented by Śruti or by Smṛti. According to the Hindu world-view, the divine is one, and it is both immanent and transcendent. It is immanently present within all that is empirically real, and yet transcends the empirical reality in the sense that the divine is more than its manifestations which form the world of human experience and understanding. Therefore, the empirical reality cannot contain and exhaust the divine. The divine is more than all that is empirically known and comprehended. This view of the divine is what is commonly shared by all the schools and sects of Hinduism even though they differ, and at times very significantly, about the nature and meaning of the divine, and its relation to the world of manifestation, including man.

Therefore to realise the divine unity or oneness of all that is empirically real by experiencing the presence of the divine within all is the meaning and end of man's religious life, according to Hinduism. And the sectarian differences within Hinduism, which are significant but are not irreconcilable, are mainly related to the nature of the divine, the nature and destiny of man, the nature of relationship between the divine and man, and man's attitude to the divine.

We find in the Smṛti tradition, in which the different sects of Hinduism find their theological development and expression, attempts to relate, reconcile and integrate the different sectarian theological beliefs and doctrines with the world-view of the Śruti, so that the various sectarian religious traditions of Hinduism are firmly grounded on the world-view or the ontological vision of Śruti, and avail or derive for themselves the authority and sanctity of Śruti. And as a result of the process of reconciliation and integration of the various sectarian theologies of Smṛti tradition with the world-view of Śruti, Hinduism has attained coherence and unity without denying religious freedom because of which several sub-religious traditions are born and developed in India. But for the unifying and integrating force of its world-view there would have been no identifiable structure or form of Hinduism apart from the sectarian forms of religious life and worship. Hinduism would then have been a conglomeration of different religious beliefs and practices without any coherence and identity. It would then have only a national or geographical identity. The world-view also prevented the various sectarian religious traditions, like Vaiṣṇavism and Śaivism, who are antagonistic to each other, from developing themselves into independent religious traditions like Buddhism and Jainism. The process of reconciliation and integration between the traditions of Śruti and Smṛti cannot be precisely dated. The fact that the Śruti literature is much older than Smṛti literature cannot be a strong reason to think that the former is very much older than the latter. The various Purāṇic texts, epics and other Āgama literature, which are composed or compiled very much later than Śruti, are only literary representation or expression of religious traditions which are as ancient as Śruti.

It is not easy to determine the relative importance of Śruti and Smṛti in the development of Hinduism. Nevertheless, we can make certain general observations which are significant and relevant in understanding the problem. In its authority and validity Smṛti is traditionally regarded as inferior or secondary to Śruti. Smṛti has to agree with or conform to Śruti in its teaching if it is to have any authority and validity. And if Smṛti simply teaches what is there in the Śruti then it cannot serve any meaningful purpose except to present the teaching or wisdom of Śruti in a manner or language which is easy and intelligible to all, including those who are excluded from the Śruti tradition, or to serve the purpose of making available the teaching or wisdom of Śruti to all irrespective of their social and cultural status. This is the traditional view or understanding of the importance and role of Smṛti in the development of Hinduism. But most of the religious ideas, beliefs and doctrines as well as the religious practices which are basic to Smṛti form of religious life are not compatible with Śruti. We cannot find in Śruti any support and justification for what is essential to Smṛti tradition. Therefore, the major concern of Smṛti is not just to present the wisdom of Śruti in a popular form so that all can have access to it, but to systematically present and justify the religious beliefs and doctrines of different sects which developed themselves independently of Śruti. The different sectarian theologies, and the various religious beliefs and practices which find their expression in the Smṛti literature, especially in the Purāṇas and Āgamas, must have been in existence long before they find their literary representation in the texts of Smṛti. Both these traditions must have developed together though the Smṛti tradition had no literary representation till the composition or compilation of epics and Purāṇas. Smṛti must have been an oral tradition as the legends, myths and the various religious beliefs and doctrines of Smṛti used to be orally transmitted from generation to generation by the *paurāṇika*s. While the Śruti tradition is preserved and transmitted with extreme care because of its sanctity and authority, the Smṛti tradition, which consists largely of myths, legends and stories is altered and modified by different sects to suit their sectarian requirements and demands. While in the case of the Veda value and sanctity are attached to the original syntax, and its literary form it is not so in the case of Smṛti literature. It is enough if the teaching or content of Smṛti is preserved, but not its form. The manner in which the different stories and myths are told and retold differ from one

Purāṇic text to another, and also from region to region. But thereby the purpose of their narration is not defeated. It is to inspire religious feelings and devotion in man, and to influence his religious life.

Another reason for the emergence and proliferation of sectarian literature known as Smṛti, is that in the Hindu religious tradition correctness of theological beliefs and doctrines is not considered essential to be religious. In the history of Hinduism it is not insisted that to be religious one should necessarily believe in a particular doctrine or theology. Doctrinal and theological differences are not therefore suppressed in favour of an official theology or creed. Supreme importance is placed on the inward experience of devotion and piety rather than on the correctness of religious beliefs and doctrine. Devotion moves a person deeply, purifies his being and reveals the nature and meaning of the divine. Inwardly experienced devotion, which is divine, may express itself in various forms, and, therefore, its nature cannot be determined in terms of any one form or concept. It cannot be conceptualised. Inwardly experienced devotion (Brahma) is the basis in human experience of the concept of divine or *Brahman*. The meaning of divine is revealed to man in the state of divinely inspired devotion (Brahma) or as devotion itself. It is commonly accepted by all the sectarian traditions of Hinduism that without experiencing devotion one cannot be religious. Devotion, which is regarded as an end in itself, is the meaning as well as the end of religion. It is divine and sacred, and in experiencing it human existence is supremely fulfilled. It is the meaning of divine as experienced by man directly and immediately. Inwardly experienced devotion transforms the being of man completely, and enables him see the divine presence within all. The Vedic vision or wisdom that the divine permeates all or is within all is based on the experience of divinely inspired devotion or Brahma. If inwardly experienced devotion is the source of man's religious life and worship, the religious or theological beliefs and doctrines are secondary in importance. They are not sufficient to make one religious. Religion finds its meaning and justification in devotion. According to the Veda, Brahma or divinely inspired devotion is the meaning of divine, or man comes to know the existence of the divine, and its nature in the state of devotion. Even in the popular form of Hinduism, based largely on the Smṛti tradition, emphasis is not placed on right theological beliefs and doctrines but on the devotional life of man. Much of Hindu religious literature is primarily intended to inspire devotion in man. The vivid and detailed narration of various myths, legends and stories which are related to God and His glory are intended to inspire devotion in man, and to promote a devotional way of life. Importance is given to devotion in Hinduism right from the beginning as to experience devotion is the same as to experience the divine. Theological freedom is, therefore, not denied in the Hindu tradition as what is really important in the religious life of a person is the birth of devotion but not his clinging to certain beliefs and doctrines. Another important reason for the theological freedom in Hinduism is its vision of the divine. All that is there is a manifestation of the divine, and, therefore, there is nothing in the universe which is divinely insignificant. However, depending upon the level of one's spiritual development and natural disposition (*pravṛtti*) one sees or understands the nature of the divine in his own way; and that alone really helps him spiritually or religiously. Since what one knows or sees is only a form of manifestation of the divine, and as it is not meaningful to set limits to the manifestation of the divine, one who has experienced devotion or is truly religious cannot find anything wrong with one who understands the divine and worships it in his own way, however, meaningless it may appear to others. Thus, the history of Hinduism is a grand attempt to reconcile, harmonise and integrate divergent beliefs, doctrines and even theologies in terms of its world-view which has no place for exclusion. The Śruti-Smṛti relationship can also be understood in the light of the Hindu world-view which is basically common to all the sects of Hinduism.

In their origin the different sects of Hinduism, like Vaiṣṇavism, Śaivism and Śāktism must have been only cults with elaborate ritual practices but without an ontology or theology to support and sustain them. Here we are not concerned whether these cults are native to some people of India, as it will not help us in understanding the meaning of Hinduism in any significant manner. However, it is historically true that though both the traditions maintain their individual identity they are in constant interaction with each other. And very significant attempts are made from time to time to reconcile them, and integrate one with the other. This has been a continuous process in the history of Hinduism as new religious cults and sects or movements come into existence, and try to find their basis and justification in the Veda. In modern times we see the continuation of the process pursued more vigorously by different sects and movements. While at the popular level Śruti or the Veda is only a term of reference and reverence, at the intellectual or philosophical level it is often interpreted to provide ontological basis and justification, sanctity and coherence to various movements and sects mainly because any religious idea or doctrine is acceptable to Hindus only if it is compatible with the Veda, or is not opposed to Vedic world-view. Therefore, all the sects of Hinduism try to find Vedic authority and justification to their sectarian beliefs and doctrines. This is not so much because they are really Vedic in origin, but because of the highest authority and sanctity the Veda enjoys in Hinduism, and the comprehensive and integral character of its world-view. Furthermore, the Śruti tradition does not place so much value and importance on theological beliefs and doctrines as on inwardly experienced devotion and piety. The idea of right knowledge (*samyag-jñāna*) which is emphasised very much in Buddhism and Jainism is conspicuous by its absence in the Śruti tradition. The term (*samyag-jñāna*) occurs only once in the Upaniṣads, and that too without any exclusive claim.[4] The Upaniṣads which present, and even discuss several views on any religious problem have not made any attempt to maintain

---

4. *Ātman* is to be attained by *samyak jñāna*. Śaṅkara interprets *samyak jñāna* as true or objective knowledge of *ātman* (*yathā bhutātma darśana*) *Muṇḍaka Upaniṣad*, 3.1.5.

an official view, as there is no conception of right knowledge or right view in the Śruti tradition. The authority and sanctity of Śruti are due to its impersonal character. Śruti makes no effort to propagate itself and its wisdom or to influence people to a particular view of truth, or to a particular way of religious life. It does not go to people with promises and rewards; it is the people who are supposed to approach Śruti if they are interested in knowing the truth. "What the Veda can do if people are not interested in knowing the truth" as the *Ṛgveda* puts it.[5] On the other hand, Smṛti promises various kinds of rewards for following it. It tries to influence or induce people to accept its teaching, and follow the religious form of life it prescribes. On the other hand, Veda stands for a vision of truth or world-view, and acts like a friend in gently persuading people to realise the truth for themselves. Traditionally the influence of Śruti is likened to the influences of a friend (*suhṛd sammita*). The Smṛti, on the other hand, talks of promises and punishments either for following or not following the form of religious life it prescribes.

Thus, Hinduism is a confluence of two major religious traditions or streams; one is represented by Śruti and the other by Smṛti. Though we find in the history of Hinduism efforts on the part of each tradition to assert itself, and establish its supremacy over the other resulting in tension between the two there has been no open hostility or conflict between them. While one is *dharma* centered, the other is faith centered. While one is impersonal, the other is personal. However, the contribution of both is significant to the growth and development of Hinduism. Therefore, any attempt to understand and determine the nature and meaning of Hinduism in terms of any one stream or tradition or to identify it with any one of them will not help us in comprehending the nature and meaning of Hinduism. Both are integral to Hinduism. And both represent Hinduism. While Pūrva Mīmāṁsā and the *dharma*-form of religious life represent one tradition, the *Bhāgavata-dharma* or devotional form of religious life represents the other. Depending upon the pre-

5. *Ṛgveda*, 1.164.39.

dominance of any one stream in the life and development of Hinduism certain ideas, doctrines and beliefs which can follow from one tradition, and are compatible with it, but not with the other dominated Hinduism. But both are Hindu or both constitute Hinduism. We cannot, therefore, assert with any authority that one is more central or fundamental to Hinduism than the other. However, depending upon the individual preferences and perspectives of the scholars and thinkers, Hinduism has been identified with one or the other tradition, and consequently the beliefs and doctrines that follow naturally from one, and are compatible with it than with the other are regarded as essential to Hinduism. For instance, doctrines of *karma* and rebirth are more natural and logically more meaningful in terms of one stream or tradition than in terms of the other.

Hinduism of the Smṛti tradition is more dynamic. It accepts growth and expansion, and is not a closed tradition though it is clear about its foundation. Hindiuism does not deny freedom to individuals to fully develop and express their spiritual possibilities. Because of religious freedom various forms of religious life and worship, different religious beliefs and doctrines as well as different paths to realise the highest end of life are developed within the Hindu religious tradition, and all are recognised as Hindu.

2
Two Traditions

ALTHOUGH, most of the modern thinkers, for various reasons, have tried to identify Hinduism with the Śruti tradition, the Smṛti tradition is in reality the basis of Hinduism as believed in and practised by almost all the Hindus. The religious life of the Hindus, in most of its aspects, is largely based on and shaped by the Smṛti tradition. Although at the theoretical level or at the level of ideas and doctrines we find tension between Śruti and Smṛti at the practical religious level Hinduism is based on or inspired by the Smṛti tradition.

Despite its diverse sects and sectarian beliefs and doctrines, which do not have coherence and unity, Hinduism as a religious tradition has a strong principle of unity in its world-view, though it is not articulated and expressed clearly at the popular level. The world-view, which is clearly reflected in the Śruti literature, has been the source of coherence and unity of Hinduism through the centuries of its existence and development. This we can discern from the history of Hinduism. Whenever Hinduism has faced a challenge, either from within or from without, it has tried to meet the challenge, and assert itself and its identity in terms of Śruti, and its world-view. The Śurti is interpreted and re-interpreted keeping in view the nature of the challenge, but without compromising its world-view. During the times of crisis and challenge the thinkers and reformers of Hinduism invariably look to Śruti for guidance and inspiration, and Śruti has been the major source of inspiration, guidance and authority for all the thinkers and reformers of Hinduism. In other words, Hinduism for its justification and validity depends on Śruti rather than on Smṛti, and invariably invokes the authority of Śruti for its defense. The means it adopts to defend itself against various kinds of challenge is to remind itself of its world-view.

While the authority of Śruti is acceptable to all the Hindus, all the Hindus do not accept the authority of Smṛti tradition. The sectarian and regional differences in theological beliefs and doctrines, forms of worship and ritual practices among the Hindus may appear to show that Hinduism lacks coherence and unity, as what unites Hinduism, and gives it its identity is not apparent to an external view. The basic source of its inspiration, which is also the principle of its coherence and unity, is its world-view, which is largely based on and shaped by the Śruti tradition. Therefore, whenever Hinduism faces a challenge or criticism, either from within or from without, in respect of its beliefs and doctrines it tries to meet such challenges and criticisms not so much by defending the beliefs and doctrines individually as by projecting its world-view and its meaningfulness. This is not, however, the case when each sect tries to establish its supremacy over other sects or when each sect defends itself against the criticisms from other sects. It is a different problem whether the world-view of Hinduism can be the source of justification for all the sects, and their sectarian beliefs and doctrines, or whether the different sectarian theologies can be reconciled and harmonised with the world-view.

Śruti and Smṛti traditions, which form or constitute Hinduism, are not completely compatible with each other. They differ in their approaches and attitudes to some of the basic problems of religion, and also about the meaning and end of realign. Nevertheless, systematic and significant attempts are made by several thinkers and saints to reconcile and harmonise Smṛti with Śruti.

Even though all the Hindus recognise the authority of Śruti, and accept its world-view as ultimately meaningful in religious or spiritual matters, most of the Hindu religious beliefs and practices are based on and developed by Smṛti tradition. However, Hinduism in its growth and development has been influenced by both the traditions. Śruti and Smṛti are independent traditions, each having its own vision about the nature and meaning of the divine, as well as about the meaning and destiny of human existence. However, it is not possible to demarcate clearly their influence in the development of Hinduism. We cannot also say with any definiteness that one tradition is represented exclusively by Śruti, and the other by Smṛti. The distinction between them is more meaningful in terms of their basic approaches to religion. While one tradition is more philosophical in its outlook and approach, the other is more religious or theological. Now, we have to admit that philosophy and religion, at least in the past, are everywhere contenders for truth. Both are basically concerned with knowing or understanding the real or true nature of the world of human experience. We are not going to discuss here whether these two traditions basically represent the intellect and emotions of man, or his head and heart, the two faculties of man. However, it is possible for the same person to be both philosophical and religious as they represent two important aspects of human reality. Both are significant ways of looking at the world, and understanding it. Therefore, instead of trying to understand them as two alternative and competing ways of knowing or understanding the divine and its nature, but as two equally significant ways of knowing the divine then intellect and emotions, which are equally significant to human life and its fulfilment, will help in revealing the nature and meaning of the divine more meaningfully and integrally. This type of thinking or understanding will be meaningful and valid if we admit that the emotional life of man, though subjective, can nevertheless help man in knowing something significant about the nature of the divine. But when man asserts that his intellect is superior to his emotions conflict between them is inevitable. And in the conflict between the two little or no importance is given to the heart of man in knowing or revealing the nature of the divine. Although we find tension and conflict between intellect and emotions of man within the Hindu religious tradition significant attempts are, however, made to reduce the tension, and achieve harmony between them.

Intellectual or rational way of understanding is more impersonal, abstract and detached, while emotional way is more personal, passionate and imaginative. It does not matter much whether both talk of ultimate reality in divine terms as the conflict between them is not a conflict between different conceptions of reality. Religious or theological understanding of the world may not be valid and meaningful from the point of view of human intellect or rational understanding of man, but is nevertheless supremely meaningful and fulfilling as far as the emotional or devotional life of man is concerned. Religiously speaking, devotional life is fulfilling in itself, or is an end in itself whether the object of devotion or *bhakti* has any rational validity or not. Similarly, intellectual or rational understanding of the world may or may not reveal the truth about the world but it satisfies the intellect or rationality of man. These two ways of understanding represent two basic aspects of man, which are integral to his being, and find their harmony and unity in him. They are the two dominant aspects of human life, and seek satisfaction and fulfilment either independently or in co-operation with each other. Their meaningfulness is for the person who is one, and in him they are integrated. But human intellect tries to guide and even control the emotional life of man, and the emotional life of man tries to influence his intellectual life and understanding.

The two approaches need not necessarily lead to or result in conflict between philosophy and religion. Usually intellect is viewed as opposed to heart, and, therefore, philosophy and religion are viewed as two different and independent activities often coming into conflict with each other. The tension between the intellectual life of man and his emotional life is mainly because of the conflict between the claims of intellect and the demands of emotional life. But within the Hindu religious tradition, sharp distinction is not made between intellect and emotions leading to conflict and opposition between philosophy and religion, which is a characteristic of Western tradition. Intellect or head is seen in the Vedic tradition as the best or supreme in man as the word *śreṣṭha* (best or excellent) is derived from the root '*sir*' which means head.[1] But the heart of man, the seat of his emotional life, is not looked down upon. On the other hand, its importance is recognised in the religious or spiritual life of man. However, tension and conflict between the two must have been experienced quite early in the Hindu tradition as it is said in the *Atharvaveda* that the seer Aṅgirasa stitched the head and heart together, and accomplished thereby harmony between the two.[2] Vyāsa who is supposed to be the author of the *Mahābhārata* and the Purāṇas, especially *Bhāgavata Purāṇa*, explicitly states that the reason for his composing the *Bhāgavata*, a religious classic, extolling the religious life of love and devotion, after composing *Mahābhārata*, which is more intellectual and analytical, is that his quest for devotional life was not satisfied by *Mahābhārata*.[3] The devotional or religious life of man does not find its fulfilment in intellectual or rational understanding of reality.

Even though the intellect (*dhī*) of man is regarded as the seat of divine inspiration in the Veda, the heart of man is also recognised as having a significant place in the religious life of man. The seers of the Veda pray that their intellect be divinely inspired, and they regard it as the best divine gift. However, they are clear that the uninspired intellect of man is not capable of knowing or comprehending the divine. It is only when the intellect of man is divinely inspired, and made divine (*divya*) it can comprehend the divine or can become a source of knowledge of the divine. Similarly, the unregenerated heart of man cannot experience pure or unmotivated love and devotion of God. To be able to experience the divine, and be devoted to it human heart is to be divinely inspired. It is only a divinely inspired heart of man that can experience pure love and devotion to God. Thus, the intellect and heart of man can become sources of divine

---

1. *Śatapatha Brāhmaṇa*, 1.4.55; see also 6.1.1.4.
2. *Atharva-veda Saṁhitā*, 10.2.26 (*mūrdhānamasya samsivyādharva hṛdaya ca yat mastiṣkādurdhvam prerayat pavamānodhi śirṣataḥ*).
3. *Bhāgavata Purāṇa*, I.5.3-5.

knowledge, and reveal the nature of the divine only when they are divinely inspired. Then they reveal the nature of the divine more fully and integrally, as what the heart of man can know, the intellect cannot, and vice versa. It is asserted in the *Bhagavad Gītā*, which is endorsed by its various interpreters, that the higher form of devotion (*parā-bhakti*), which is an end in itself, is not different from higher knowledge (*parā-jñāna*) which is also an end in itself. *Parā-bhakti* is the same as *pārā-jñāna* as what is revealed in and through both the states is the same divine reality.[4]

In the Hindu tradition the heart of man is recognised as a faculty by means of which he experiences or comes to know the nature and meaning of love, devotion, sympathy, compassion, etc. Though thinkers, like Śaṅkara, find it difficult to reconcile and harmonise the claims of intellect with the demands of heart, relegating thereby the religious or devotional life of man to a lower level, the thinkers like Rāmānuja and the author of *Bhagavad Gītā* and *Bhāgavata* do not find it difficult to reconcile and harmonise them. Pure or unmotivated devotion to God (*parā bhakti*), according to them, is not different from higher knowledge (*parā-jñāna*). Pure devotion to God is spiritually as significant and fulfilling or emancipating as higher knowledge or *parā-jñāna*. The nature of the divine is revealed in and through both the states; their revelatory value is the same. Therefore, one does not depend for its justification and validity on the other. And as they are not seen as antagonistic or opposed to each other, the claims of one are not sought to be judged and validated in terms of the other. Both higher knowledge and higher devotion are due to divine inspiration as without being divinely inspired the intellect and heart of man cannot reveal

4. *Para-bhakti* means to realise that Vāsudeva is all (*vāsudeva sarvamiti*). It is to seek and realise God in His true nature (*tatvataḥ*). *Bhagavad Gītā*, 7.16-19; 18.55; 12.20. In the *Bhāgavata-purāṇa parā-bhakti* is also known as *nirguṇa* or *ātyantika bhakti* — *Bhāgavata*, 3.29.12-14. *Parā-bhakti* is disinterested and supreme (*nirapekṣa* and *parā*) — *Bhāgavata Purāṇa*, 11.20.35.

the divine. Just as higher knowledge (*parā-jñāna*) is not the same as ordinary intellectual or rational understanding, pure devotion is not simple emotional satisfaction. The intellect and heart of man become sources of divine revelation only when they are divinely inspired. Uninspired intellect and heart of man tend to oppose each other as they pursue different ends or forms of life, and seek different kinds of satisfaction and fulfilment. Because of the opposition between them, at the empirical level, one cannot be employed to justify and validate the claims of the other. However, the conflict or opposition is not experienced at a higher level or when they are divinely inspired. Though the manner of response to divine inspiration, on the part of intellect and heart, and the manner in which the state of inspiration is expressed by them may not be same, both find their supreme fulfilment in being divinely inspired. In the state of divine inspiration one does not experience antagonism or conflict between them. There is no conflict among the various organs of man, though each is distinct from the other, both structurally and functionally, as they find their harmony and unity in man, their guide and controller. They are enlivened and inspired by the same person whose purpose they serve. Otherwise, each is distinct from the other, and have their functional autonomy. They cannot, therefore, provide validity and justification to the claims of each other as their functions and objects are not the same. Nevertheless, they reveal and express different aspects of human reality as well as different aspects of the reality they reveal. Thus, inspired intellect and heart of man help in revealing different aspects of the divine. Though their unity is not possible at the functional level they find their harmony and unity in the divine, the ultimate source of their inspiration as well as their ultimate object.

In the Hindu religious tradition, both human intellect and heart are regarded as seats of divine inspiration though in the Śruti tradition emphasis is placed more on the intellect. In the Smṛti tradition the emphasis is more, and even exclusive, on the heart of man. However, both intellect and heart of man are recognised by both the traditions as the sources of divine knowledge or wisdom. Although subtlety (*aṇu*) and sharpness of intellect are praised in the Śruti tradition they are not, however, considered as sufficient to know the divine. To be able to receive divine light, and reveal the nature of the divine the intellect is to be divinely inspired, and made divine (*daivyā dhiya*).[5] It is only an inspired intellect that can reveal the divine which otherwise it cannot though it strives to know the divine. And it is repeatedly asserted in the Smṛti tradition that unless the heart of man is divinely inspired or without the grace of God man cannot experience pure love and devotion, and surrender himself to God totally and unconditionally. Ordinary devotion, which is emotional and motivated, can culminate in higher or disinterested devotion which is an end in itself. While ordinary devotion is a means, higher or pure devotion is an end in itself. In ordinary devotion or emotional attachment to God it is the devotee who is active, and tries to attach himself to God, while in higher devotion, which is the consummation of man's religious life, it is God who is active, and becomes attached to the devotee, and liberates him from his self-centred existence. Thus, though as means *jñāna* and *bhakti* are different, in their pure form the difference between them is obliterated. Both are divine, and are regarded as ends in themselves. However, in terms of the difference between intellect and heart as faculties of knowing the divine, different aspects of the divine are revealed. Thus, the difference in the nature of intellect and heart, as sources of knowledge of the divine, may give rise to different conceptions or views about the nature and meaning of the divine, and different forms of religious life and worship.

The two distinct ways of knowing the divine, and its nature, which are broadly speaking represented by Śruti and Smṛti, did not, however, give rise to two distinct world-views. They share the same world-view despite the difference in their understanding about the meaning and end of man's religious or spiritual life. Thus, even though Hinduism represents two

5. *Ṛgveda*, 10.176.2.

distinct forms of religious life and worship, and two distinct ways of understanding the nature and meaning of religion, it is informed by the same world-view. The basic difference between the two major forms of Hindu religious life is mainly due to difference in man's approach and attitude to the divine which is due to the importance given either to intellect or heart of man in knowing the divine. A child may not have intellectual or conceptual understanding of its mother but its love and attachment to her is more intense when compared to that of a grown-up who may know more about his or her mother, but may not have child-like attachment or love for her. Both love their mother, but that aspect of a mother which a child experiences more intensely does not come into conflict with the understanding of a grownup. Intellectual understanding of the divine may not give rise to love and devotion, and in terms of inwardly experienced devotion one may not know much or all about the divine. Therefore, intellect may not be able to understand and appreciate the sweetness of attachment to God or love and devotion to God, and, therefore, it may not be able to grasp and appreciate that aspect of the divine which is experienced in the state of devotion or as devotion itself.

In the Hindu religious tradition the intellect and heart are not seen as opposed to each other, as both are regarded as capable of knowing the nature of the divine. And even though we find tension and conflict between them in the development of Hinduism, attempts are made by most of the thinkers and saints of Hinduism to reconcile and harmonise them, and the richness and integral nature of Hinduism is due to such efforts. The tension and conflict between intellect and heart, and several attempts to reconcile them has been a prominent feature of the development of Hinduism. Almost all the major thinkers and theologians of Hinduism faced the problem of their reconciliation. However, some of the thinkers consider that the Śruti tradition of Hinduism, especially the Upaniṣads, stands for intellectual insight and understanding, and, therefore, they tried to subordinate the heart of man to his intellect. According to them, devotion and love are subjective, and, therefore, do not have the value of knowledge (*jñāna*), and objective validity. However, intellectual or rational approach to the divine will be more intelligible, significant and valid than emotional or devotional approach to the divine if one's view of the divine is impersonal. One's preference or commitment to an intellectual or rational approach to the divine presupposes one's preference or commitment to the view that the divine is impersonal. And if one's view of the divine is impersonal then his attitude to the divine would be significantly different from the one in which the divine is viewed as a personal being or is identified with God. When one is committed to the view that the divine is personal his attitude towards intellect and its place and value in knowing the nature of the divine, and, therefore, its place of importance in the religious or spiritual life of man would not be positive and significant. Instead, greater importance and value would be attached to the heart of man in knowing the divine and its nature, and is, therefore, given a place of importance in the religious life of man. Faith is more a matter of heart than of intellect.

Śruti gave rise to basically different interpretations and philosophies, like Pūrva Mīmāṁsā, on the one hand, and different schools of Vedānta, particularly Advaita Vedānta, on the other. They have very little in common except the fact that both of them are Śruti based, and accept its authority. The different schools of Vedānta also differ among themselves significantly in terms of their understanding the nature and meaning of the divine or *Brahman*. The problem whether *Brahman* is personal or impersonal or both or neither has engaged the attention of all the *Vedāntin*s. And generally speaking personal or theistic conception of the divine or *Brahman* overweighs or dominates the impersonal conception of *Brahman* in the Vedānta tradition.

Although the Purāṇas, particularly the *Bhāgavata Purāṇa*, and the Vedānta differ very significantly in their understanding of the divine one thing is commonly accepted by both of them. They accept that the divine, in the ultimate analysis, is impersonal or rather transcends the personal-impersonal dichotomy. Though the Smṛti tradition in general, and the Purāṇas in particular, identify the various sectarian deities, like Śiva and Viṣṇu, with the divine, yet they accept the ontology of the Upaniṣads which is not clearly and definitely theistic. The sincere and significant attempts made by several Smṛti thinkers to reconcile and harmonise sectarian theologies with the Vedāntic ontology show that the Smṛti tradition does not accept the theistic claims of different sects as ultimately meaningful and valid. This is not, however, the case with those *Vedāntin*s who are avowedly theistic, and are opposed to Advaita, as according to them *Brahman* is clearly personal, and is the object of higher devotion which is not different from higher *jñāna*. If we look to the Veda or Vedic *Saṁhitā*s in trying to understand the problem whether the divine is viewed by them as a personal being or as an impersonal reality permeating all that is, we have to admit that though both the views are present in the Vedic literature, the Veda is more in favour of the view that the divine is impersonal. But whether the divine is viewed as personal or impersonal devotion is regarded as the most appropriate response to the divine on the part of man. The divine is the ultimate source of inspiration of devotion in man. It inspires in man the sense of divine, and evokes in him devotion, piety and surrender. The Vedic hymns, which are primarily prayers and praises addressed to various deities, either individually or collectively, express spontaneous devotion and child-like attachment of the Vedic seers to the divine. They express devotion which is spontaneous and soul-stirring as well as the finest and sublime emotions or feelings which devotion brings forth in a person. The divinely inspired devotion stirs or moves a person as wind the forest, and he becomes attached to the divine as spontaneously as a child is attached to its mother or as water seek declivity.[6] The devotion of the Vedic seers to the divine or the deities is as passionate, intense and pure as devotion to God expressed in some of the classical Smṛti texts, like the

---

6. *Ṛgveda*, 10.39.1; 8.32.23; 1.114.9; 8.61.12; 8.6.34.

Bhāgavata. The only difference between them is that the nature of the divine revealed during the state of devotion or as devotion itself is represented or expressed in personal terms in the classical *Bhakti* tradition. While, according to the Vedic tradition, divine light or divine inspiration is essential to know the divine and its nature, the grace of God is essential to experience pure love and devotion, according to *bhakti* tradition. Basically both the traditions are religious in the sense that in both man is moved or stirred by the divine, and in this regard there is no fundamental difference between them.

If the divine is viewed as impersonal the relationship between the divine and the world, on the one hand, and between the divine and man on the other will be significantly different from the relationships if the divine is viewed as a personal being or God. According to the impersonal conception of the divine, the divine has become all that is by way of self-manifestation, or all that is there is a self-manifestation or self-expression of the divine. Therefore, to know the divine is to know it as being present within all that is there, including man. And as all that is there is a self-manifestation of the divine the divine is the unity or oneness of all that is. The divine is that which is being manifested or expressed in and through all that is. But to see the divine within the world of manifestation is not to identify the divine with any one phenomenon of nature but to see or realise it as the common source as well as the inner unity of all that is. To see the unity of all that is there is not to arrive at the idea of what is common to all, as is done in speculative metaphysics, but to see or experience the divine as that because of which everything is what it is, and is sustained. In other words, it is to know the *ātman* or essence of all, including man. The divine sustains all, and reveals itself as the essence or *ātman* of each and every phenomenon, including man. It is the essence or *ātman* of fire, water, earth, or all that is there, including man. In becoming several objects gold does not lose its essence, and to see gold in all that is made of gold is to see it as the essence and unity of all that is made of gold. This is possible only when one knows the nature of gold so that he can see gold in all that is made of gold. The divine in manifesting itself in the form of the world has not lost its nature or essence, and, therefore, to know the divine is to know it in and through all the forms of its manifestation. To know or realise that all that is there is a manifestation of the divine is to know the divine as that which is being manifested in and through all the forms of its manifestation. In other words, the divine in itself cannot be known at the level of manifestation, as the divine cannot be identified with any one or all the forms of its manifestation. It is more than its manifestations. But as the divine has not lost its essence or nature in manifesting itself it can be known in and through the forms of its manifestation as that which is commonly revealed in and through all the forms of its manifestation. And in knowing the essence of all that is direct knowledge of one's own essence or self is highly significant and valuable. If the same reality has become all that is, including man, then what is there outside of man is also present within man, and, therefore, what forms the essence of the world is also the essence of man or his *ātman*. If what is present within man is also present without him, direct and immediate knowledge of one's own essence or *ātman* will help man in knowing the essence of the word. Though the divine is the essence of all that is there the way it manifests itself in each phenomenon will be different. The essence of water is not the same as that of fire or air. The essence of man is not the same as the essence of an inanimate thing or phenomenon. Therefore, to know the essence of the manifested world is not to know what is abstractly common to all the phenomena, but to know that because of which every thing or phenomenon is what it is, and is sustained. Without its essence a thing or phenomenon cannot be what it is.

The divine is not a material or physical reality with a determinable nature so that its nature or essence will remain the same in all the forms of its manifestation. The divine in its absolute freedom, for its creativity is the same as its freedom, is not guided and controlled by another reality. In its creativity it manifests or expresses itself in infinite forms. It is not possible to determine the nature of divine creativity, or to set limits to its capacity to express itself in varied forms. The capacity of the divine to express itself is infinite. It can express itself in infinite forms, and, therefore, to see the divine in and through the forms of its expression is to know it as that which is being expressed in and through all the forms of its manifestation. It is the essence and inner unity of all the forms of its manifestation. Whether different phenomena can have a common essence is more a philosophical problem. But to see the divine as the essence or nature of all is to know the divine as the ultimate source as well as the reality that sustains all. Just as a phenomenon is what it is because of its essence, the whole world is what it is because of the divine, the ultimate source of its existence as well as its inner unity or oneness. This is a matter of divine inspiration. Or it is the ontological vision or world-view of Hindu religious tradition. It is more a matter of vision, and an object of faith. It cannot be demonstrated either empirically or rationally though people try to find empirical evidence and rational justification in its favour. Such an ontological vision or the world-view has given rise to or inspired a major form of religious life within the Hindu tradition which we may identify as the religion of *dharma*.

Dharma and *svabhāva* (nature) refer to the same thing. For instance, the capacity to burn is the *svabhāva* or nature of fire, and burning a thing is its *dharma*. *Dharma* is the manifestation of *svabhāva* or the manifestation of *svabhāva* is known as *dharma*. *Dharma* refers to the dynamic aspect of a thing or a phenomenon. And in the case of natural phenomena, *dharma* and *svabhāva*, are used interchangeably, though they are viewed as distinct. The *dharma* of a thing depends upon the *svabhāva* of the thing. A thing or a phenomenon cannot manifest that which is not inherent within itself. Though *dharma* is used to signify the nature of a thing or a phenomenon it is mostly used to mean the nature of a thing in its manifested form. Therefore, *dharma* is the law of a thing or a phenomenon which it cannot violate. As the laws of nature flow from the *svabhāva* of nature to see the divine within nature is to know it as that which governs nature thorough its own laws. Since the laws of nature are an expression of the divine they are sacred.

In the Vedic context *ṛta*, which is the forerunner of the concept of *dharma*, is both identified with and distinguished from *satya* or Truth. *Ṛta* is distinct from *satya* in the sense that it is the *satya* as revealed within creation or within the realm of manifestation, whereas *satya* refers to the truth in its unmanifested state. Though the word *ṛta* is used to mean Truth or Reality (*ṛtam bṛhat*) in majority of the cases of its usage in the Veda it refers to truth as revealed within creation or within the realm of manifestation. It reveals itself in and through all the deities or in and through the varied workings of nature. It is that which is commonly revealed by all the deities; it is their defining principle or what constitutes the divinity of the deities (*viśve devatvam nāma ṛtam*).[7] It is the supreme form of the deities (*devānām śreṣṭan vapu*).[8] It encompasses the whole world, but is not encompassed by any other principle or reality. It is enveloped by itself, and is the sole controller of the whole world. It is self-governed or it is its own controller (*ṛtena ṛtam niyatam*), but it regulates and governs the whole world. The deities are the manifested forms of *ṛta*, and are, therefore, the source of its revelation. The deities know *ṛta* as it is the source of their being. All the deities are addressed in the Veda as the source of revelation of *ṛta* or they reveal *ṛta* (*ṛta bhodi* or *ṛta cit*).[9] They are also addressed as its protectors and leaders (*gopa* and *radhya*). They observe *ṛta*, and further the manifestation of *ṛta* or help its increase or extension. As they are born of *ṛta* their truth depends on their being the manifestations of *ṛta*. They are naught without *ṛta* or have no existence independently of *ṛta*. They are born of *ṛta* and are governed by it as well. They delight in *ṛta* which is their abode, and in their own individual ways spread or extend it, and help in its fulfilment. *Ṛta* is the nature of the divine as it reveals or manifests itself within the

7. *Ṛgveda*, 10.35.8; see also 1.68.2.

8. *Ibid.*, 5.62.1; see also 4.7.7.

9. *Ibid.*, 7.76.4; 4.47.8; 5.58.8; 5.66.1.

realm of manifestation. It is divine, and can inspire devotion, worship and prayer in man. It can open the deaf ears of man to divine influence, and its light can destroy the sins of man.[10]

The knowledge of *ṛta*, which is due to its own inspiration, makes or transforms a person into a *kavi* or a *ṛṣi*, terms which refer to divinely inspired state of human existence. Human intellect that is not inspired or influenced by *ṛta* cannot help man in knowing the truth or in knowing the divine nature of the world. Ordinary or uninspired intellect of man can only help man in knowing or understanding the phenomenal aspect of the creation, but not its hidden divine aspect. It is because of divine inspiration one can see the world in its divine aspect or as a manifestation of the divine, and can realise the divine as the inner ruler and oneness of the world. The seers are candid in admitting that while they were groping in darkness not knowing the truth it is the light of *ṛta* or the light born of *ṛta* that led or helped them in knowing the truth. They are then able to see nature in its divine aspect or as a creative manifestation of the divine. They are then known as *kavi* or *ṛṣi*. They are the knowers of *ṛta* (*ṛtacit*), and are filled with *ṛta* or are full of *ṛta* (*ṛtavan*).[11]

Ṛta is the manifested form of *satya*, or *ṛta* is *satya* as revealed within the world of manifestation. It is divine, and comprehends within itself the whole world, and governs it. And to know *ṛta* is to live it and uphold it, and help in its increase or extension. To live in accordance with *ṛta* or to extend it to one's life is not to follow something or some laws which are extraneous to man, but to live in accordance with *ṛta* as it reveals itself within one's own being or within one's own nature. Though man can conceptually distinguish and even detach himself from nature, and view himself as different from nature, in reality, he is an integral part of it. He belongs to nature, and is controlled and governed by the same reality which governs nature. In his

---

10. *Ṛgveda*, 4.23.8.
11. *Ibid.*, 2.23.15; 4.3.4; 7.76.4.

uninspired or unillumined state of existence man thinks of himself as different from and unrelated to nature. It is the divine light of inspiration that helps him realise the divine nature of the world, and his oneness with it. The divine lives within man and sustains his existence as it dwells within the world and sustains it.

R̥ta manifests and reveals itself in man as *dharma* or righteousness. Therefore, to be divine is to be righteous or to live the life of *r̥ta*. And to be righteous is to participate in the divine process (*yajña*) involved in the creation and sustenance of the world. The divine process of creation is expressed by the concept of *yajña* which stands primarily for the act whereby the divine has become all that is, or has manifested itself in the form of the world. The primordial divine *yajña* enacted by the divine *puruṣa* whereby the world has come into existence is being enacted by the various deities at the cosmic level. The deities are born of divine *yajña*. They participate in the process of divine *yajña*, and extend it in their own characteristic ways at the cosmic level or at the level of nature, and help in fulfilling the divine purpose of realising itself in and through all that it has become.

The divine *yajña* is to be extended by man at the human level. Every act of man attains the significance of *yajña*, and serves the divine purpose if it is done by him in imitation of the primordial *yajña* enacted by the divine, and is being perpetuated by the deities at the cosmic level. It is to participate in the divine process involved in creation, and serve thereby the divine purpose. In most of the cases of its usage it is said that *yajña* is to be extended (*tan*) (*yajñam atanvata*) but not performed as it is in the case of *yajña* ritually performed. *Yajña* that is ritually performed is a symbolic act in which all the elements or components employed are symbolic representation of cosmic reality.

The Vedic sense of *yajña* or its original meaning is well represented in the *Bhagavad Gītā* in which it is not seen as a ritual act. *Yajña* is any act done as an offering to God. An act done as an offering to God is *yajña*, and culminates in the realisation that the life of man is itself a *yajña*. It is meant to serve and fulfil God's purpose in creating the world. Then all the actions of man or rather the whole life of man is seen as serving and fulfilling the divine purpose. As expressed in the *Bhagavad Gītā*, the act of offering, the offering, the person who offers and the deity to whom it is offered, Agni into which the offering is made as well as the object of its attainment are all *Brahman*.[12] While the actions performed with the intention or purpose of serving or satisfying one's self or ego will have no divine significance or the significance of *yajña*, and bind a person, the same when performed in the spirit of *yajña* or as an offering to God will acquire divine significance, and liberate the person. Even the intellectual life of man acquires religious or divine significance when it is consecrated to the divine, or when the thoughts and wisdom of man are directed towards the divine, and are offered to it as an act of worship. It is then known as *jñāna-yajña*. In the *Mahābhārata* it is said that a śūdra can attain the highest and be liberated when he regards his ordained duty of service as his *yajña* (*sevā-yajña*).[13] The *sevā-yajña* of a śūdra will have the same significance as *jñāna-yajña*. The socially assigned duties differ from caste to caste, and also according to one's station of life, but all of them will gain spiritual significance and become means of divine realisation when they are performed with the sense of *yajña*, or as an offering to the divine, or as an act of worship of the divine.

According to this view of religion as *dharma*, there are no specific or special acts which are religious, and whose performance will help man in realising the highest end of life or the divine. Depending upon one's social identity and station of life one performs certain duties; and when they are done as one's form or mode of *yajña* or one's offering to the divine they become

12. *Bhagavad Gītā*, 4.24. The idea is present in the *Ṛgveda* when it is said that one should act with *haviṣmata manasa* or with a sense of (offering) *yajña* — *Ṛgveda* 7.67.1; 7.12.2.

13. *Sevā-yajña* is also known as *paricāra-yajña* in the *Mahābhārata* — *Mahābhārata*, Śānti-parva, 238.12; Anuśāsana-parva 141.57,60.

his means of divine realisation. When one acts with the realisation that everything is a manifestation of the divine the acts become an offering to the divine or attain the sanctity and significance of worship. It is said that a person becomes spiritual or religious, and his life attains divine significance when he enjoys the fruits of his actions as a remnant or left-over of *yajña* (*yajña avaśiṣṭa*) or as sanctified by *yajña*.[14] One's existence is due to divine *yajña*, and, therefore, has the significance of *yajña*. The ultimate meaning of life, according to this view of religion, is to realise the divine in what one is and does. In other words, the meaning and end of religion conceived as *dharma* is to realise the divine in what one is and does, or to regard one's life as a *yajña*. Keeping this end in view, several religious acts are prescribed, which are of symbolic significance and value only, but are helpful in realising the highest end of life. Thus, *yajña* as a ritual act performed out of a sense of duty (*dharma*), and the *yajña* that is divine worship are different. The former is a means to the realisation of the latter which is an end in itself. The latter is not an act having religious significance and value, but is a form of life lived in imitation of the divine *yajña*. *Yajña* is divine, and is an end in itself. It is the form of religious life and worship for those who follow the tradition of the Veda. To worship the divine is to participate in the divine process involved in the creation of the world. We do not find the concept of *mokṣa* as the meaning of human existence either in the Vedic *Saṁhitā*s or in the Upaniṣads.[15] *Yajña* is a religious concept central to the

14. The idea that *dharma* consists in enjoying everything as a left over of *yajña* or as sanctified by *yajña* occurs very frequently in the Śānti and Anuśāsana parvas of *Mahābhārata* — *Mahābhārata* Śānti-parva, 11.24. In the *Bhagavad Gītā*, which is an integral part of *Mahābhārata*, it is said that one who enjoys everything as a left over of *yajña* (*yajña śiṣṭāmṛtabhujo yānti brahma sanātanam*) attains *Brahman* (4.31); one who enjoys everything as *yajña śiṣṭa* is free from all sins (*yajña śiṣṭāsina santo mucyante sarva kilbiṣaiḥ*) (3.13).

15. The concept of *mokṣa* as developed in the schools of Vedānta is absent in the Upaniṣads. In almost all the major Upaniṣads the realisation of truth is seen as an end in itself. Śaṅkara endorses the same when he says that the knowledge of supreme *Brahman* is never utilised for

→

Veda, and signifies the meaning and end of Vedic form of religious life. The Upaniṣads also do not talk of *mokṣa* directly. It was introduced, and given importance or prominence by the interpreters of the Upaniṣads. The Pūrva Mīmāṁsā which has developed a form of religious life based on or inspired by the Veda, and is older than the Vedānta, has no real concern either for God or for *mokṣa* or liberation. Its primary or major concern is for *dharma* understood as religious action.

Dharma is central to Vedic form of Hinduism, and to an extent it also represents the Smṛti form of Hinduism as reflected and represented by the epic texts of *Rāmāyaṇa* and *Mahābhārata*, particularly the latter. As pointed out earlier, *dharma* is a development of Vedic *ṛta*, and both are based on or are inspired by the same world-view. The world-view that gave rise to the concepts of *ṛta* and *yajña* is also shared by the Smṛti tradition. The Vedic concept of *ṛta* and the Smṛti concept of *dharma*, as represented in the epic text of *Mahābhārata*, are based on or inspired by the same world-view. Both represent a similar type of thinking or understanding about the nature and meaning of religion. According to the tradition that gave birth to the concept of *dharma*, the meaning and end of religion is to live a life of *dharma*, and *dharma* comprehends the whole life of man, including his social life. The perfect state of *dharma* is figuratively expressed in the Smṛti literature as *dharma* standing, as it were, on its four feet. It is only when the hold of *dharma* on people or their faith in it gets weakened, the other major form of Hinduism, according to which *bhakti* or passionate love and devotion to God is the meaning and end of religion, gains ascendancy. The ideal state of perfection of human life and civilisation is represented by *satya-yuga* or *kṛta-yuga* (an epoch that is accomplished by human effort) in which *dharma* flourishes and prospers completely or stands, as it were, on its

→ attaining human ends (*tad vijñānasya kecit puruṣārtha sādhane aviniyogāt*) — Śaṅkara's commentary on the *Bṛhadāraṇyaka Upaniṣad*, 1.4.10. Except in the *Śvetāśvatara Upaniṣad* (6.16) the concept of *mokṣa* is absent in all the major Upaniṣads.

four feet. When the *dharma* form of religious life gets weakened more and more in successive ages they are described in terms of the relative strength of *dharma*. With the decline in the *dharma* form of religious life, the devotional form of religious life has gained ascendancy or has become the dominant form of Hindu religious life. And the *dharma* form of religious life, and the ontological vision that gave rise to it are more or less replaced by the *bhakti* form of religious life based on the theistic vision of the divine. However, both are equally significant, and are major forms of Hindu religious life though they differ basically in their understanding or vision of the nature and meaning of the divine, and man's attitude to the divine. It is said in the *Bhāgavata Purāṇa* that when *jñāna* (knowledge or wisdom) and *vairāgya* (detachment or renunciation) become old and weak, *bhakti* becomes young and strong.[16] The Smṛti classification of historical time into four aeons (*yuga*) or ages which is done in terms of the relative strength and prosperity of *dharma* in each age shows that till the dominance of Smṛti tradition, the meaning of Hinduism was defined in terms of *ṛta* or *dharma*, or *dharma* had been the meaning and end of Hindu religious life. And with the decline in the *dharma* form of religious life, *bhakti* form of religious life gained ascendancy and popularity.

Dharma is conceptually akin to *ṛta*, and is even identified with it. The only difference between *ṛta* and *dharma* is that the meaning of *dharma* is defined more in relation to man and his conduct at all levels. *Ṛta* is also conceived as moral law but it is defined primarily as the divine law that is immanent within the whole of creation, regulating and governing it. No realm of reality is excluded from its influence and control. All the realms of creation, like *ādhidaivika*, *ādhibhautika* and *adhyātmika* are under its sway though the manner of its manifestation, and, therefore, its meaning differs from realm to realm. *Ṛta* is the natural order that reveals itself in and through the world or

16. *Bhakti* is portrayed as a young and healthy mother, and *jñāna* and *vairāgya* are portrayed as her two decrepit and fallen sons — *Bhāgavata Purāṇa*, *māhātyam*, 1.1.38-45.

nature, and reveals itself as moral law within man, regulating and governing human conduct at all levels. *Dharma* is also ontological in its conception; it holds together and sustains all that is there.[17] However, it is used more significantly to mean the law or principle that regulates and governs human conduct at all levels. It holds together and governs all that is human. *Dharma* is *ṛta* as it manifests itself within the human realm, and gains its significance in relation to human conduct at all levels. *Dharma* is also cosmic and divine as *ṛta* is, but its primary significance is in relation to man. However, in the Smṛti tradition of Hinduism the cosmic meaning of *dharma* is not given so much importance as its human significance and value. While *ṛta* is both cosmic and human, *dharma* is more human than cosmic.

Our concern with the concept of *dharma* in this chapter is not to analyse and understand the general meaning of *dharma*, but to understand it as a form of religious life or its meaning as religion. Hinduism, for most of the Hindus, means either Hindu *dharma* or Sanātana *dharma*. To understand Hinduism or Hindu *dharma* as Sanātana *dharma* is to view it as emanating ultimately from the divine, and is, therefore, timeless. Every religion is timeless as the source of origin of every major religion is ultimately God or the divine. In elucidating the nature of *dharma* it is commonly asserted in the Smṛti literature that it is timeless or Sanātana (*esa dharmaḥ sanātanaḥ*). It amounts to saying that all laws, including social and moral laws, are ultimately related to the divine or flow from the nature of the divine. Though every *dharma* appears to have been propounded by someone he is, however, not regarded as the real author of it. He only claims to himself the agency of transmitting or communicating the *dharma*, which he has received from some deity, to future generations. The origin of every *dharma*, howsoever, mundane it seems to be, is traced to a deity who is regarded as its ultimate source. But, the moral laws are regarded

17. *Bṛhadāraṇyaka Upaniṣad*, 1.4.14; *Mahānārāyaṇa Upaniṣad*, 78.6; 79.7. In the *Bhāgavata Purāṇa* Viṣṇu is addressed as *dharma svarūpa* (3.16.22).

as eternal as they flow from or are based on human nature which in its essence is unchanging, though man in his wisdom understands their significance differently while adapting them to his changing needs and circumstances. And in the process of adapting them to new circumstances they are at times modified or are given a new meaning and value.

While Buddhism is the *dharma* as discovered and propounded by the Buddha, Hinduism, at least conceptually, is not propounded by any one person or group of persons though several persons played a very significant role in its formulation and development. Although the Hindu *dharma* is not known after a person, the names of several persons are associated with its articulation and development. In other words, *dharma* as flowing or emanating ultimately from the nature of the divine is eternal. Within the Hindu tradition no one has claimed to himself the authorship of *dharma*, either in its universal form or in the particular forms of its manifestation. The names of all those persons associated with *dharma*, either in its universal form are in its particular forms of manifestation, are only its enunciators or at the most interpreters.

What is *dharma* or what is the nature and meaning of *dharma* as a form of religious life? What is the meaning of *dharma* as religion or more specifically Hinduism? *Dharma* as in the case of *ṛta* is also identified with Truth or *satya*. In the *Bṛhadāraṇyaka Upaniṣad* it is said that there is nothing higher than *dharma* (*dharmāt param nāsti*).[18] That which is *dharma* is also the truth (*yo vai dharmaḥ satyam vai tat*), and, therefore, one who knows *dharma* knows the truth, and vice versa.[19] *Dharma* is the sweetness or delight as well as the sustaining principle of all that is. It is regarded as supreme because all the worlds or all that is there is established or founded on *dharma* (*dharmaḥ visvaśya jagataḥ pratiṣṭhā*).[20] *Dharma* comprehends

18. *Bṛhadāraṇyaka Upaniṣad*, 1.4.14.
19. *Ibid.*, 1.4.14.
20. *Mahānārāyaṇa Upaniṣad*, 79.7.

all the worlds, and all the worlds are held together by *dharma*. It is ontological as it is based on Truth or is an expression of Truth. Nevertheless, it is not the same as or identical with truth as in that case there will be no need for a separate understanding of the nature of *dharma* as understanding the nature of truth will be sufficient to understand the nature of *dharma*. Knowing or understanding the nature of truth, though helps in understanding the nature of *dharma*, is not the same as knowing or understanding the nature of *dharma*. However, both are interrelated as what is *dharma* in any given situation or context can be known only in relation to the conception of truth one holds. Divine and *dharma* are related as ultimately *dharma* is defined in terms of the divine. The meaning of *dharma* follows from the conception of the divine, or the meaning of *dharma* is conceived in relation to the meaning of the divine. And the ultimate object of *dharma* is to lead one to the realisation of the divine.

Dharma is defined as regulating and governing the conduct of man. It is primarily concerned with the conduct of a person either as an individual or as a member of a community or society. It is that which inspires man to act (in a particular way or in accordance with a tradition). Conduct is the defining characteristic of *dharma* (*ācāra lakṣṇaṇo dharmaḥ*).[21] In view of the several meanings given to the word *dharma* or the various definitions of it, it is really difficult to ascertain the primary or basic meaning of *dharma*. It can mean morality, righteousness, code of conduct, either individual or social, which depends upon the social status and station of life of an individual. It can mean the nature or character of a thing or a phenomenon, and also the various elements of nature. It can also mean justice. However, in its functional aspect signifying duties of an individual, individual or social, its meaning is liable to modification or change from time to time, depending upon the social and individual circumstances. In this sense *dharma* is

21. *Mahābhārata*, Anuśāsana-parva, 104.9; Śānti-parva, 132.15.

not universal as the same *dharma* is not valid in relation to all the castes and stations of life as well as to all the ages. It can be changed, modified and even suspended in times of crisis or emergency. And as the nature of a thing, it is the same as the defining characteristic of a thing. What is *dharma* has exercised the great minds of Hinduism, and no one definition of it is accepted as the definition of it. In the *Mahābhārata*, considered primarily as a treatise on *dharma*, several definitions of it are attempted and discussed, and in all of them the meaning of *dharma* is understood in relation to right conduct of man. Some of the definitions of *dharma* that received final approval and are considered universal are: "*Dharma* is what one does not expect it to be done to himself he should not do to others,"[22] "*dharma* is that which promotes the welfare of all".[23]

All other texts that deal with *dharma*, like the various Dharma-śāstras, are not so much interested in defining *dharma* as in specifying its content and meaning in relation to various contexts and situations, either individual or social. However, they agree that the meaning and validity of *dharma* in relation to the conduct of man change according to the changing circumstances. The various texts on *dharma*, therefore, try to define or determine the meaning and value of *dharma* in relation to changing circumstances of man, both individual and social. But, all these texts accept the basic meaning of *dharma* even though they differ in its interpretation and application. And when it is asserted that the *dharma* of an individual depends upon his nature (*svabhāva*), which is in accordance with the three *guṇa*s that constitute his nature, no significant attempt is made to understand whether there is something universal in human nature so that what is meaningful and valid with regard to a person or group of persons can be valid universally. The Dharma-śāstras somehow tend to think that there is no *dharma* which is

22. *Mahābhārata* Anuśāsana-parva, 113.8; see also Śānti-parva, 259.25-26; *Bhāgavata Purāṇa*, 6.16.9.

23. *Ibid.*, Śānti-parva 259.25.

universal and unchanging, and, therefore, meaningful and valid to all. Such a view of *dharma* entertained in the Dharma-śāstras gave rise to the view that the meaning of *dharma* is relative, and its validity is situational or contextual. But this view that the meaning and validity of *dharma* depend more on the situation or context than on human nature goes against the basic meaning of *dharma*.

Is it possible to determine or define the nature of *dharma per se* or in itself? The problem of understanding the nature and meaning of *dharma* in itself or *per se* is meaningful because when a tradition tries to determine the nature of *dharma*, according to the context or situation of an individual or society, the tradition must have an understanding of the nature of *dharma* as such so that what it can mean in a given situation or context, or how to interpret it in relation to a given situation or context can be determined. Unless there is a clear and definite understanding of the nature of *dharma* as such the meaning and validity of *dharma* in relation to a given situation or context, whether individual or social, cannot be decided or determined. We cannot say justifiably that the nature of *dharma* is situational or contextual, or *dharma* has no nature or character of its own independently of a given situation or context, for in that case we cannot even understand and determine the meaning of *dharma* in a given situation. At the same time, we cannot say that *dharma* is something abstract or metaphysical, and is, therefore, eternal and unchanging. What is *dharma* in itself? What is its religious significance or value or how to understand *dharma* as religion? Just as the nature of *ṛta* is conceived in ontological terms or in terms of the divine, *dharma* is also defined in ontological terms. *Dharma* is that which flows from the nature of the divine or is in accordance with the nature of the divine. The meaning of *dharma* depends ultimately upon the view or conception of the divine, and the way it is related to the world and man. If the divine is conceived as a personal being or God who can reveal His will and intention in creating the world, then His word will acquire the character of *dharma*. In other words, the word of God will be the *dharma* for those who believe in the personal nature of the divine. But according to Hinduism of Śruti tradition, *dharma* is not the word of God for in the Śruti tradition, the divine is not clearly viewed as a personal being. The divine is immanent within creation, and reveals itself in and through creation, its own creative self-expression or manifestation. There is no conception of a special revelation in the Hinduism of Śruti tradition. The divine can be known by all those who want to know it. According to the *Ṛgveda*, all see it and hear it though very few people are aware of that fact, or while seeing and hearing it, people do not see it and hear it.[24] Many people do not know it though in reality it is being seen by them. As the divine is immanent within creation anyone who wants to know it can know it. Our knowledge of the divine does not, therefore, depend on the special revelation of the divine. What is an act of self-expression or manifestation to the divine is an act of revelation to man. The divine is self-evident as it is essentially spiritual. Therefore, the object of all religious preparation, according to Hinduism, is to get rid off or overcome that which prevents one from seeing or knowing the divine which is eternally self-revealing. However, as the world of manifestation is infinitely rich and varied the nature of the divine that is revealed in and through any one phenomenon will not be the same as it is revealed in and through other phenomena. Similarly, within the human realm also the divine reveals itself in various ways, or the manner or mode of its revelation may not be same in all human beings. Human nature is as variegated as the nature outside of him. It is not easy to define or determine human nature, as man is a creative being. There is nothing fixed about human nature, so that what is meaningful and valid to someone is meaningful and valid to all.

Although Hinduism cherishes certain values like kindness, non-violence, compassion as universally valid, what is really religious or divine about *dharma* is the recognition that all that a human being is and does is a manifestation of the divine. Therefore, when one realises that one's way of worship of the

24. *Ṛgveda*, 10.71.4.

divine or his *yājña* consists in performing one's duties, his life and conduct attain divine significance. When one sees within oneself and in one's nature the manifestation of the divine whatever one does will be his form of worship of the divine, or his form of *yajña*. Whatever one is capable of doing and achieving will acquire religious or divine significance and value when one sees in one's life the manifestation of the divine. Then all of man's actions will gain the significance of *yajña*, and become his means of divine realisation. What is spiritually or religiously significant is not what one does, but the sense or attitude with which he acts. Whatever a man does will gain the status of *dharma* or acquires the significance of *yajña* when it is done as ultimately serving the purpose of the divine. On the other hand, when one acts to achieve either his own purpose or that of society it cannot mean *dharma* in the religious sense. Just as every act can be an act of *yajña* if it is offered to the divine, or when one sees in his actions the means of serving and fulfilling the divine purpose, similarly what one does can attain the significance of *dharma* if one acts with the realisation that one's nature is a manifestation of the divine. Without such realisation the actions cannot acquire the significance or character of *dharma*, and become a means of divine realisation. *Dharma* is to do one's duty, which is in accordance with one's nature, with the realisation that in doing one's duty one is serving the divine purpose. It is the sense or attitude with which one acts that distinguishes an ordinary act from that of *dharma*. If one sees in one's actions the means of fulfilling one's own purposes such actions cannot gain the significance and value of *dharma*. But the same when performed with the sense or realisation of serving the divine purpose (*yajña*), they will acquire the significance and value of *dharma*.

With the dominance of Smṛti tradition a major shift had taken place in the life of Hinduism affecting its meaning and development. We do not find in the Śruti literature any emphasis on doing something other than one's duty or something special which is regarded as specifically religious or as having religious value. To be religious is to follow one's *dharma* as *dharma* is the meaning of religion. Although the meaning of *dharma* varies from situation to situation and from community to community, and also from time to time which is mostly due to change in the mode of man's understanding and circumstances there is no radical change in the basic idea that *dharma* means doing one's duty as an act of worship (*yajña*) of the divine, or one's way of serving and fulfilling the divine purpose in creating the world. In other words, *dharma* means doing everything with the sense and realisation of serving and fulfilling the divine purpose, or as an act of divine worship. Society is also a form of divine manifestation, and in serving it one serves the divine provided one sees the society (*virāṭ*) as a manifestation of the divine. In this sense *dharma* is not fundamentally different from *ṛta*; only *dharma* is mostly conceived in human terms, and is related to human conduct at all levels. *Ṛta* is *dharma* as it reveals itself within human nature. *Ṛta* is conceived as controlling the movements of the sun and other planets. It manifests itself in and through all the laws of nature, but *dharma* is not so described. Otherwise, *dharma* is also seen as saving man from sin, just as *ṛta* does. In the story of Dharmavyādha, an ascetic who acquired some supernatural powers due to his austerities and penance is not considered a knower of *dharma* or as religiously virtuous when compared to a dutiful housewife or a butcher. The latter are regarded as greater than the ascetic because of their truthfulness to *dharma*. It is said in the *Bṛhadāraṇyaka Upaniṣad* that because of *dharma* an ordinary and weak citizen can hope to defeat a king or be equal to him as it is the *dharma* which is supreme, and rules both the strong and the weak or the king and his subjects.[25]

The specific duties of individuals and communities may change from time to time and from place to place, but thereby they do not lose their dhārmic character and value if they are done with the sense of serving the divine purpose or as an act of worship of the divine. Hinduism of Smṛti tradition accepts the

---

25. *Bṛhadāraṇyaka Upaniṣad*, 1.4.14.

Sāṁkhya categories of *prakṛti* and *puruṣa* without accepting its dualistic ontology with a view to explaining the differences or multiplicity. *Prakṛti* and *puruṣa* are not viewed as ontologically independent, as in Sāṁkhya, but as forming the two-fold nature of the divine. They are conceived as forming the body and self of the divine or God. Therefore, the multiplicity is equally a manifestation of the divine as *prakṛti* or the physical or material side of creation forms the body of the divine. The idea or the vision that all the varied forms of manifestation that constitute the world are equally the manifestation of the divine is central to the concept of *dharma*, as without such a vision *dharma* loses its religious significance and value. Such a vision of the divine is the foundation of *dharma* as a religious way of life. Therefore, to be divine or to realise the divine which one is already, as everything is a manifestation of the divine, one has to realise consciously that all that he is and does is divine. According to this view, there is no religious form of life which is completely different from or other than the ordinary or mundane form of life. Ordinary or mundane form of life gains religious significance and value when one's vision or understanding is divinely transformed. It is said in the *Ṛgveda* that when the divine is realised every act of man will be an act of *yoga*, and becomes a means of praise and glorification of the divine. Even the ordinary act of harvesting will then become an act of *yoga* and a praise of the divine (*yoge yoge tava staram*).[26] We do not find in the Śruti tradition of Hinduism a demand to renounce or give up the ordinary life to lead a different kind of life which is regarded as religious. What is required to be religious is to bring about a total change in one's vision or understanding. Ordinary vision of differences is to be transformed into a vision of divine oneness, so that one sees the world as a manifestation of the divine, and regards every act of his as an act of worship of the divine, or as his *dharma*.

Before we discuss the second major and dominant stream or tradition of Hinduism we have to keep in mind one or two

---

26. *Ṛgveda*, 1.30.7.

important things. In the formation and development of Hinduism we can discern the influence of two streams of thought and two major forms of religious life and worship. The intention here is not to maintain that the two traditions of Śruti and Smṛti developed themselves independently of each other, each maintaining its own individual identity. However, many scholars on Hinduism subscribe to the view that Hinduism proper emerged long after the close of Śruti tradition which they prefer to identify as Brāhmaṇism. Some even tend to think that Hinduism consists of two alien traditions, one developed by the Āryans, and represented by the Śruti tradition, and the other by the Draviḍian people, and represented by the Smṛti tradition. Though theoretically speaking the two traditions are independent and distinct, and are not completely compatible with each other, both of them constantly interacted with each other, and each has significantly influenced the other. Also each has tried to reconcile itself with the other so as to achieve harmony between themselves. And the Hinduism as we know it, or the Hinduism as it is believed in and practised by almost all the Hindus is not developed exclusively on the basis of either Śruti or Smṛti, but is a result of the process of reconciliation and harmonisation between the two traditions. However, occasionally each tradition has tried to dominate, and even submerge the other. We find a subtle form of tension between them due to the attempts on the part of each to prove or establish its own superior meaningfulness and validity. It is a fact that in the development of Hinduism each tradition has tried to dominate the other. Though the tension between them has not resulted in disharmony and open conflict, yet the tension between them has remained a feature of Hinduism which has greatly contributed to its growth and development.

Now, instead of viewing Śruti and Smṛti as representing two distinct religious traditions belonging to two distinct ethnic groups and cultures, each trying to maintain its individual identity, we can view them and their origin, as pointed out earlier, in terms of the two major faculties of man. They represent the two dominant aspects of human life, one representing human intellect and the other the human heart, or one representing the rational and even scientific outlook of man, and the other the emotional or devotional side of man. The head and heart of man are in conflict with each other not only within the Hindu religious tradition but also in other religious traditions of the world. The conflict between the head and heart of man is universal. It is more or less a conflict between man's rational and scientific outlook and his emotional or devotional attitude to the world. In the Indian tradition it is the tension between *dhi* or *buddhi* or intellect, the seat of reflective or rational understanding in man, and *hr̥daya* or heart, the seat of emotional and devotional life of man. One stream or tradition is based more on man's intellect, and tries to understand the nature and meaning of the world in a dispassionate and detached way, while the other in which heart plays an important role in understanding the nature and meaning of the world is more passionate and involved. But both can be sources of religion or both can give rise to religious way of life if they are divinely inspired. Then without being indifferent or antagonistic to the claims of each other, they can find their harmony in the divine. An uninspired intellect finds itself in conflict with an uninspired heart, and vice versa. Though one cannot provide validity or justification for the claims of the other, both can reveal the nature of the divine more integrally when they are divinely inspired. This is not the proper place to discuss whether the claims of an inspired heart can have any cognitive value, and whether an inspired intellect can give birth to a life of love and devotion.

Within the Hindu religious tradition the heart is seen as the source of knowledge of love, devotion, faith, kindness, compassion, etc., which human intellect cannot know and appreciate. And if the ultimate reality or the divine is viewed as a substance devoid of inner life or subjectivity then that form of religious life which is more passionate and devotional, and is inspired by human heart will be seen as purely subjective having no basis in objective reality. Then rational or scientific understanding of man or his intellect can be the only means of knowing or comprehending the nature of the ultimate reality. And if we consider that the subjective or the inward life of man as purely human it will have no significance and relevance in understanding the nature and meaning of what is objectively real. Then that form of religion which is centred round a personal conception of the divine or God, with devotion and love as appropriate means of realising Him will have no objective validity. But, if the divine is viewed as the ultimate source and ground of all that is, including human reality, then it would be more meaningful to view it as personal. One way of understanding this problem is to understand the nature of consciousness which is regarded as constituting the essence of both man and the divine. Is consciousness intrinsically personal or impersonal? The problem whether consciousness, as it reveals itself in man, is intrinsically personal or impersonal will help us in understanding the problem whether the divine is personal or impersonal or both or neither. However, these problems shall engage our attention when we discuss the nature of the divine in a separate chapter.

Conception of the divine as a personal being, and pure love and devotion to God as the meaning and end of religious life are as much integral to Hinduism as an impersonal conception of the divine, and a form of religious life in which the concepts of *ṛta*, *dharma* and *yajña* occupy a central place. In the Vedic tradition, human heart is given importance in revealing the nature of the divine as it is also regarded as a seat of divine inspiration. Divinely inspired heart is also a source of the knowledge of the divine. As a source of knowledge of the divine, human heart reveals that aspect of the divine which human intellect cannot grasp. However, the Vedic tradition which is a major source of Hinduism, is more intellectual than emotional. It gives more importance to knowledge and action than to love and devotion. *Ṛta*, *yajña* and *dharma* are the concepts central to the Vedic form of Hinduism. To be religious is to imitate and participate in the divine *yajña*. Pūrva Mīmāṁsā with its exclusive emphasis on *dharma*, and Uttara Mīmāṁsā or Vedānta with its emphasis on 'knowledge' (*jñāna*) are born of the same kind of thinking and understanding, or are based on the same vision of the divine. They consider that the divinely inspired intellect of man is the source of knowledge of the divine, and seek to attain objective knowledge of the divine.

The Smṛti tradition, which includes different Āgamas, represents the other major stream of Hindu religious thought and life. It is as ancient as the Śruti tradition though the various Smṛti texts are composed or compiled much later. Most of the Smṛti texts are only compilations or collections (*Saṁhitās*) in which the different theistic religious beliefs and doctrines are articulated and justified. The Purāṇas, which represent different religious traditions of Smṛti, are sectarian in their outlook, and are not systematic and coherent in their presentation of various ideas and doctrines. Their main object is to propagate sectarian religious beliefs and doctrines, and to provide for them a sort of intellectual or metaphysical justification. However, there is no justification to think that with the emergence of Smṛti tradition there is a radical shift within Hinduism. As pointed out earlier, the Smṛti tradition represents the religion of the common people or the religious beliefs and practices of the non-twice-born. It also represents the emotional or devotional aspect of Hindu religious life. Śruti and Smṛti, representing two major and dominant traditions of religious thought and life must have developed and flourished side by side, interacting with each other and influencing each other. It may not be true to say that the Smṛti tradition emerged and developed as a reaction to too much or even exclusive importance given to human intellect in knowing or understanding the nature of the divine, and the meaning and end of human life, because the emphasis placed either on intellect or heart is not exclusive and dogmatic in either of the traditions. The Upaniṣads favour intellectual or contemplative form of religious or spiritual life, and the emotional life of man is not generally recognised as having any place of importance in man's spiritual life. The emotional life of man is not encouraged or is even sought to be subordinated to and controlled by the human intellect so as to lead a life of detachment and contemplation. Human emotions are seen as a hindrance to spiritual growth of man. Therefore, it may not be meaningful to think that the Smṛti tradition is developed mainly to popularise the Śruti tradition or to make it available to those who are denied access to it. Smṛti is an independent tradition representing a major form of Hindu religious life and thought. It is more universal when compared to the Śruti tradition of Hinduism which is limited, both in principle and in practice, to the twice-born of Indian society. Furthermore, the meaning and end of religion as developed in the Smṛti tradition is clearly different from the meaning and end of religion as developed in the Śruti tradition. The Śruti and Smṛti are distinct traditions, and on certain important problems of religion they do not agree with each other, and are even opposed to each other.

While in the Śruti tradition the divine is not conceived as a personal being, the Smṛti form of religion is clearly theistic, and a personal form of the divine is central to it. However, Śruti is not opposed to a personal conception of the divine though it is more in favour of an impersonal conception of the divine. Though Śurti recognises the possibility of the divine being personal it has not been fully developed in the Śruti tradition. The Śruti concept of *puruṣa* indicates a personal conception of the divine though His relation to the world, and man's attitude to Him are not strictly speaking theistic. The Upaniṣads also recognise the possibility of the divine being personal (*puruṣa vidaḥ*).[27] They address and describe the divine in personal terms though the Upaniṣadic conception of the divine is predominantly impersonal. However, the dominant trend or tendency of the Śruti tradition is to view the divine as transcending personal-impersonal dichotomy. The divine can be personal, but is not avowedly conceived as a personal being. The divine is more often addressed and described in personal terms though it is viewed as transcending the categories of personal and impersonal. *Brahman* cannot be viewed as a personal being though the possibility of its being personal is not repugnant to the concept of *Brahman*. The Upaniṣadic definition of *Brahman* as *sat-cit-ānanda* is meaningful only in relation to a personal being, as

27. *Bṛhadāraṇyaka Upaniṣad*, 1.4.1; *Taittirīya Upaniṣad*. 2.3.1.

only a person can be a conscious being, and can experience bliss. But the will which can give *Brahman* individuality and personal character is not regarded as a defining characteristic of *Brahman*. Though the Vedic deities are known for their *kratu* or *ākuti*, will or intention, they are not viewed as individual divine beings. They are the primary and cosmic manifestations of the divine, which as the ultimate source of all, including man, is not conceived in clear personal terms or as a personal being. The divine manifests itself in the form of deities who represent different phenomena of nature, and though they possess individual identity they are not strictly speaking personal, as man is personal.

The Hindu understanding of man though recognises his personal character is not clear about his personhood, as man can transcend his consciousness as a person or his identity as a person in realising his oneness with the divine, and all. Whether consciousness regarded by most of the Hindu thinkers as the reality or essence of man is personal or impersonal is crucial in understanding the problem whether man is essentially or intrinsically personal or impersonal. Also important in this context is the problem whether consciousness, in the ultimate analysis, is devoid of personal character. Man is personal, but can we say that he is essentially or inalienably personal. If man, the crown or epitome of creation or the near culmination of the process of self-manifestation of the divine, is essentially or intrinsically personal, and cannot, therefore, transcend his identity as a person or his personal character, then the divine must be a personal being. Then it would be meaningful to identify the divine with God. On the contrary, if the category of person is not essential to understand the nature of human reality, as in reality he can transcend it, then the divine need not necessarily be conceived as a personal being or in personal terms.

Whether the divine is personal or impersonal, or is both or neither depends ultimately on the conception of the divine which in turn depends on the manner of its revelation to man. If the divine is viewed as being immanent within the world, or if the world is seen as a manifestation of the divine then it is not so much meaningful to think of the divine as a personal being. According to the world-view of Hinduism, the divine is immanently present within all, and, therefore, it is not meaningful to identify the divine with God, a personal being. If the divine is personal, then it is not intelligible to think of its becoming all, and dwelling within all, including physical nature. This problem attracted the attention of those who conceive *Brahman* as a personal being or identify it with *Īśvara* or *Bhagavān*. If God is personal, and has an individual identity of His own how to conceive Him as being immanently present within all or becoming all that is there. A person without losing his personal identity cannot become all that is, and be present within all, including physical or material nature. On the other hand, if the divine is identified with God only His will can prevail everywhere, and He can guide and govern the course of the world without Himself becoming the world, or being within it. The immanence of a personal being within the world is not intelligible if we understand by person something unique and unanalysable, or as a category by itself. The presence of a person within all, like the presence of gold within all the objects made of gold, is unintelligible. Therefore, it is not meaningful to think of God, a personal being, becoming all, and being present within all. It is only an impersonal reality or a reality which transcends personal-impersonal dichotomy, be it matter or spirit, that can manifest itself in the form of the world, and be present within all. It is only a reality that can manifest itself in various forms can be immanent within them all without thereby losing its nature or essence.

The divine is spiritual, and the spiritual need not necessarily be personal though the idea of being personal is not incompatible with the idea of the divine. The divine can become personal or manifest itself in the form of a person though in itself it is neither personal nor impersonal. Divine, spiritual and personal need not necessarily go together, and at the same time they need not be opposed to each other. To admit the possibility of the divine being personal is not the same as to assert that it is essentially personal, or to say that the idea of the divine is not incompatible with the idea of person is not the same as to identify the divine with God. But the immanence of the divine within all is not compatible with the conception of the divine as a personal being. We cannot, therefore, determine the nature of the divine in personal or impersonal terms. The divine manifests itself in man as a personal being, but man can transcend his identity as a personal being. Thus, the Śruti conception of the divine cannot be consistent with the theistic concept of God who is essentially personal.

The Smṛti form of Hinduism insists on the personal character of the divine, or the divine, according to it, is a personal being. Even though the Smṛti tradition adopts the concepts and categories of Śruti they are theistically interpreted to suit its theological needs. Smṛti accepts the Vedāntic concept of *Brahman*, but interprets it in personal terms, and identifies it with *Bhagavān* or God. The term *bhagavān* means one who is adorable or worshippable (*bhajanīyam*). The other terms preferred by the Smṛti tradition to indicate the divine are: Vāsudeva, one who lives within all, and *parameśvara*, the Supreme Lord or God. Man also, according to the Smṛti tradition, is essentially personal, and cannot transcend his identity as a person. Personal nature of man is not something contingent or accidental but substantive. However, the world-view of Śruti which the Smṛti has adopted is not strictly speaking compatible or consistent with the personal conception of the divine. But the Smṛti tradition lays more or less exclusive emphasis on the personal nature of the divine, because the personal character of the divine is revealed to a divinely inspired heart, and such a conception of the divine can alone satisfy and fulfil the emotional or devotional life of man. And the devotional life of man is as much human as rational or intellectual life of man, and man seeks the fulfilment of both. However, as Smṛti does not give up the idea of God being immanent within creation, it does not subscribe to the idea of creation. The Hindu world-view which is based on or inspired by the Śruti tradition is completely accepted by the Smṛti tradition.

What distinguishes Smṛti from Śruti is its conception of the divine as a personal being, and its theistic form of religious life and worship. The Smṛti form of religion is basically Hindu, as it accepts the world-view of Śruti though it rejects most of the religious beliefs and practices of Śruti. Smṛti represents the theistic form of Hinduism which is clearly formulated and fully developed in some of the major Purāṇas, like the *Viṣṇu* and *Bhāgavata*. According to the Smṛti form of Hinduism, known as *Bhāgavata-dharma*, the divine is clearly personal or is identified with God, and love of God, which is considered as an end in itself, is the meaning and end of religion. Love of God, and total surrender to Him are not considered possible for man without the grace of God as they involve total denial of himself which man on his own cannot achieve. The divine grace has no explanation (*nirhetuka*). However, ordinary religious life of devotion and worship, which is open to all, can lead to or culminate in love of God. Religious life of devotion and worship is only a preparation to receive the grace of God.

Although the meaning and end of religion as envisaged in both the traditions may seem to be the same, that is to realise the divine unity or oneness of all that is there, in real terms their impact on the Hindu religious life is not the same. The attitudes of both the traditions to certain basic human values, like knowledge, place and importance of rational understanding and the value of human effort in the religious life of man are basically different. While these are depreciated in the Smṛti tradition, they are positively encouraged in the Śruti tradition. As total and unconditional surrender to God is the end of religious life, according to Smṛti, even one's quest to know and understand the nature and meaning of the divine is not encouraged, as ultimately not only human ignorance but also knowledge (*jñāna*) is regarded as a hindrance to total devotion and surrender to God. Any effort to know or understand the nature and meaning of the divine, and other religious problems mean an assertive attitude on the part of man, and that stands in the way of total surrender to God. The concept of *vidvat-*

saṁnyāsa as enunciated in the *Bhāgavata Purāṇa*, means giving up or renouncing ultimately ones knowledge and wisdom about God , which from the point of view of God are a sort of ignorance.[28] One has to give up or surrender oneself totally to God as God is all. One has to deny one's individual identity totally, and realise that one is nothing before God to receive the grace of God. This form of religious life which gained ascendancy with the decline in faith in the *Brāhmaṇa* form of Hinduism is projected as the real meaning of Hinduism by most of the Smṛti thinkers and saints. Although the Smṛti form of Hinduism is the most dominant and popular form of Hinduism, it cannot be construed as the meaning of Hinduism, because the Śruti form of Hinduism, its vision and values have at no time lost their meaningfulness and validity in the life of Hinduism though they have been occassionally submerged by the Smṛti form of Hinduism.

The Śruti form of religious life with its more or less exclusive emphasis on *ṛta* and *yajña* was the meaning of Hinduism till the dominance of Smṛti form of religious life which is traditionally signified as the beginning of *kali-yuga* or dark age. Śruti form of religious life is not open to all, and is also difficult to follow by all when compared to Smṛti form of religion which is easy and open to all. The vision that gave rise to the Smṛti form of religious life, at least theoretically, envisages a social order and cultural values that are not strictly speaking the same as those that are based on or inspired by the Śruti tradition. The Smṛti form of Hinduism, especially as reflected in the epic text of *Mahābhārata*, is based on a vision, according to which all that is there is permeated by the same divine reality or God, or all that is there is a varied manifestation of the divine. Although every person is a manifestation of the divine yet in terms of his nature (*svabhāva*) which is determined by the *gúṇa*s and their dominance each individual is different from others. Just as each phenomenon of nature has its own nature, and laws that govern it, which differ from phenomenon to pheno-

28. *Bhāgavata Purāṇa*, 11.19.25-26; see also *Devī Bhāgavata*, 8.32.

menon, so also the human beings are not alike in their nature (*svabhāva*). Each individual is different from others in terms of his *svabhāva* or nature or character which determines one's social and religious life. Nevertheless, all can be religious or spiritual if they see in their nature the manifestation of the divine which has become varied in the forms of its manifestations. What is, therefore, meaningful and valid for one need not be so for others. But these differences should not be construed as pointing to spiritual inequality. Inequality is a valid concept only at the empirical level or at the level of manifestation, as all the manifestations are not alike or similar in their forms and functions. Therefore, even a butcher can be a knower or follower of *dharma* (religion) than a brāhmaṇa ascetic provided he sees in his *svabhāva* the manifestation of the divine. When one realises that one's nature is a manifestation of the divine, then doing one's duty, born of one's *svabhāva*, will be his form of religious life and worship. Service (*sevā*) to others, the *dharma* of a śūdra, will be his form of religious life and worship (*sevā-yajña*), according to *Mahābhārata*.[29] The oneness or unity of humankind is valid only at the non-empirical or transcendental or divine level, but not at the level of manifestation. Therefore, no one form of religious life and worship need be meaningful and valid to all. Thus, religion as *dharma* need not uniformly be same to all, for religion as *dharma* depends for its meaning and validity more on the nature of an individual than on abstract theological understanding. *Dharma* is divine though the nature of it differs from person to person depending more upon the nature or character of a person. At the practical level, *dharma* is not one and the same for all though the meaning of *dharma*, which comprehends all its specific and functional meanings, remains the same. The whole of Hindu life is based on or inspired by the vision that the divine, the source of all that is empirically real, is one, and all that we experience at the empirical level is its manifestation. The divine can, therefore, be realised without denying reality to the differences by realising the divine as that

---

29. *Mahābhārata*, Śānti-parva, 238.12; Anuśāsana-parva, 141. 57 and 60.

which is being expressed in and through all the differences. In other words, one need not cease to be oneself to realise the divine as one can see in one's *svabhāva* a manifestation of the divine.

Dharma is dynamic in the sense that its meaningfulness and validity are in relation to the conduct of a person. It is to regard one's duties, which are in accordance with one's nature, as one's form of religious life and worship. The nature is one not because all the phenomena of nature follow the same laws, but because all the phenomena of nature are the manifestation of the divine. Similarly, all the human beings are one not because they are governed by the same *dharma*, but because they are a manifestation of the same divine reality. Such vision of the divine encourages the full growth and development of an individual. Each individual has to grow and develop, and reach perfection in accordance with what one is capable of growing into; and that acquires spiritual or religious significance if one sees in all what one is and does the manifestation of the divine, or if one regards what one is capable of doing as his form of *yajña* or as his *dharma* or his form of worship of the divine. In this form of religious life there is no significant place for God who can fulfil human existence. Man is autonomous though he has to gradually evolve to reach perfection, and realise the meaning of *dharma* or *yajña* in his life.

Dharma form of religious life recognises each person as a self-conscious participant in the process of divine manifestation. As an individual manifestation of the divine, and as one who is capable of realising that fact, man is not helpless in shaping the course of events, either at the collective or at the individual levels. Man shares the divine power of creativity, and in his creativity, which is a sign of his divine nature, he can self-consciously and actively participate in the process of divine creation. Thus, to realise the divine as the source of diversity as well as the oneness of all that it has become is the ultimate meaning of human existence. As expressed in one of the *Brāhmaṇa* texts, the object of the Veda is to reveal the unity of the divine which it has lost, as it were, in becoming many or in the process of creation, and the one who sees the divine unity of all that is there is a *ṛṣi*.[30] In the process of realising the divine or divine unity of all that is there knowledge and understanding of one's own reality plays a crucial role. Unless one knows what is divine one cannot see all that is there as a self-manifestation of the divine. To see gold in all that is made of gold one has to first know the nature of gold as otherwise one cannot see gold in all that is made of gold. To see the divine in all that is one has to know what divine is. And the presence of the divine is revealed clearly in one's own reality when one is divinely inspired.

According to the Vedic *Saṁhitā*s, we come to know the presence of the divine in nature because of divine inspiration of which nature is the immediate source. Nature is capable of revealing the divine which it does by inspiring man divinely. And though nature is divine yet that aspect of the divine which is revealed to man within his own reality is not revealed to him in nature. The divine that is known as it reveals itself within the reality of man, a self-conscious being, is more perfect and comprehensive than the divine that reveals itself in and through nature. The spiritual nature of the divine reveals itself to man within his own reality, and to realise one's spiritual nature is to see himself in all his self-expressions, and yet realise himself as transcending them all. All the expressions of man reveal himself or his reality as they are his self-expressions, and yet as the source of all the expressions man transcends them. The reality of man cannot be contained and exhausted by any one or all of his self-expressions. It cannot be equated or identified with its expressions, as at any given time of his existence man realises that his reality is more than its expressions. Man realises at every stage of his growth and development that he is more than

30. In the *Ṛgveda* though both *ṛṣi* and *kavi* are regarded as divinely inspired they are distinguished in terms of the nature of their wisdom. While a *kavi* is one who sees the divine in the forms of its manifestation, a *ṛṣi* is one who sees the divine as the unity underlying all the forms of its manifestation. While a *kavi* sees the creative aspect of the divine, a *ṛṣi* sees the unitive aspect of the divine — *Ṛgveda*, 10.130.5; 10.71.3; 10.130.6.

what he is or has become. He is not the sum total of his expressions. Therefore, man's knowledge of himself involves an awareness of himself as transcending all that he has become as well as all that he would like to become. His reality is a mystery to himself as he does not know at any time of his existence all that he is capable of becoming or the full or perfect nature of his being. In this sense, the divine *puruṣa* is all that is, and yet transcends all that he has become or all the forms of his manifestation. His manifestations reveal his glory, and he exceeds or transcends his own glory as the *Puruṣa-sūkta* expresses.[31] In Himself *puruṣa* is really infinite as no one can measure the fullness of his being.

The divine has become all that is in terms of its creative power, which is inherent within itself, and, therefore, to realise the divine is to see it in all its manifestations, and yet to realise the futility of comprehending the nature of the divine in terms of any one definition or concept. All the conceptions and definitions of the divine express the reality of the divine though none can contain it and determine its nature fully. In itself the divine transcends all the meanings and definitions as no one definition or meaning can comprehend its nature, and contain its being. Therefore, to assert that the divine is personal or impersonal is to determine its nature, and to measure its being which is measureless. Nevertheless, to conceive the divine as a personal being is more meaningful than to conceive its nature in impersonal terms on the basis of its manifestation at the level of physical nature, as the human person is the near culmination of the process of self-manifestation of the divine.

We may discuss here the reasons why the divine is viewed as transcending the categories of personal and impersonal within the Hindu religious tradition. If we accept the view that the divine is all that is, including man, it is meaningful to say that the personal character of man, which is unique about man as only man is personal, is the highest form of self-manifestation

---

31. *Ṛgveda* 10.90.1 (*Puruṣa Sūkta*).

of the divine. The flower, its beauty and fragrance though are less tangible than the roots, trunk and other parts of a tree are nevertheless the culmination of the growth of a tree. The divine realises its being more fully in the reality of man, or man is a near perfect form of self-manifestation of the divine. We cannot understand the beauty and fragrance of a flower in terms of the trunk and roots of a tree which also form the tree, and are integral to it, and seem to be more real than the beauty of its flower because of their more tangible nature. The flower and its beauty are the culmination of a tree's growth. Can we then say that though the divine is present within all yet within the self-conscious being of man it finds its best form of self-expression or realises itself more fully and perfectly? If man is the best form of divine self-manifestation (*sukṛta*), then it is more meaningful to think that the divine is personal, as otherwise it cannot express or manifest itself in the form of man, a personal being. In man the divine attains or realises the object of its self-manifestation or self-expression, and more so in a fully evolved state of human existence. According to such a view or understanding of the divine it is more meaningful to think that the divine is personal, as the human person is the best form of its self-expression or the near culmination of its self-manifestation and self-realisation. Man is personal or what is unique about man is his personal character. But is man intrinsically or essentially personal? Is it possible for man to transcend his identity as a person or his person-hood? Or is it the case that though man is personal which is his greatness, yet being personal is not the ultimate truth about man ? Can we understand the reality of man without the category of person? Is it meaningful to think of the reality of man in impersonal terms? If man is essentially or intrinsically personal, and cannot, therefore, transcend his personal character, we cannot, meaningfully think of the divine in impersonal terms as man is the best possible form of its self-manifestation or in man the divine has realised itself more fully.

Although within the Śruti tradition of Hinduism the reality of man is viewed in personal terms, and is regarded as the best form (*sukṛta*) of divine manifestation, the personal character of man is not considered to be the ultimate truth about man, as he can transcend his identity as a person. The essence of man or his *ātman* is identified with consciousness, and consciousness need not necessarily be personal. Though consciousness, at the empirical level, is tied up with the concept of self which is personal, it can transcend its personal character. There is no contradiction in denying selfhood to consciousness. If it is intelligible to talk of consciousness, the essential being of man, in impersonal terms then the divine need not necessarily be personal, or being personal need not be an essential and defining characteristic of the divine. If it is meaningful to think of human reality as transcending personal identity then it is equally intelligible and meaningful to think of the divine as transcending the concept of God viewed as a personal being. Somehow man's self-understanding plays an important role or acts as a paradigm in understanding the nature of the divine. All talk of God is anthropomorphic, and man's self-understanding influences and even determines his understanding of the divine. And there is no universally meaningful and valid definition or understanding about the nature of human reality. Furthermore, whether the divine is personal or impersonal is not really a problem as conceptually there is nothing which is not possible for the divine. Therefore, the divine need not necessarily be identified with God, a personal being. However, the problem is meaningful in relation to human understanding as his self-understanding influences his understanding of the divine. Thus, for those who consider man to be inalienably personal the conception of the divine as a personal being or God is highly meaningful and valid. And the religion based on such an understanding or vision will be significantly different from the religion based on the vision or understanding that human reality is not essentially personal. It is, therefore, meaningful to think of the divine as transcending the concept of God as human reality is not ultimately tied up with the concept of person. However, at the empirical level it is not meaningful to talk of man in impersonal terms as the impersonal character of man is meaningful only at the transcendental level. In transcending his identity as a person man also transcends the ordinary religious categories and limitations.

Whether human reality is personal or impersonal is really a problem of mysticism. However, religious life in the ordinary sense is not meaningful without accepting the personal character of man. In asserting that human reality is not really or ultimately personal, Hinduism does not deny the essential spiritual nature of human reality. Human reality is essentially spiritual, but to be spiritual is not the same as to be personal. Spirituality of man cannot be equated with his identity as a person. Furthermore, man's capacity to transcend his personal character or identity is to be admitted on the evidence of such states as *turīya* and *nirvikalpa samādhi*. Consciousness is identified as the essential nature of the divine, and it is perfectly intelligible to think of consciousness in impersonal terms. In other words, the concept of person involves consciousness, but consciousness does not necessarily involve the concept of person. Consciousness can be personal though it is not essentially personal. Pure consciousness, as absolute freedom, can manifest itself in the form of a person. Thus, though man is personal he has the capacity to transcend his identity as a person. However, religion in the ordinary sense is meaningful in terms of man as a person or it is concerned with man as a personal being.

Both the conceptions about the nature of the divine as well as about the nature of man are present within the Hindu religious tradition, though in its popular or Smṛti form, Hinduism is theistic. Nevertheless, those who maintain that the divine is essentially personal, and those who think that the divine is not essentially personal do not differ in their basic conception of the divine, that it is both immanent and transcendent. The Smṛti tradition which is avowedly theistic, and identifies the divine with God (*Bhagavān*) accepts the immanence of God, and the Śruti tradition which is more inclined towards the impersonal character of the divine accepts the transcendental aspect of the divine. In its transcendental aspect the divine is beyond all the human conceptions and categories, and, therefore, anything that is said about the divine will invariably be meaningful and valid only in terms of its immanence. And anything that is said about the divine in its transcendental aspect is said on the basis or in terms of its immanence in nature, and, therefore, need not be true of it in its transcendental aspect. To accept the transcendence of the divine is to admit the limitations of human understanding and experience in comprehending the nature of the divine, and, therefore, any attempt to determine the transcendental nature of the divine in terms of any concept or definition is to deny transcendental character of the divine. The divine is beyond or transcends all possible conceptions and categories about it, including its being personal. Therefore, it is not a dogma with the Śruti tradition either to deny something about the divine or to dogmatically assert something about the nature of the divine. The Śruti is not dogmatic in maintaining the impersonal nature of the divine. It is more philosophical as anything that can be said about the divine need not be true of the divine in itself or of the divine in its transcendental aspect, and at the same time everything that is said about the divine can be true of it though not in an absolute sense. And all that is said about the divine in the Śruti tradition is said by way of praise, but not by way of definition.

The possible relationship between the divine and the world on the one hand, and the divine and man on the other depends upon the conception of the divine. The divine immanence is more meaningful in terms of its impersonal conception. It is not meaningful to think of the immanence of God, a personal being. If the divine is personal it cannot be present within all, including the physical or material world. It is also not meaningful to think of God, a personal being, becoming the world or manifesting Himself in the form of the world. He can only be conceived as the creator of the world, which as an act of His wisdom and will can only reveal His wisdom and glory, but not His being. His being will then be completely outside the created world though the world can have no existence independently of God. God can either create or dissolve the world at his will, and the realisation that one's very existence and that of the world depend upon God's will is sufficient to make one surrender oneself to God or to make him feel his absolute dependence upon Him. Man's true welfare or the true meaning of his existence consists in the realisation that his existence is completely dependent upon God. God as a personal being can be pleased and displeased, and can be loved and hated. Such language which is meaningful in relation to a human person will be appropriate to describe God also. Then God cannot be viewed as being indifferent to human values and aspirations or as transcending them. The conception of the divine as a personal being or God is more meaningful to man as long as he cannot transcend his subjectivity, and as the meaning of subjectivity differs from person to person what is meaningful and valid to one person may not be so for all. And human subjectivity plays an important role in all the conceptions of the divine. The qualities and values in terms of which God is conceived and described vary from tradition to tradition depending upon what qualities and values each tradition cherishes, and regards as most meaningful and supreme. And they are reflected in man's subjective or inward life. In so far as human subjectivity plays a significant role in conceiving the nature of the divine, the nature of the divine is conceived predominantly in human terms. But the moment man realises that the divine transcends every conception of it, howsoever, meaningful and valid it may be to man, then he sees the futility of identifying the divine or determining its nature in terms of any concept or definition. But consciousness when compared to other subjective feelings and values of man is objective and universal. Therefore, in identifying the divine with consciousness we do not limit the nature of the divine to what is subjective and changing in human nature.

If the divine is conceived as impersonal, or rather as transcending the dichotomy of personal and impersonal, the world will not be an act of creation on the part of the divine. It will then be a matter of self-manifestation or self-expression of the divine which is spontaneous or natural. The manifestation of the divine, which is natural or spontaneous, does not involve any kind of activity on the part of the divine, and, therefore, will have no causal explanation for its existence. And as the world, including man, is a manifestation of the divine, the world is divine though the divine and the world are not one and the same. They cannot be identified as conceptually they are distinct, and do not have the same meaning. Although the divine is present within the world it is more than the world. Therefore, the divine transcendence is not compatible with the concept of pantheism. According to this view of the divine, the ultimate fulfilment of human existence consists in realising the divine unity or oneness of all that is. As the divine is present within all its manifestations though in itself it transcends its manifestations, to realise the divine one need not deprecate and renounce the world, as he can realise the divine by being within the world. One's individuality will not then be a burden but a means of divine realisation. One need not give up oneself or surrender oneself to God, as in the other form of Hindu religious life, as the divine is not something completely other than and different from oneself and the world. To worship the divine is to actively participate in the process of divine manifestation, and to extend the meaning of divine *yajña* to his own life. It is to realise in one's own life the manifestation of the divine, and, therefore, to consecrate it to the divine, or to adopt it as his means of divine realisation. An intellectual can be religious if he can see in his intellectual life, and its varied forms of manifestation, the manifestation of the divine, and its wisdom. If one can see in all his faculties, including his will, the play of the divine, it liberates one from the sense of ego or his ego-centric existence, which is what is really opposed to the divine. Then one realises that the divine is the ultimate guide and controller of himself and his actions or the divine is the real agent of all his actions. Such realisation is not the same as to deny oneself to assert the glory and greatness of God.

While the Śruti tradition gave rise to *dharma* form of religious life, the Smṛti tradition is the source of theistic form of religious life in which devotion and surrender to God are central. Though they are different conceptually, and also in terms of their influence on man's religious life they are integral to Hinduism. Therefore, Hinduism cannot be identified exclusively with one or the other form of religious life and worship. However, in the growth and development of Hinduism we find each form of religious life and worship trying to assert itself and prove its superior meaningfulness and validity over the other. But the theistic form of religious life proved itself to be more influential and popular in the Hindu religious life. But, both the forms of religious life with their theological traditions are integral to Hinduism though occasionally one or the other gained ascendancy and popularity. Therefore, the nature and meaning of Hinduism cannot be determined in terms of the one or the other as both the forms of religious life are integral to the nature and meaning of Hinduism.

The development of Hinduism is full of efforts to reconcile both the forms of religious life or the traditions of Śruti and Smṛti, and integrate them in terms of its world-view. Hinduism is an integration or a harmonious blend of both the traditions with their diverse beliefs, doctrines and even theologies, and *Bhagavad Gītā* excels all other attempts in reconciling and harmonising them. Whether both the major forms of religious life and their theologies can really be reconciled or not is a different problem, and has engaged the attention of almost all the Hindu religious thinkers and saints. However, because of its integral character Hinduism may seem to lack theological or doctrinal coherence and unity as it has not sacrificed doctrinal or theological differences to achieve coherence and unity at the level of beliefs and doctrines. Hinduism is an unending process of integration in which different and even mutually opposed trends of religious thought, and different theological beliefs and doctrines are sought to be reconciled and harmonised in terms of its world-view which can comprehend and integrate all without excluding or rejecting any.

The two streams of religious thought and life which differ

in their understanding about the nature and meaning of religion are represented by two different models or paradigms. While the seers like Vāmadeva, Yājñavalkya, and almost all the seers of the Veda, including the Upaniṣads, represent one way of understanding the meaning and end of religion or spirituality, the other is represented by the devotees like Prahlāda, Nārada and Ambarīṣa, the representatives of *Bhāgavata dharma* or the devotional form of religious life. These two basic trends co-exist in Hinduism. And each has influenced and enriched the other. Each helped the other in becoming more comprehensive and integral. Hinduism is not one stream or one tradition, but a confluence of two major traditions and two different forms of religious life, and what we have tried in this chapter is to present the two basic forms of religious life within the great tradition called Hinduism.

3

Hindu World-View

What distinguishes Hinduism from other religions of the world, and what is commonly shared by all the sects of Hinduism and different schools of Hindu religious thought, which are otherwise quite distinct from each other, and are even antagonistic to each other, is its world-view. The Hindu world-view which is based on and shaped by the Śruti tradition is the major source of unity of all the diverse sects and sub-traditions of Hinduism. Vaiṣṇavism, Śaivism and Śāktaism, and other minor sects of Hinduism are all different forms of Hinduism not so much because they are born and developed in India but because they commonly share the same world-view. The world-view which can be discerned at a deeper level is what is common to all the sects of Hinduism. However, at the surface level of beliefs, doctrines and practices, the sects are so diverse, and are even antagonistic to each other, it is difficult to find out what they have in common, or what makes them Hindu. Though in their theological beliefs and doctrines some of the sects of Hinduism appear nearer to other theistic religions, like Christianity, they basically differ from them in terms of the world-view, which not only gives them their Hindu identity but also integrates them with Hinduism, and the other forms of Hindu religious life. The world-view gives diverse sects of Hinduism their Hindu identity and character. What distinguishes Hinduism, which is a federation of faiths, from other religions of the world, and gives it its identity, is its world-view. To express the same in the traditional Hindu manner, while the different sects with their distinctive religious beliefs, doctrines, and forms of worship are based on Smṛti or are Smārta in their origin and development, the basic vision or world-view which is commonly shared by all the Hindu sects and schools of religious thought is based on Śruti. It may appear trivial but is nevertheless significant that all the sects of Hinduism, though accept the authority and sanctity of Śruti, differ significantly among themselves, and also from Śruti in respect of their religious beliefs and doctrines. All the schools of Hindu religious thought, and all the sects of Hinduism adopt the world-view of Śruti. Hinduism as it is commonly known or in its popular form is mostly based on and developed by Smṛti. There is no Śruti authority or justification for all that is known as Hinduism, or for all the Hindu beliefs and doctrines. However, the various sects of Hinduism claim the authority of the Veda for their various sectarian beliefs and doctrines. And all the sects claim that the vision or world-view of Śruti is the real basis or source of inspiration for their theological views and doctrines. We may, therefore, say that while Smṛti represents the body of Hinduism, Śruti is its soul or spirit.

The world-view of a religion is the real and ultimate justification of its various beliefs and doctrines which they may not have individually or by themselves. Therefore, without comprehending the world-view of a religious tradition, and be in sympathy with it one may not be able to find meaning and justification for all those ideas and beliefs which are developed on the basis of or are inspired by the world-view. On the other hand, one who has faith in the world-view, and to whom the world-view is meaningful and valid the lack of individual justification for the beliefs and doctrines does not destroy one's faith in them. A world-view is the real and ultimate source of justification and validity for the various ideas and beliefs of a religion as they are developed on the basis of the world-view or are inspired by it. The same ideas and doctrines may be present in more than one religion, but they do not have the same meaning and justification as the world-view in terms of which they derive their meaning and justification differs from religion to religion. And as long as the world-view of a religion has not lost its meaningfulness and validity to its followers, or their faith in it is not destroyed the various ideas and doctrines, which are in a sense the working out of the world-view or are inspired by it, remain meaningful and valid. A world-view can give birth to or inspire various ideas, beliefs and doctrines, and the loss of meaningfulness and validity of an idea or doctrine, therefore, does not destroy the meaningfulness and validity of the world-view. Thus, all the Hindus may not accept the meaningfulness and validity of any particular idea or doctrine, and consequently the value of a particular religious form of life and worship, but they remain Hindu, and are free to develop their own religious beliefs, doctrines and forms of worship as long as they have not lost their faith in the world-view, and the world-view has not lost its meaningfulness to them. In the long history of Hinduism several beliefs and forms of worship came into existence and dis-appeared, and newer beliefs and forms of worship are developed. In other words, in the historical development of Hinduism, theological beliefs, doctrines, religious practices and forms of worship have undergone significant changes, and some of them are even given up, and yet Hinduism has not lost its coherence and identity mainly because of the stability of its world-view.

What is the place of importance of a world-view in the life of a religion? Does a world-view also change along with the changes in the theological or religious beliefs and doctrines? Generally speaking, world-views are not totally rejected, but are interpreted from time to time with a view to adapting them to changing circumstances and challenges giving thereby rise to new ideas and doctrines. Interpretation of a world-view does not mean its rejection. It is only when the meaningfulness of a world-view is recognised it is interpreted and re-interpreted. Thus, all the interpretations of Śruti accept its meaningfulness and validity as otherwise there is no need to interpret it. The interpretations differ, and in certain cases very significantly, and this is the case with all the religious traditions. Interpretation is an attempt to grasp the meaning of a world-view in relation to changing circumstances, as well as to satisfy the growing intellectual demands of the community. It is a creative act, as an interpreter may be able to find out a new meaning of the world-view which its earlier interpreters could not see. And an interpretation may, therefore, give birth to a new sect or movement. A world-view is not clearly definable. We cannot define or determine its nature and meaning in clear and precise intellectual terms. However, the influence of a world-view in the life of an individual or a community is more profound, and comprehensive. It is the real source of meaning and justification of a religion. A world-view is more a matter of lived and shared experience of a community, and finds its most effective expression in the life of an individual or that of a community. Broadly speaking, a world-view represents the meaning given by a tradition to human existence and the world. Different religious traditions conceive the meaning of human life differently, and the meaning given to human life is related very significantly to the meaning given to the world. Although each person is capable of finding for himself the meaning of his life and the world, in reality most of the people accept the meaning given by the tradition to which they belong. Thus, though the world in which we live and experience is the same the meaning we give to it is not the same. Different people live in different meaning-worlds or their world-views differ significantly. Our attitudes to the world, and our views about it or the meanings we give to it are not the same. There are several meaning-worlds or world-views. Therefore, when different religions talk of the world they really talk about their views of the world, or what the world means to them. In the formation and development of a world-view the entire personality of man gets itself actively involved. Man's feelings, intentions, hopes, fears and aspirations influence in shaping the world-view.

The Hindu world-view is reflected fully and comprehensively in its Śruti literature and tradition. It is the Śruti that is interpreted to make the Hindu world-view more and more meaningful in terms of changing circumstances and modes of human understanding. And Smṛti is not an interpretation of

Śruti though all the Smṛti texts claim that their teaching is based on or inspired by Śruti. The different sectarian traditions of Smṛti tradition are drawn to the Vedic world-view mainly because of its integral nature. And they try to provide the authority and sanctity of Śruti to their different sectarian theological claims. Another important reason why the Smṛti tradition adopts the world-view of Śruti is to provide ontological basis and stability to its sectarian theological beliefs and doctrines which they do not have otherwise. In other words, the Smṛti tradition adapts the world-view of Śruti to serve or suit its sectarian theological needs.

Śruti talks of so many things, and represents various philosophical and religious views and ideas, but what is of enduring value in it that can be discerned through its influence in the development of Hinduism is its basic ontological vision or its world-view. The Hindu world-view is shaped and expressed fairly clearly in the texts of Śruti by which I mean the Vedic *Saṁhitās* and the Upaniṣads. What is Śruti or what texts constitute Śruti has no clear and definite answer. All the views about the Veda or about its meaning and validity are the views of different interpreters of Śruti, including the authors of different Smṛti texts, and for most of them we do not find any basis or justification in the Śruti literature. Several claims that are traditionally made about Śruti are not made by Śruti itself. And in the Hindu tradition we find different views not only about the meaning of Śruti, but also about its authority and validity. Almost all the Smṛti texts, especially the Purāṇas, claim that everything that is expressed in them is based on the authority of the Veda, or is consistent with the wisdom of the Veda. Most of the popular Hindu beliefs and doctrines that find their expression only in the Smṛti texts are, however, attributed by them to the Veda. For instance, in the Śānti-parva of *Mahābhārata*, which reflects the wisdom of *Mahābhārata*, and represents the wisdom of several thinkers on various problems, it is often asserted that the *Mahābhārata* represents the wisdom of the Veda, or its ideas and doctrines are based on or inspired by the wisdom of the Veda.[1] And if we do not compare the teaching of Smṛti with that of Śruti, it may appear that Smṛti is only trying to represent the wisdom of the Veda, and express it in a language that is more simple and direct. The various theological ideas and doctrines that are expressed and discussed in the Smṛti texts, have no basis or justification in the Veda. They find their expression in the Smṛti tradition only, and rest entirely on the authority of Smṛti. There is no authority of Śruti for all the theological or religious beliefs and doctrines that are enunciated in the Smṛti literature. Smṛti even goes against the spirit of Śruti, and rejects most of the ideas and doctrines of Śruti. However, the basic vision or the world-view of Śruti is adopted by almost all the Smṛti texts or the Smṛti tradition in general. The different sectarian traditions of Smṛti adapt the world-view of Śruti to serve or suit their theological needs. They also try to reconcile and harmonise their theological positions with the Vedic world-view. But how far the Smṛti tradition could succeed in reconciling and harmonising its sectarian theologies

---

1. It is traditionally believed that Vyāsa, who arranged or classified the Vedas, is also the author of the *Mahābhārata* and the Purāṇas. And he composed the *Mahābhārata* and compiled the Purāṇas to make available the wisdom of the Veda to those who are denied direct access to the Veda, like the śūdras and women. It is said in the *Vāyu Purāṇa* (1.38) that Vyāsa churned the ocean of the Veda with the churning rod of his intellect, and produced the moon in the form of the *Mahābhārata*. With the help of a significant analogy the Purāṇas claim that their wisdom represents the fruit of the Veda. The same sap though is present throughout the tree it is more sweet in its fruit. Thus, the Purāṇas relate themselves to the Veda as a fruit to the tree. The Purāṇas are considered to be an extension or expansion of the truth contained in the Veda. Śruti and Smṛti are regarded in the Smṛti tradition as two eyes of God. The Smṛti texts claim to themselves the same authority as that of the Veda for they think that their main object is to express the meaning of the Veda in a manner intelligible to all. In the Smṛti tradition Vyāsa is regarded as one who had known the truth of the Veda directly. And just as a tree proliferates into many branches after reaching fertile soil and in congenial season, the tree of the Veda spreads itself out after reaching Vyāsa — *Vāyu Purāṇa* 1.39.

with the world-view of Śruti is a different problem, which we shall discuss elsewhere. However, the efforts of Smṛti in reconciling and integrating itself with Śruti or in adapting the ontology of Śruti to suit its sectarian theological claims gave rise to certain distortions and confusions within Hinduism. Most of the Hindu intellectuals and thinkers have recognised the tension and conflict between Śruti and Smṛti, and have made sincere and significant efforts to achieve harmony between them, without discarding or rejecting the basic positions of either. All this will be meaningful only if we admit that Śruti and Smṛti are two independent traditions, but developed together without much conflict and antagonism. And it has been the endeavour of several Hindu thinkers and saints to reconcile and harmonise both the traditions without overlooking their basic positions, and individual identities. In the process of reconciliation and harmonisation for which the initiative has come from Smṛti, it is the Smṛti tradition that has benefited itself most, and enriched itself. While the Śruti is a closed tradition, Smṛti is not a closed tradition. Smṛti is a continuously developing or evolving tradition, and includes the contributions of all the enlightened Hindus to the growth and development of Hinduism. It continues to evolve or develop as long as Hinduism remains meaningful as its purpose is to interpret the world-view of Hinduism with a view to adapting it to the changing circumstances and challenges, from both within and without.

What distinguishes Smṛti from Śruti is its basic theological character. While Smṛti is religious or theological in its approach and attitude, in its approach and attitude the Śruti is not religious or theological if we exclude from Śruti all the *Brāhmaṇa* texts, and accept only the *Saṁhitā*s and the Upaniṣads as constituting Śruti. The truth or wisdom of the Vedic *Saṁhitā*s and the Upaniṣads is really revealed or is divinely inspired. They do not promise any rewards, either here or hereafter, for accepting them and following them, which is not, however, the case with the Smṛti literature in general. This is the reason why Svāmī Dayānanda, a modern interpreter of the Veda, refuges to recognise the *Brāhmaṇas* as constituting Śruti.[2] *Brāhmaṇas* are a motivated literature. They are an attempt to adapt and employ the truth or wisdom of the Veda (*Saṁhitās*) to serve or suit the practical religious needs of man. Smṛti literature is also highly motivated, as its chief object is to justify and propagate different religious sects, and their sectarian theologies. The different Smṛti texts, particularly the Purāṇas, the real source of popular form of Hinduism, constantly talk of possible rewards for accepting and following their teaching. Smṛti tradition is intended to justify different sectarian religious beliefs and doctrines, and their forms of religious life and worship. The object of different Purāṇic texts is to present and justify different sectarian forms of religious life, and to influence or motivate people for following them. Śruti, on the other hand, does not talk of rewards, and makes no promises for accepting its teaching or wisdom. It is, however, religious in the sense that its central concern is with devotion, spontaneous response on the part of man to his experience of the divine, which is an end in itself. Some of the Smṛti texts, like *Bhāgavata Purāṇa*, also speak of devotion to God as an end in itself, which is, however, an exception. As Dayānanda Sarasvatī points out that while Śruti texts start with *oṁ* and end with *śānti-pāṭha*, the Smṛti texts start with a prayer to a sectarian deity, and end with a promise.[3]

The *Brāhmaṇas* are the manuals for the performance of various rituals, and contain detailed instructions and directions for their performance, and mention the results that follow their performance. They are an attempt to develop a religious form of life on the basis of Vedic revelation, and are the first to interpret the Vedic *Saṁhitās* with the purpose of adapting the wisdom of the Veda to serve the practical religious needs of man. However,

---

2. According to Dayānanda Sarasvatī, who opposed the Smṛti form of Hinduism, the *Brāhmaṇas* do not constitute Veda or Śruti. According to him, only the *Saṁhitās* constitute the Veda, and are, therefore, infallible and authoritative. They are truly revealed.

3. *Satyārtha Prakāśa* (Light of Truth), pp. 198-9.

this is not the case with the *Saṁhitā*s and the Upaniṣads. While the Vedic hymns (*Saṁhitā*s) are a poetic expression of divinely inspired devotion, the *Brāhmaṇa*s, which are mostly liturgical texts, are an attempt to adapt and employ the wisdom of the Veda to serve the religious needs of man. All the rituals developed and elaborately described in the *Brāhmaṇa* texts along with their possible results are intended to encourage and influence people to follow a particular form of religious life and worship. This led Pūrva Mīmāṁsā, which follows the *Brāhmaṇa* interpretation of the Veda (*Saṁhitā*s), to define *dharma* (religion) as that which impels one to (religious) action, and their rejection of the Upaniṣads as having no religious use or application.[4] On the other hand, we do not find either in the *Saṁhitā*s or in the Upaniṣads any promise of rewards for knowing the truth. The Vedic seers declare that they have known the truth which is beyond the darkness of ignorance. Truth is an end in itself. And the Veda pleads its helplessness if people are not interested in knowing the truth or in knowing the true meaning of the Veda.[5] The end of devotional life is to repay one's debt to the divine for the gift of divine inspiration, and to praise and glorify the divine. Divinely inspired devotion, the consummation of man's religious life, is regarded as an end in itself by the Vedic seers. Since the Śruti is not interested in the application or employment of truth for achieving human ends, either mundane or heavenly, we cannot say that the Śruti tradition in its intention is religious if we mean by religion a

---

4. According to Pūrva Mīmāṁsā the Upaniṣads are only *arthavāda*. And the object of the Veda is religious action or *dharma*. Therefore, only the *vidhi* (imperative) statements represent the Veda. The Upaniṣads, which have no application (*viniyoga*) in any rites and rituals developed in the *Brāhmaṇa*s, are intended to persuade or induce people to observe *dharma*. The Upaniṣadic statements are not, therefore, objectively true. Their validity lies in their capacity to persuade or induce one to practice *dharma*. An *arthavāda* statement is not literally true as, for example, when someone says to the other that a particular cow is good the intention of the speaker or the statement is not to describe the cow but to induce the other to buy it.

5. *Ṛgveda*, 1.164.39.

fruitful or useful human activity aimed at attaining some of the higher ends of man. Śruti stands for a divinely inspired vision of truth or divinely inspired knowledge of the divine which I prefer to call a world-view.

A world-view influences the life of an individual and that of a community comprehensively and profoundly, and it is what is stable and enduring in the life of a religion. It is of foundational importance or value to a religion, and endures as long as the religion survives. It is the real or ultimate source of meaning and justification of a religion, and its beliefs and doctrines. Therefore, criticism and rejection of some of the beliefs and doctrines of a religion do not really undermine the meaningfulness and validity of a religion as long as its world-view has not lost its meaningfulness to its followers. Thus, all the representative thinkers and saints of Hinduism refer to Śruti, and its world-view when they talk of Hinduism, and it is what is commonly acceptable to all the Hindus even though they disagree among themselves on some aspects of Hinduism. Even though much of Śruti tradition is modified by way of interpretation, its world-view which gives Hinduism its character and identity has remained stable. Śruti represents that aspect of Hinduism which has been the source of inspiration for various thinkers and saints in all times, or the Hinduism that is a vision or a world-view. And it has not undergone any significant change throughout the existence of Hinduism. However, the manner of its formulation and expression differs from school to school. In other words, the basic vision of Hinduism, which is the basic characteristic of Hinduism and distinguishes it from other religious traditions, has remained more or less stable and unchanged, while that aspect of Hinduism which is represented by Smṛti tradition has undergone changes and modifications, and much of it has even been rejected by some of the Hindu thinkers. Śruti represents the inner strength and vitality of Hinduism, and one's acceptance of its authority and sanctity is, therefore, the only criterion to be a Hindu. On the other hand, a Hindu is free to accept or reject partly or fully any of the Smṛti beliefs and doctrines without ceasing to be a Hindu. Such freedom is not, however, allowed in the case of Śruti and its world-view, as to reject it is to cease to be a Hindu. However, freedom is allowed to interpret the Śruti tradition.

We now try to present and understand the world-view of Hinduism or the basic vision on which Hinduism is founded. What strikes one about the Śruti literature, which fully reflects the world-view of Hinduism, is the absence of dichotomy and opposition between divine and mundane, or sacred and secular, or spiritual and material. However, these distinctions are made, and are considered meaningful and valid only for the purpose of a conceptual understanding of the world. They are not seen as having any ontological status and validity. According to the world-view of Hinduism, there are no two ontologically distinct realities corresponding to our concepts of divine and mundane or spiritual and material, or sacred and secular. What is ultimately or ontologically real is one only, and that is the source of existence of all that is there, and, therefore, it constitutes the unity or oneness of all that is there. All that we know and experience is a varied manifestation of one and the same reality which in terms of its inherent creativity manifests itself in various forms. The world with all its diversity and richness is a creative manifestation of the same divine reality. Therefore, knowledge of the distinctions and differences, which are revealed to man's ordinary or empirical knowledge and understanding, does not make one religious or spiritual. To see or realise the divine unity or oneness of all that is empirically known and experienced is the meaning and end of religion, or the realisation that all that is there is a creative manifestation of the divine makes one religious. The divine is the ultimate source of existence as well as the inner unity or oneness of all that is empirically real. Therefore, to know the divine is to realise it as the oneness of all that is there, and that is the consummation of man's religious or spiritual life. The divine reveals itself in and through all the forms of its manifestation, and, therefore, the world of manifestation is the source of our knowledge of the divine. To know the divine is to know it in and through all the forms of its manifestation known as the world. Our knowledge of the divine is not possible outside the realm of its manifestation, though the divine transcends the world of its manifestation. But to see the world as world is not the same as to know it as a manifestation of the divine, and to know that the world is a manifestation of the divine is to experience the divine oneness or unity of the world. What is it to experience or realise the divine oneness or unity of the world? For instance, matter is conceived as the unity of all that is physical or material, just as gold is the unity of all that is made of gold. And to see gold in all that is made of gold or clay in all that is made of clay is to see gold or clay as the unity of all that is made of gold or clay. However, conception of matter as the unifying principle of the world has not given rise to religion. One does not become religious by accepting the material unity of the world. And there are different views as to what constitutes the unity of the world.

What is it to see or realise the divine unity or oneness of all that is there? According to the Hindu world-view, the divine is the unity or oneness of both matter and spirit, and the divine is not just a metaphysical idea or concept. The sense of the divine or its presence within nature is revealed to man by the divine itself as man comes to know the divine not because of his own efforts and understanding but due to divine inspiration. The way the divine is known to man influences his understanding of the nature and meaning of the divine, as well as his attitude towards the divine. The vision of the divine influences not only the religious life of a person, but his whole life. The Hindu world-view influenced the classical Indian culture and civilisation. Nature is the primary source of revelation of the divine to the Vedic seers. It reveals the divine by inspiring man divinely or by inspiring devotion in man which is divine as man comes to know the nature and meaning of divine in experiencing devotion. Therefore, nature is seen as a creative manifestation of the divine by the Vedic seers. The divine that is present in nature acts on the divine that is within man, and that is the moment when man sees the divine presence within himself as well as in nature. Man's response to his awareness of the divine is to spontaneously bow down in reverence (*namaḥ*). Man experiences divine in the state of divinely inspired devotion or as devotion itself. And as the vision of the divine so experienced is expressed through the hymns of the Veda, the Veda is divine and sacred. As the Veda (hymns) is an expression in language of divinely inspired vision of the divine it is the basic source of Hinduism. And because of its revealed character the Veda or Śruti is regarded as the supreme or ultimate authority for Hinduism, and is regarded as both impersonal and infallible. It is impersonal in the sense that it does not represent the wisdom of any one person or group of persons, and for the same reason it is also infallible.

The Smṛti tradition is not, strictly speaking, an interpretation of Śruti. The Smṛti texts do not refer to any text or passage of the Veda in support or justification of its views or teaching. On the other hand, most of the Smṛti texts claim that the source of the wisdom they represent are the various sectarian deities of the Smṛti tradition. But for the world-view of Śruti, which the Smṛti tradition adopts, there is little or nothing in common between Śruti and Smṛti. Śruti and Smṛti are not completely compatible with each other in respect of certain basic religious ideas and doctrines. Their differences are basic, and they are even opposed to each other in their understanding of the nature and meaning of religion. However, Smṛti tradition has adopted the world-view of Śruti, and has made significant attempts to reconcile and harmonise its sectarian theologies with the world-view of Śruti. The world-view integrates Smṛti with Śruti, and gives it its Hindu character and identity. Otherwise, Smṛti protests though in a subtle way against Śruti, and has even rejected much of Śruti tradition. We find tension between Śruti and Smṛti which at times has resulted in open conflict between them. However, the tension between Śruti and Smṛti, and the constant attempts to reconcile and harmonise them helped in enriching Hinduism, and making it more comprehensive and integral. While the universal outlook of Hinduism, and its openness to new ideas are due to its world-view, its development as a religious tradition, its theological character and emotional appeal are the contribution of Smṛti tradition to Hinduism. And it is the Smṛti tradition which has made significant attempts to harmonise and integrate the popular form of Hinduism with the Śruti tradition.

Smṛti has no distinct world-view of its own. It accepts the world-view of Śruti, and adapts it to suit its theological needs. And unless we admit the independent origin of the Smṛti tradition we cannot satisfactorily explain certain facts about Hinduism as believed in and practised by almost all the Hindus. Much of Hinduism or most of the Hindu beliefs, doctrines and practices are not compatible or consistent with the world-view of Śruti. There is no Śruti authority and justification for all that is known and accepted as Hinduism or for most of the Hindu beliefs, doctrines and practices. In other words, most of the Hindu religious beliefs, doctrines and practices cannot be explained and justified on the basis of Śruti. Hinduism is largely a creation of Smṛti tradition, as most of its beliefs, doctrines and practices have their origin and development only in the Smṛti tradition. The Smṛti tradition is the authority as well as the justification for most of the Hindu religious beliefs and practices. The various sectarian theologies of Smṛti cannot be reconciled and harmonised with the world-view of Śruti though for various reasons Smṛti claims that it is a creative extension and development of Śruti. The Smṛti form of Hinduism is theistic though under the influence of Śruti it sees the limitations of a purely theistic conception of the divine, and, therefore, tries to transcend its theism in comprehending the nature of the divine without, however, giving up its basic theistic position. Because of the influence of Śruti the theistic tradition of Smṛti is distinct in certain important aspects from other theistic traditions. We find in the development of Hinduism a constant tension between the theism of Smṛti and the Vedāntic conception of the divine. However, by adopting the Śruti world-view the Smṛti tradition could not significantly change the character of Hinduism, at least at the popular level. This is evident from the fact that the various reform movements within Hinduism are basically an attempt to remind Hinduism of its basic world-view, and to interpret it in the light of its world-view.[6] As pointed out earlier, Hinduism is a confluence of two major streams or traditions represented by Śruti and Smṛti, and though they are distinct and independent traditions we find constant interaction between them in which each tried to influence the other.

The basic vision or the world-view of Hinduism is expressed through such Śruti statements like 'all this is *Brahman*', 'all that is there is permeated by the divine', 'one who sees the (same) *ātman* in all, and all in the *ātman* is wise, and is freed from all misery and sorrow'.[7] The vision that all that is there is a creative self-manifestation of the divine, and, therefore, the divine is the inner unity or oneness of all that is there is the foundation as well as the consummation of Hindu religious life. However, we find within the Hindu tradition significant differences about the nature of the divine, the manner or mode of its manifestation, and the nature of the relationship between the divine and the forms of its manifestation. But all the sects of Hinduism and the different schools of Hindu religious thought accept the oneness of the divine, and its immanence within creation. All that is there or the world of empirical experience and understanding is a creative manifestation of the divine. But how to adapt this ontological vision to the practical religious life of

---

6. The modern movements of Hinduism, like Ārya Samāj and Brahmo Samāj, are based on or inspired by the Śruti tradition of Hinduism. While the Ārya Samāj rejects the authority and relevance of Smṛti tradition in knowing or understanding the nature and meaning of Hinduism (*Ārya-dharma*), the Brahmo Samāj is not so open in its rejection of the Smṛti tradition. Dayānanda has opposed the Smṛti form of Hinduism, and the various Smṛti beliefs and practices, like idol-worship, exclusion of certain sections of society from practising the Śruti form of Hinduism. While the Brahmo Samāj is based on the Vedānta texts, the Ārya Samāj is based on the Vedic *Saṁhitās*. Generally speaking, most of the modern Hindus do not regard the Smṛti form of Hinduism as real Hinduism, and it is the Smṛti form of Hinduism that has been the object of attack and criticism.
7. *Īśavāsyopaniṣad*, 1.1.

man, or what form of religious life the world-view of Śruti can give rise to are some of the problems on which there is no agreement among the various sects and schools of Hinduism. Although Hinduism is theoretically one, and has an identity of its own, as in reality there are different forms of religious life and worship within it with their distinct religious beliefs and doctrines, one may find it difficult to identify the principle of unity that runs through all the sectarian differences. But all the sects of Hinduism and the different schools of Hindu religious thought accept the divine unity or oneness of all that is there. Therefore, the world of empirical experience is not only a source of divine revelation but is also a means of divine realisation. The divine in its creativity manifests itself in varied forms, and all the forms reveal the nature of the divine. And, therefore, to be devoted to and worship any form of divine manifestation, which has its appeal and significance to an individual, is religiously as significant and meaningful as worshipping any other form of the divine. What different people are devoted to and worship are one or the other form of the divine, and the divine in itself, which transcends all the forms of its manifestation, and cannot, therefore, be identified with any form, is not an object of worship. Though the divine is known in and through the forms of its manifestation its nature cannot be determined on the basis of such knowledge. However, to worship any of the forms of its manifestation is to worship the divine if it is based on the realisation that the divine is present within all the forms of its manifestation.

To see or realise the divine in and through some of the pre-eminent forms of its manifestation is one aspect of religious life which, however, remains incomplete until one sees the divine in all the forms of its manifestation. It is to see the divine in all that is there or in all the forms of its manifestation, and yet realise that the divine transcends all that is there. According to Hinduism, whether it is based on Śruti or on Smṛti, the realisation that all is *Brahman*, or Vāsudeva is all (*vāsudeva sarvamiti*) is the consummation of man's religious life, as well as the meaning and end of religion.[8] Such vision of the divine is central to Śruti tradition, and the Smṛti tradition adopts it, and tries to reconcile and harmonise its sectarian theologies with it. In other words, the Smṛti tradition tries to integrate itself with the Śruti tradition by means of adopting the world-view of Śruti. Therefore, Hinduism as it is known to us, and is believed in and practised by almost all the Hindus, is the result of the process of reconciliation and integration between the traditions of Śruti and Smṛti. It is not based completely either on the Śruti tradition or on the Smṛti tradition. We are not concerned here with the problem whether the two traditions can really be reconciled and integrated with each other or not. But almost all the creative Hindu thinkers and saints, down to the present day, are alive to the problem of their reconciliation, and in their own characteristic ways have tried to reconcile and integrate the world-view of Śruti with the Smṛti form of Hinduism. The Śruti tradition recognises the importance of the Smṛti tradition in the development of Hinduism, and its authority and validity are not generally questioned as long as its theological or religious beliefs and doctrines do not come into conflict with Śruti, and its world-view. This is obviously the standpoint of those who accept the supreme authority of Śruti, while the thinkers of Smṛti tradition are, generally speaking, apologetic and defensive in their attitude to Smṛti tradition, and try to find the authority and justification of Śruti for their theological beliefs and doctrines. And when they fail to find any basis or justification in Śruti for their beliefs and ideas they adduce the argument that that portion or text of Śruti which is supposed to be the source of justification and authority for their theological views and ideas might have been lost. Thus, generally speaking, the

8. The realisation that God is all (*vāsudeva sarvamiti*) is the end and meaning of religion, according to *Bhāgavata dharma*. God is identified as Vāsudeva as He lives within all (*vāsanād vāsudevasya*). All beings abide in Him, and He in all beings. He is identified with the Vedāntic *Brahman*. *Viṣṇu yasyābhinnam idam jagat* — *Viṣṇu Purāṇa* 1.19.82; *sarvam brahma mayam jagat* — *Kūrma Purāṇa* 14.64.

Smṛti thinkers are apologetic and defensive in their attitude towards the status and validity of Smṛti tradition. But it is a fact that Śruti and Smṛti are not completely compatible with each other in their approaches and attitudes to the basic problems of religion. They also differ in their understanding of the nature and meaning of religion. This is reflected in the history of Hinduism in which attempts are made to reform, and even to reject Smṛti as something un-orthodox (un-Vedic) or even un-Hindu as in certain important aspects Smṛti does not only agree with Śruti, but even goes against it.[9] To an extent this is also true of Smṛti's attitude towards Śruti. It is critical of Śruti, and its teaching, and in a very subtle manner tries to undermine the authority and validity of Śruti. However, we do not find any open conflict and antagonism between Śruti and Smṛti, as it is in the case of Hinduism and Buddhism. This is largely due to the fact that Smṛti accepts the world-view of Śruti, and tries to reconcile and integrate itself with the Śruti tradition.[10]

---

9. Although the Smṛti tradition claims to itself the authority of the Veda as it thinks it represents the wisdom of the Veda, its authority is traditionally regarded as only secondary to that of the Veda. Though most of the sectarian Purāṇas claim independent validity to themselves, the general view of the Smṛti tradition is that it derives its authority from the Veda. However, in modern times most of the reform movements of Hinduism have rejected the authority of the Smṛti tradition. Even some, like Ārya Samāj, have opposed the Smṛti tradition. Though most of the Hindu religious beliefs, doctrines and practices are Smṛti based, most of the Hindus in modern times, tend to identify Hinduism with the wisdom of the Upaniṣads. As most of the Hindus try to understand the Purāṇas literally they find it difficult to justify and defend the Purāṇic form of Hinduism. However, Purāṇas do not subscribe to the view that what is said in them is literally true. Their main intention is to give birth to and develop in the hearers devotional form of religious life and worship. *Bhāgavata* is a religious classic, and is fully conscious of the possible criticisms against its approach and attitude to religion, and tries to meet such criticisms in a very meaningful manner.

10. Smṛti tradition is integral to Hinduism primarily because of its acceptance and adoption of the Śruti world-view. Otherwise, in some of its basic beliefs and doctrines it is not wholly compatible with the

→

Smṛti is basically a religious tradition, and theism in one form or other is central to it, whereas Śruti cannot be identified as a religious tradition though Hinduism is primarily based on its authority. However, the Smṛti tradition claims that its theistic position is consistent with the wisdom of Śruti. As it has been pointed out earlier the tension between Śruti and Smṛti, and the various attempts to reconcile and harmonise them has been a dominant feature of the development of Hinduism. The dominant concern of most of the Hindu thinkers right from the epic period down to the modern times is how to reconcile and integrate both the traditions, one predominantly philosophical and monistic or even absolutistic, and the other religious and theistic. While the Śruti form of religious life, which is limited, both in theory and in practice, to elite sections of society, had been the dominant form of classical Hinduism, the Smṛti form of religion, but as influenced by the world-view of Śruti, which is open to all the sections of society, has been the dominant form of religious life of the Hindus.

The Smṛti also represents a tradition of reconciliation of the sectarian theologies of various religious sects of Hinduism on the basis of the world-view of Śruti. The different sectarian theologies of Smṛti tradition try to appropriate for themselves the authority and sanctity of Śruti, and the object of Smṛti in claiming the authority of Śruti to its theological beliefs and doctrines is to claim to itself the status of Śruti. The Smṛti tradition finds in the philosophy of Sāṁkhya, particularly in its metaphysics, a philosophical basis for achieving reconciliation and harmony between its theism and the ontology of Śruti. It adopts Sāṁkhya metaphysics without its dualism as it sees in

---

→ Śruti tradition. We find even a subtle form of criticism of Śruti tradition within the Smṛti tradition. However, because of its acceptance of the Śruti world-view it was not rejected by the Hindu tradition. Had Buddhism and Jainism accepted the meaningfulness and validity of the Śruti world-view they would not have been rejected by Hinduism. Here the intention is not to say that the Smṛti tradition has accepted the world-view of Śruti for practical reasons. It has fully adopted the world-view of Śruti because of its integral character.

Sāṁkhya philosophy a meeting point between itself and Śruti. The basic idea of the Smṛti tradition that the creation or the world is the body of God or Viṣṇu, which was developed philosophically by Rāmānuja, and theistically by the authors of Purāṇas, especially the *Viṣṇu* and *Bhāgavata*, finds its original expression in *Rāmāyaṇa*, a work earlier to both Purāṇas and Rāmānuja.[11] While the creation is seen as the body of God, who is variously identified in the Smṛti tradition as Viṣṇu or Vāsudeva or Śiva, His soul or self is seen as the source of all that is spiritual. As the ultimate source of all that is there, both physical and spiritual, the person of God is the unity of both. In the person of God both matter and spirit are integrated, and find their unity. God is present within all creation, including matter, as both matter and spirit constitute the person of God. He is one without a second, and is personal. He is the supreme object of love, devotion and worship.

The *Brahman* of Śruti tradition, which is more impersonal than personal or rather transcends the dichotomy of personal and impersonal, is identified with God, a personal being, in the Smṛti tradition. *Prakṛti* and *puruṣa* which are ontologically independent and are unrelated in the philosophy of Sāṁkhya are conceived in the Smṛti tradition as constituting the person of God. While *prakṛti* forms the body of God, *puruṣa* is His self or soul. *Prakṛti* and *puruṣa* constitute the person of God, and as a person He is more than *prakṛti* and *puruṣa*. And as the body of God *prakṛti* is not simple matter because it is enlivened by the spirit or self of God. According to the understanding of Smṛti tradition, the body and self, though can be distinguished, cannot be separated as either of them cannot be conceived without the other. They are inseparable, and though they are distinct they are not two. While, according to Smṛti tradition, God is the oneness or unity of *prakṛti* and *puruṣa*, *Brahman* is not conceived as the unity of *prakṛti* and *puruṣa*. While *Brahman* is more impersonal than personal, God of Smṛti tradition, even in His

11. *Rāmāyaṇa*, Yuddha-kāṇḍa 117.26.

identification with the *Brahman* of the Upaniṣads, is viewed as a personal being. The difference between Śruti and Smṛti in their basic positions and concerns, and the continuous efforts to reconcile and integrate them helped the growth and development of Hinduism. The intellectual openness of the Hindu tradition, and its deep religious or spiritual significance and appeal are due to constant interaction between the two traditions, and their influence on each other. The Hindu world-view helped in reconciling and integrating the philosophical insights of Śruti, particularly of Vedānta, with the devotional form of religious life of the Smṛti tradition, though at times each tried to marginalise the importance of the other.

The major problem faced by several thinkers in their attempts to reconcile and integrate the world-view of Śruti with the theistic tradition of Smṛti is how to reconcile the concept of *Brahman* with that of God (*īśvara* or *bhagavān*). It is not easy to reconcile the Vedāntic concept of *Brahman* with the Smṛti concept of God. However, the various problems such attempts gave rise to, and constant efforts to resolve them form the theological or religious development of Hinduism. The attempts to reconcile and integrate both the traditions, whatever may be the historical or sociological reasons behind such attempts, mark the birth or beginning of Hinduism, and its development as a religious tradition. Therefore, Hinduism is not based completely either on Śruti or on Smṛti. And their contribution to the growth and development of Hinduism is substantial and significant. It is not, therefore, easy to determine which of them is more basic and significant in understanding the nature and meaning of Hinduism. And as both the traditions are so integrated in the life of Hinduism it is difficult to isolate the contribution and influence of each in the development of Hinduism. Even the most philosophically-minded Śaṅkara was not averse or indifferent to Smṛti aspect of Hinduism as is evident from his devotional compositions in praise of various deities of the Smṛti tradition, and the theistically oriented philosopher like Rāmānuja was keen on developing philosophical basis and justification for theism. Rāmānuja is not opposed to rational or philosophical understanding of religious problems as Śaṅkara is not opposed to devotional form of religious life. Furthermore, the fact that there is little or no antagonism between philosophical understanding and devotional way of religious life within the Hindu religious tradition, as it is exemplified in the lives of most of the saints, philosophers and religious thinkers of Hindu tradition, shows that both the traditions are well integrated and balanced in the life of Hinduism. A world-view without giving rise to a religious or devotional way of life, and a life of religious faith and devotion without a clear intellectual or philosophical understanding to sustain it will not help in integrating the human person, and help his spiritual growth and fulfillment.

4

Dharma as Religion

THERE are several definitions of religion in all of which attempts are made to understand what is essential and common to all the religions of the world. And in all such definitions what is peculiar and unique to each religion is overlooked, and that aspect of a religion which it has in common with all other religions is highlighted. Our present purpose in trying to understand the nature and meaning of religion is not to attempt a new definition of religion, but to understand the meaning of religion on the basis of Hinduism which may or may not be meaningful and valid with regard to other religions of the world. What is true of Hinduism is also to an extent true of other religions, and what is true of other religions is also to an extent true of Hinduism. Therefore, instead of trying to understand the nature and meaning of Hinduism in terms of any one definition of religion an attempt is made to understand the meaning of religion on the basis of Hinduism. Though most of the beliefs and doctrines that are considered essential to religion are also present within Hinduism, they are not considered essential to Hinduism, and, therefore, they may not help us in understanding the nature and meaning of Hinduism. There are certain characteristics of Hinduism which are essential to it, but they are not to be found in other religions of the world. And these characteristics also help us in distinguishing Hinduism from other religions of the world.

What is Hinduism or what is it to be a Hindu? According to the traditional definition of Hinduism, which is formal and minimal, a Hindu is one who accepts the authority of the Veda or Śruti. But this definition of Hinduism is meant to distinguish Hindus from those who do not accept the authority of the Veda. All those who do not believe in the truth or wisdom of the Veda, and accept its authority are not Hindu. This definition, which is post-Buddhistic, is meant to distinguish Hindus from non-Hindus. It is formal, and insists on a minimum condition to be a Hindu. One has to accept the authority of the Veda to be a Hindu, whatever may be his interpretation of it. The Buddhists and the Jains, and people belonging to various other minor religious traditions of India are highly religious, but they are not considered Hindu as they do not accept the authority of the Veda in religious or spiritual matters. This definition of Hinduism does not say anything about the beliefs, dogmas and doctrines one has to accept to be a Hindu. This may also be true about other religions. For instance, all those who believe in monotheism need not be Christian or Muslim though belief in monotheism is essential to both Christianity and Islam.

What is it to accept the authority of the Veda? Is it to accept any beliefs and doctrines supposed to be Vedic in origin and character? All those who accept the authority of the Veda differ significantly in their beliefs and doctrines, and in certain cases the differences are even basic. Therefore, a formal acceptance of the authority of the Veda is not sufficient to be a Hindu. To accept the authority of the Veda is to accept the world-view that is fundamental or central to the Vedic or Śruti tradition. The Veda or Śruti does not represent the wisdom of any one person or group of persons. Without entering into the controversy whether the Veda is beginningless (*sanātana*) and impersonal (*apauruṣeya*), we can say that it represents the divinely inspired wisdom of several seers belonging to different periods of time. And most of the views about the Veda, such as that it is eternal, infallible and impersonal, are not entertained by the Veda itself, but by different interpreters of the Veda. Therefore, they do not have the same validity and sanctity as of the Veda. They can be discussed, modified, and even rejected without affecting thereby the authority and sanctity of the Veda. However, the Veda is eternal in the sense that the truth or wisdom it represents is not the wisdom of a person or group of persons. The divine is self-luminous, and is, therefore, eternally self-revealing. Furthermore, it is not meaningful to talk of truth as having an origin or beginning as truth in the ultimate analysis is not different from the divine. According to Hinduism, truth as the self-revelation of the divine is co-eternal with the divine. As the self-revelation of the divine truth can have no origin or beginning. And as the divine is self-luminous and eternally self-revealing anyone who wants to know the divine can know it. Our knowledge of the divine involves self-revelation on the part of the divine, as otherwise there can be no knowledge of the divine. The divine reveals itself in and through the forms of its manifestation, or the world, and, therefore, to know the divine is to know it in and through the forms of its manifestation. The idea or notion of the divine in itself is mostly logical and speculative, and is intelligible and meaningful only in relation to the manifested state of the divine. It is only when the divine is known in and through its manifestations the problem of knowing it in itself arises. To think of the divine in itself is to understand the nature of the divine prior to its manifestation, or the nature of the divine in its un-manifested state of existence. And if the divine has not manifested itself the problem of knowing the divine in its un-manifested state of existence or in itself will be superfluous. Our knowledge of the divine based on its revelation in and through the forms of its manifestation is presupposed in all our attempts to understand the divine in itself or in its un-manifestated state of existence. Furthermore, we cannot think of the divine without its self-manifestation, as it would not be meaningful to think of the divine, which is essentially spiritual, without its self-manifestation or self-expression. If the divine is essentially spiritual it cannot be without its self-expression or self-manifestation as to be spiritual is to be creative. The divine and its self-expression or manifestation go together, and, therefore, the idea of the divine in itself is a demand of reason, but not an object of direct knowledge or experience. On the other hand, our knowledge of the divine in and through its manifestations is a matter of direct experience. All that we know and experience is a manifested form of the divine or its self-manifestation or expression. The divine in itself or in its un-manifested state of existence cannot be an object of direct knowledge or experience, because without the manifestation of the divine there can be no existence of the world, and, therefore, the possibility of knowing the divine in itself. The notion of the divine in itself is a matter of logical understanding based on our conception of the divine in terms of its manifestations. There are several conceptions of the divine in all of which certain manifestations of the divine are given supreme importance and value; and it is only on the basis of them we can think of the divine in itself. What each person or each religious tradition knows about the divine is based on certain forms of its manifestation, and, therefore, there can be several conceptions of the divine based on different forms of its manifestation We cannot also deny the role of human understanding and its limitations in knowing or conceiving the nature of the divine. Depending upon the differences in human understanding, and other subjective factors there can be several conceptions of the divine, even though all of them are based on one or the other form of manifestation of the divine. But to say that human understanding is limited and conditioned is to admit that it has the capacity to know its conditioned nature, and, therefore, an ability to transcend it. Otherwise man cannot hope to transcend his limitations, or his conditioned state of existence. Similarly, man's ability to know that the divine is more than or transcends all our conceptions of it, or no conception of the divine is adequate to represent the nature of the divine truly and perfectly, shows that somehow man has the capacity to know the divine. To admit that man has the capacity to know that the divine transcends all the conceptions of it is to admit that man has the capacity to know the divine. Otherwise, we cannot also explain the fact of growth or development in human understanding about the nature of the divine in which process it transcends several conceptions of the divine, and yet is not certain about the true nature of the divine. This gives rise to a sense of mystery about the nature of the divine.

According to the Hindu world-view, all that is there is a manifested form of the divine. All the conceptions of the divine in which some aspect of the divine as revealed either within the reality of man or in nature is high-lighted and emphasised, are true of the divine as they reveal something about the divine though the nature of the divine cannot be determined in terms of any one or all the conceptions. This is because the possible forms of divine manifestation are infinite. Therefore, all the views or conceptions of the divine only reflect its greatness and glory. This kind of understanding, though is skeptical about man's ability to know the divine in itself, yet helps man in recognising the meaningfulness of all the conceptions of the divine. The divine in its creativity is dynamic. It can manifest itself in infinite forms, and, therefore, it is not meaningful to determine the nature of the divine in terms of fixed concepts and definitions. Man also in his attempts to understand himself or his reality forms various views about himself, and yet realises that no one view is adequate to know the reality of himself. He is more than all the views about himself. This is because man is also essentially spiritual and creative. There is development in the self-understanding of man. And, therefore, all the views or concepts of man, though reveal something about the reality of man, cannot determine his reality.

It is almost a dogma with Hinduism, which is shared by almost all the sects of Hinduism, and different schools of Hindu religious thought, that the world is a manifested form of the divine, whether the divine is conceived in personal or impersonal terms. The world is the cosmic (*virāṭ*) form of manifestation of the divine, and as a manifestation of the divine it is divine. And logically speaking the process of self-manifestation or self-expression of the divine because of its inherent power of creativity can have no beginning, and, therefore, no end. It is said in one of the major Upaniṣads that the divine (*Brahman*) manifests itself for the purpose of self-realisation (*ātma prabodhanārtham*).[1] The divine realises itself in and through all the forms of its manifestation, and there can be no other purpose for the self-manifestation of the divine. The divine manifests itself as spontaneously as a spider weaves a web.[2] And, therefore, the divine is not completely other than and different from the world of its manifestation, and at the same time it is not the same as the world of its manifestation. The terms 'divine' and 'world' do not mean the same. They do not refer to the same reality, and at the same time they do not refer to two ontologically independent realities. The Upaniṣadic statement, 'I am the creation';[3] expresses the relation of oneness between the divine and the world of its manifestation. The divine and the world are not one and same, and yet they are not different. This vision of the divine, which is fundamental to the Veda or to Śruti tradition, is central to Hinduism, or Hinduism is founded on such a vision of the divine. Therefore, to accept the authority of the Veda is to accept its vision of the divine. Though a personal conception of the divine is not basically inconsistent with the Vedic vision of the divine, what is essential to the Vedic vision of the divine is its immanence. Therefore, without accepting the Vedic vision of the divine one cannot be a Hindu though in details concerning the nature of the divine, the mode or manner of its manifestation, and its relation to its various manifestations, including man, complete agreement is not insisted upon in Hinduism. The different sects of Hinduism and schools of Hindu religious thought differ in their understanding of the nature of the relationship between the divine and the world on the one hand, and between the divine and man on the other. The basic Hindu approach and attitude to various problems concerning religion, including its nature and meaning, are directly influenced by its vision of the divine. All the creative thinkers of Hinduism, and its saints and sages share the same ontological vision though they differ among

1. Śaṅkara's introduction to *Aitareya Upaniṣad*, 2.1.1.
2. *Muṇḍaka Upaniṣad*, 1.1.7.
3. *Bṛhadāraṇyaka Upaniṣad*, 1.4.5.

themselves in its articulation and expression, as well as in working out its implications. Even the avowedly theistic sects of Hinduism accept the Vedic vision of the divine.

One can be devoted to and worship any form of the divine as the divine is immanently present in all the forms of its manifestation. And at the level of manifestation the divine can be worshipped only in its forms of manifestation. The world of empirical experience and understanding is a manifestation of the divine, and as the source of manifestation, the divine transcends all the forms of its manifestation. The various forms of its manifestation reveal the glory of the divine, and the divine is more than its glory as the *Ṛgveda* puts it.[4] Therefore, to identify the divine exclusively with any of the forms of its manifestation is not consistent with the Hindu vision of the divine. Every conception of the divine, which is based on some of the pre-eminent forms of its manifestation, is selective, and excludes from itself some aspects of the divine. No conception of the divine can comprehend the nature of the divine fully, and, therefore, no conceptions of the divine is adequate to know or understand the nature of the divine. Such realisation gives rise to negative description of the divine, the intention of which is to show that the divine is all inclusive.[5] The realisation that all the forms of the divine are equally divine, and, therefore, devotion to and worship of any form of the divine is religiously meaningful and fulfilling is central to Hinduism. On the other hand, to identify the divine with any one or more forms of its manifestation, or to understand its nature in terms of any one form of the divine, though may be meaningful from the point of view of practical religious life, is to miss the all-inclusive and integral nature of the divine.

How do we know that the world, and the various creations of human creativity are the forms of manifestation of the divine, or how do we recognise their divine character? Not only nature

4. *Ṛgveda* 10.90 (Puruṣa Sūkta).
5. *Bṛhadāraṇyaka Upaniṣad*, 2.3.6 and Śaṅkara's commentary on it.

in its diverse phenomena, but also human reality is a manifestation of the divine. Being a manifestation of the divine each phenomenon of nature can reveal the divine, or the divine reveals its nature in and through all the forms of its manifestation. The divine reveals itself as the essence and inner unity of all that is there, including man. Each phenomenon of nature has its essence or nature (*dharma*) which it expresses and follows. If we can discern the essence of a phenomenon we can know the nature of the divine as it is the essence of all that is there. For instance, the principle of heat or warmth is the essence of fire though fire manifests itself in various forms, such as the ordinary fire, the lightening in the firmament, the heat in man, animals and plants that helps their growth. In other words, in whatever thing or phenomenon heat in any form is discerned, Agni, a manifestation of the divine, is present. All the phenomena of nature and man are governed by their essence or nature (*svabhāva*), or the whole world, including man, is guided and governed by its own nature or *dharma*. Although the manner of manifestation of *dharma*, the revelation of the divine within the realm of manifestation, is not the same in all phenomena, yet they all manifest *dharma*. The *dharma* of a phenomenon is also the principle of its unity. In this sense *dharma* not only governs every phenomenon of nature, but also forms the unity of every phenomenon, and, therefore, the unity of all that is there. The manner or mode of manifestation of *dharma*, as the essence of a thing or a phenomenon, differs from phenomenon to phenomenon, but as that which governs, sustains and units *dharma* is inherently present within all phenomena. And this basic characteristic of *dharma* is common to all the meanings of *dharma*.

The word *dharma* is used in many senses or it has several meanings which can be discerned in terms of the context of its usage. It is used to mean the rightful conduct of man, either individual or social, or as that which sustains, governs and unites the world, or as the nature of a thing or a phenomenon. What is basic to all its senses or what characterises *dharma* in whatever context it is used is its power or capacity to hold together, sustain and unite. What sustains, governs and unites a thing or a phenomenon is *dharma*. Each phenomenon is unified, sustained and governed because of *dharma*. The world is ordered, and is a unity because of *dharma* that is immanent within it. As the essence of each and every phenomenon *dharma* is the unity of every phenomenon. This is the primary or Vedic meaning of *dharma*. All that is there is grounded or founded on *dharma*, or *dharma* is the ground or foundation of all that is there (*dharme sarvam pratiṣṭhitam, dharmaḥ viśvasya jagataḥ pratiṣṭhā*).[6] All that is there is comprehended by *dharma* (*dharmeṇa sarvamidam parigr̥hati*).[7] In this sense *dharma* is not different from *r̥ta* as everything is ordered and governed by *r̥ta*. *Dharma* is that which holds together and sustains, and this meaning of *dharma*, as pointed out earlier, is the basic characteristic of *dharma* which is reflected in all its usages. Everything in the world, or the world as a whole follows *dharma* in the sense that everything is governed by its *dharma* or its own laws or nature (*svabhāva*). All the phenomena of nature and all the planets follow *dharma* and uphold it as well. *Dharma* constitutes their nature or essence which they cannot violate. In this sense *dharma* is not different from *r̥ta*. Both are ontological. *Dharma* is also identified with truth (*yo vai sa dharmaḥ satyam vai tat*).[8] However, while *r̥ta* is explicitly identified with the divine in the Veda, *dharma* is not so identified. Although *r̥ta* and *dharma* are almost identical in their natures, meanings and functions, *dharma* is given more prominence in the Smr̥ti form of Hinduism.

Dharma is beginningless as it is not a custom or a code of conduct or a religion that is established or propounded by someone. It flows from the nature of the divine or is the nature of the divine as it reveals itself within the realm of manifestation. Like *r̥ta*, *dharma* is also a manifestation of the divine within

---

6. *Mahānārāyaṇopaniṣad*, 78.6; *Br̥hadāraṇyaka Upaniṣad*, 1.4.14.
7. *Ibid.*, 79.7.
8. *Br̥hdāraṇyaka Upaniṣad*, 1.4.14.

nature. In this sense *dharma* is ontological, and is co-eternal with the divine. It has no origin. As that which sustains, governs and unites *dharma* is immanent within all. The laws of nature reveal themselves in nature, and are inherent in nature.

What is the meaning of *dharma* in relation to man or in the context of human reality? Is it something fixed as it is in the case of nature and animals, which he cannot violate, or is it something which man can decide for himself either individually or collectively? Can we identify *dharma* in relation to man with morality? Is *dharma* natural to man or is it something conventional? While in other religious traditions *dharma*, conceived either as morality or as religion, is viewed as something God-given, in the Hindu tradition, as succinctly expressed in the *Kaṭha Upaniṣad*, both *śreya* and *peya* or what is ultimately good and what is sweet or pleasant, are given to man in his nature.[9] They come to him naturally, in the sense that man is naturally endowed with the sense of what is good and what is sweet or pleasant. To express it in the language of the Smṛti tradition, both *pravṛtti* (attachment to ordinary or sensuous form of life and enjoyment) and *nivṛtti* (detachment from ordinary or sensuous form of life) are in the nature of man.[10] Man has no fixed or determinable nature which he cannot violate. At no stage of his existence man is satisfied or content with what he is. He knows the world that is given to his sense-experience, and yet not being satisfied with it, he aspires to know what is not so given or what transcends the reality of his empirical experience . He knows the present, and wants to know the future.[11] As the sense of what is desirable or good is inherent within himself his attachment to the world of sense-experience or its hold on him is not total and absolute. His desire to

9. *Kaṭha Upaniṣad*, 1.2.l.

10. *Bhāgavata Purāṇa*, 1.1.26; *Kūrma Purāṇa*, 1.2.61; *Mahābhārata* Śānti-parva, 241.14; *Viṣṇu Purāṇa*, 19.70; see also Śaṅkara's introduction to his commentary on the *Bhagavad Gītā*.

11. *Vājasaneya Saṁhitā*, 34.4; *Aitareya Āraṇyaka*, 2.2.3.3.

transcend the world of his sense experience, and his ability to detach himself from it show that man is not just a physical reality with a determinable nature. Man is not satisfied or content with his ordinary or empirical state of existence, and seeks to know the truth whereby all his desires and aspirations are supremely fulfilled. He seeks to know the truth which can liberate him from his conditioned state of existence. The constant tension and strife between his two dispositions, one seeking what gives pleasure, and the other because of which man is not happy or content with his ordinary or empirical state of existence distinguishes man from the rest of creation. The desire to transcend his ordinary state of existence is due to the fact that man is aware, though dimly, of his divine nature, the real source of his perfection and happiness. Thus, man's need for religious or spiritual perfection and fulfilment is as natural to him as his need for the fulfilment of his physical and psychological desires and needs. Man experiences within himself tension and conflict between the two dispositions, or he is torn, as it were, between his two dispositions not knowing what is his true nature. As Śrī Aurobindo puts it, man is abnormal when compared to other creatures as he does not know what is his normal being.[12] This is what is symbolically represented as a fight between the divine and demoniac or undivine forces within man (*sura* and *asura*), as Śaṅkara interprets the mythological fight between the gods and demons (*deva* and *dānava*).[13] The Vedic analogy of two birds living on the same tree, one seeking pleasure or what is sweet, while the other simply looks on also points to the conflict within man between his two dispositions.[14] Thus, there is tension within man between what he is and what he aspires to be or between what he is and what he cherishes to be. This tension or conflict

12. *Life Divine*, chapters on Man and the Evolution and Man in the universe.
13. Śaṅkara's commentary on *Bṛhadāraṇyaka Upaniṣad*, 1.3.1; *Chāndogya Upaniṣad*, 1.2.1.
14. *Ṛgveda*, 1.164.20; *Śvetāśvatara Upaniṣad*, 4.6; *Muṇḍaka Upaniṣad*, 3.1.1.

is the source of man's misery as well as his greatness. Man is not happy with himself or is not content with what he is, when compared to animals, as he does not know what constitutes his real happiness, and at the same time it reveals his greatness as it can lead him to further growth and perfection. However, in Hinduism there is no notion of a reality that is other than and opposed to the divine, and, therefore, the conflict is not between what is divine and what is undivine. Therefore, the problem is not how to conquer or overcome what is undivine, but how to explain man's ignorance of his divine nature which results in his misery. If the divine nature of man is ontological, and cannot, therefore, be explained away, how to account for the fact that man is most of the time ignorant of his divine nature. The divine in man manifests itself in various forms and ways. Man's unhappiness or discontentment with himself, and, therefore, a desire to transcend his ordinary state of existence, is an indication or a sign or a form of manifestation of the divine within himself. The sense of mystery which man feels about himself when he experiences tension and conflict between his two dispositions is an indication that he is more than what he ordinarily thinks of himself. Man is more than physical as he is not happy or content with his mere physical existence. He is aware, though dimly, of his spiritual or divine nature, which he seeks to realise more clearly and fully. As expressed in the *R̥gveda*, though seeing man does not see, and though hearing he does not hear.[15] He knows the world, and yet does not know it in the sense that he does not know its true or divine nature which is hidden as it were to his ordinary experience and understanding. Similarly, man knows himself, and yet he realises that he is a mystery to himself.

Man overcomes his misery caused by the tension between his two dispositions when he realises the divine within himself fully, or when he sees clearly the divine light within himself. The divine is known and realised more and more clearly and

---

15. *Ṛgveda*, 10.71.4

fully when the darkness of ignorance that seemingly prevents its realisation is destroyed. Then man's vision gets divinely transformed, and enables him to see the presence of the divine within all. And the practical religious life of man is only a preparation (*sādhana*) which helps him in overcoming the ignorance which prevents him from realising his divine nature. The mist (*nihāra*) like power which clouds man's vision, and prevents him from seeing the divine is identified as sin (*pāpa* or *agha*) in the Veda, and as *māyā* or *ajñāna* in the Upaniṣads.[16] The object of man's religious life is to overcome it, and realise thereby his inherent divine nature.

We may wonder in what sense such a state of realisation of the divine, or the religious life based on such realisation can be viewed as *dharma*? As pointed out earlier, *dharma* is that which holds the world together, and sustains it. It is the nature of the divine as revealed within the world of manifestation. And as to see or realise the divine is to see it in all that it has become, including human reality, every action of man, whatever may be his social status, when done with such realisation is known as *dharma*. On the other hand, an action done without the sense of divine though it may be conventionally moral cannot be regarded as *dharma*. In this sense *dharma* is not conventional morality though it is not opposed to morality. In Hinduism *dharma* is not explicitly identified with morality though in a limited sense *dharma* means morality. We cannot, therefore, understand the nature and meaning of *dharma* without understanding its relation to the divine. *Dharma* is divine, as it flows ultimately from the nature of the divine. Therefore, any action done as an act of worship of the divine, or as serving the divine purpose acquires the meaning and value of *dharma*. Otherwise, whatever may be its social or moral value it cannot be considered *dharma*. On the other hand, an action which may appear to be morally deficient, according to the ordinary standards of morality, but is done without any sense of ego, and

---

16. *Ṛgveda*, 10.82.7.

as an act of worship of the divine is regarded as *dharma*. Then every act of man will gain the meaning and value of *yajña*, and serving the divine purpose will be its object. The same idea is expressed more significantly when it is said in the *Mahābhārata* that man can enjoy everything as a left-over of *yajña* (*yajña-avaśiṣṭa*) or as sanctified by *yajña*.[17] In other words, every action done in the spirit of *yajña* will acquire the character of *dharma*.

For a man of realisation his whole life or all that he does is *yajña*. However, for those who have not realised the divine, the meaning of *dharma* is decided by those who have known the meaning of *dharma*, and the purpose of it is to turn man away from the life of attachment (*pravṛtti*) to one of detachment (*nivṛtti*), and help him in realising the meaning of *yajña* in his own life. *Yajña* encompasses the whole life of man. And the Hindu ideal of life is to live a life of *yajña* or *dharma*. According to Hinduism of the Śruti tradition, *yajña* is the meaning of human life. Manu also refers to the vision of the divine or the world-view of Śruti as the ultimate justification, at least theoretically, for all the rules of conduct he formulates to different castes and stations of life.[18] *Bhagavad Gītā* also refers to the vision of the divine as the basis and justification of its teaching. As an integral part of the *Mahābhārata*, which is known as a treatise on *dharma*, *Bhagavad Gītā* is basically concerned with *dharma*. In this sense, *dharma* is more than morality or righteousness though morality and righteousness derive their final justification and value from *dharma*. The Veda or Śruti is the ultimate source of *dharma*, and Śruti is not basically a work on morality; it is not a moral code. It is the basis or the foundation of *dharma* as it provides the basic vision or world-view from which is born the concept of *dharma*, and, therefore, the Vedic vision of the divine is the real basis, and the ultimate source of meaning of *dharma*. It is also the final justification of *dharma*, and, therefore, we cannot understand

17. *Bhagavad Gītā*, 4.31; 3.13 see also Anuśāsana and Śānti-parvas of *Mahābhārata*.

18. *Manu-saṁhitā*, concluding (xii) chapter verses 116-125.

the meaning of the one without understanding the meaning of the other. But what would be the meaning of *dharma* in specific situations, either individual or social, is to be determined or decided upon keeping in view or consistent with the *dharma* that is divine.

Hinduism is often termed by some of its followers as *sanātana dharma*, that is, *dharma* or religion without a beginning, and, therefore, eternal. But in a very significant sense every religion is *sanātana* as no religion is an invention on the part of man, but is founded on truth which is either revealed or discovered. Most of the major religions of the world, like Christianity and Islam, are founded on the truth revealed by God, and are, therefore, eternal or beginingless. And the religions in which there is no concept of revelation, like Buddhism and Jainism, are founded on the truth discovered by their founders. The truth or wisdom of the Veda is in a sense revealed to the Vedic seers. The seers of the Veda have seen or known the truth because of divine inspiration which they acknowledge as a divine gift. Thus, no religion thinks that it is founded on human wisdom or understanding, and, therefore, the truth it represents is not conditioned by time and space, and other human limitations Though the event of revelation is dated its content or wisdom is timeless. This is also the case with Hinduism. It represents the timeless wisdom of the divine as seen or known by the seers because of divine inspiration. It is the timeless wisdom of the divine as known or discovered within the framework of time and space. It is interesting to note one or two points in this connection. In the major Smṛti texts, like the *Mahābhārata* and *Bhāgavata Purāṇa*, a distinction is made between the divine that is known through Śruti (*śabda*), *śabda-brahman* or *vācya-brahman*, and the divine or *Brahman* that is known directly or without being mediated by any text or tradition.[19] Likewise, the *dharma* that flows from the nature of the divine, and is eternal, and the *dharma* that is discerned by man within the context of

19. *Mahābhārata*, Śānti-parva, 232.30.

a situation are conceptually different. The latter though is a manifestation of the *dharma*, that is timeless or *sanātana* is, however, conditioned by time and space, and other human limitations. Its validity is, therefore, conditioned by time and space; it will not have unconditional and universal validity. However, it is the eternal *dharma* but as conditioned by the limitations of human understanding. As the *Ṛgveda* expresses, the divinely inspired truth or wisdom is expressed in speech by different seers according to the levels of their understanding.[20] The divine wisdom is objective and universal, but as understood and interpreted by human beings, who differ in their levels of understanding, it will not be completely objective and universal. Therefore, the meaning of Hinduism as *dharma* need not be the same for all people and for all times. The meaning of *dharma* can change from time to time or from age to age. What is *dharma* in the *satya-yuga* (ideal epoch) also known as *kṛta-yuga*, need not be the same in other ages. It is not only the ethical and social codes that change from time to time and from place to place, but also the meaning of Hinduism as *dharma*. It need not remain, and as a matter of fact, it has not remained the same through the centuries of its existence. But the basic meaning of *dharma* as living and conducting oneself in all situations in accordance with *ṛta* has almost remained the same.

What is peculiar to the Hindu conception of the divine is that the divine in its creativity manifests itself in varied forms, and there is no limit to divine creativity. It is not possible to set limits to the possible forms of expression of the divine creativity, unless one thinks of the divine as having a determinable nature. We cannot determine the nature of divine wisdom and creativity, and, therefore, set limits to the forms of their manifestation. It is, therefore, un-divine not to see the divine in any of the forms of its manifestation. Time (*kāla*) itself is a manifestation of the divine, and, therefore, to think that the divine has nothing to do with time, or the changing circumstances of man and history is

---

20. *Ṛgveda*, 10.111.1.

not really divine.[21] Though the divine is the source or ground of all change in its essence it remains the same, as otherwise it cannot be recognised. Therefore, to see the divine in all the newer forms of its manifestation, and in the ever changing circumstances of human history is the meaning and end of religion conceived as *dharma*. It is, therefore, not so much the correct theological conception of the divine that is really significant for the religious life of man as devotion to and worship of the divine in any form one likes. One may be attracted or drawn to a form of divine manifestation and be devoted to it, but not to recognise the divine in other forms of worship is not to be religious. Thus, Hinduism which attaches supreme importance and value to inwardly experienced devotion does not try to limit the meaning of the divine to any definition or conception of the divine. The nature and meaning of the divine cannot be determined on the basis of some of its manifestations to the exclusion of other forms of its manifestation. What is religiously meaningful and fulfilling, and helps man to lead a divine life is to realise the divine within himself or to inwardly experience devotion, rather than to hold on to certain religious beliefs and doctrines. Hinduism does not, therefore, insist on the uniformity of theological ideas and doctrines, but attaches utmost importance to inwardly experienced devotion. A saint or a devotee is not one who clings to certain theologically correct beliefs and doctrines, but whose life is divinely transformed. And at that stage of human perfection all the theological disputes and controversies fade into insignificance.

What would be the meaning of Hinduism as *dharma* if *dharma* is conceived in dynamic terms, or if the forms of its manifestation go on changing? Just as there is tension and conflict among different religions of the world because each religion identifies the divine with one or the other form of its manifestation, there is tension and conflict within the Hindu

21. In the Veda Prajāpati is identified with *kāla*; *Bhāgavata Purāṇa* 3.29.36-37; 3.6.35. Viṣṇu is addressed as Kālātmaka, *Viṣṇu Purāṇa*, 3.17.25.

religious tradition between those who conceive religion as *dharma* and those who regard unconditional love and devotion (*bhakti*) to God as the meaning and end of religion. However, the traditions of Smṛti and Śruti though significantly differ in their understanding of the nature and meaning of religion, both of them constitute Hinduism, and represent Hinduism. What unites and integrates the two traditions of Hinduism, as discussed in the previous chapter, is its world-view. It is the world-view that is basically common to both the traditions, and gives them their Hindu identity. While the concept of *dharma* is central to one form of Hindu religious life, pure love and devotion to God are central to the other form of Hindu religious life. Though we find tension between them, both at the doctrinal level and at the level of practice, they have developed a common identity because of the world-view, and its integrating force. The saints and creative thinkers of Hinduism, in their attempts to achieve harmony and coherence among the various sects of Hinduism, have, therefore, paid more attention or placed more emphasis on the world-view of Hinduism rather than on theological beliefs and doctrines. This is clearly reflected in the Smṛti tradition and literature. God (*bhagavān*) identified either as Viṣṇu or Śiva in the major Smṛti texts like *Bhāgavata*, *Viṣṇu* and *Śaiva* Purāṇas, is also identified with *Brahman* of the Vedānta tradition. The attempts to identify Viṣṇu or Śiva with *Brahman* and *Brahman* with Viṣṇu or Śiva are highly significant in integrating the Smṛti or *Bhāgavata* form of religion with the Śruti form of religion. The meaning and end of religion, according to Smṛti form of religion, known as *Bhāgavata-dharma*, is to see the presence of God within all (*vāsudeva sarvamiti*). God is addressed as Vāsudeva because He resides or lives within all in terms of His two-fold nature.[22] Smṛti tradition tries to reconcile and integrate its conception of the divine (*bhagavān* or Vāsudeva) with the Śruti or Vedāntic vision of the divine (*Brahman*) in terms of Sāṁkhya philosophy or metaphysics. Within the Smṛti tradition, the divine is conceived as a personal

22. *Viṣṇu Purāṇa*, 2.15.35; 6.5.80,82; *Bhāgavata Purāṇa*, 11.5.39-40.

being, and is identified as Viṣṇu or Śiva or even as Śakti, the different sectarian deities of Hinduism. Therefore, Smṛti tradition sees in unconditional love and devotion to God, identified as Viṣṇu or Śiva or Śakti, as the meaning and end of religious life.

While the physical aspect of the world (*prakṛti* or *kṣetra*) is identified as the body (*śarīra*) of God, the spiritual side of creation is viewed as representing the spiritual nature or self of God. Thus, both the aspects of the world, physical and spiritual, are integrated and united in the person of God. Though *bhagavān* (God), one who is worshippable or adorable (*bhajanīyam*), is loved and worshipped in several forms by different sects of Hinduism, love of God, which is regarded as an end in itself, is regarded as the true meaning of religion. Love of God, which is an end in itself, is the supreme meaning of human life (*parama puruṣārtha*), and is even regarded as superior to *mokṣa*.[23] While in *mokṣa* the individual is concerned with his spiritual liberation, love of God is an end itself. Love of God is self-fulfilling; it is not a means to an end. *Bhāgavata-dharma* means unconditional or pure love of God, and to love God or Vāsudeva is to love His creation, especially those who are in need of love and help, and to share the joys and sorrows of others.[24] To love God is to surrender oneself totally and unconditionally to Him, including the burden of his own individuality. One who loves God sees His presence within all, including those who hate him and oppress him. Prahalāda, a great *Bhāgavata*, or a paradigm of *Bhāgavata-dharma*, points to his father, who wanted to kill him for his devotion to God (Viṣṇu), that a *Bhāgavata* will have no enemies as he sees God's presence within his enemies also.[25]

---

23. *Bhāgavata*, 11.19.24; *Viṣṇu Purāṇa*, 12.100.

24. *Ibid.*, 6.1.17; 8.7.43; I do not seek from the Almighty Lord the highest position attended with eight spiritual powers (*aṇimā*, *garimā*, etc.) nor emancipation from *saṁsāra*. I would rather prefer to dwell in all beings and undergo sufferings for them, whereby they may be free from miseries. (Rantideva's prayer) *Bhāgavata Purāṇa*, 9.21.12.

25. *Viṣṇu Purāṇa*, 12.115.

Others may consider a *Bhāgavata* as their enemy, but as a *Bhāgavata* sees the presence of God within those who hate him and oppress him, he cannot have enemies. To know God is to love Him, which is really a gift of God. God is love itself (*parama prema svarūpa*),[26] and, therefore, one loves God with the love one receives from God as a gift. Love of God is a gift of God or is due to His grace (*anugraha* or *prasāda*). Love of God and total surrender to Him are not due to one's effort. They are not attained because of one's religious beliefs and doctrines. Love of God has no explanation (*nirhetuka*), and has no other end in view. It is the consummation of man's religious life. According to the Smṛti tradition, *Bhāgavata* form of religious life is open to all, including those who are not Hindu or are outside the fold of Hinduism.[27]

The most important characteristic of the *Bhāgavata-dharma* is its sole or exclusive emphasis on love and devotion to God. Love of God, and disinterested devotion to Him reveal that aspect of the divine which intellectual or rational understanding of man cannot apprehend and appreciate. The sense of uncertainty, which is a characteristic of man's intellectual life, and the sense of burden one feels about one's own individuality are overcome by surrendering oneself to God totally, even without caring for his own liberation or salvation. While the seers like Vāmadeva and Yājñavalkya represent the Śruti form of Hindu religious life, Prahlāda, Rantideva, Ambarīṣa, Nārada and the *gopī*s of Vraja represent the Smṛti form of Hinduism or *Bhāgavata-dharma*. The consummation of religious life of love and devotion is to become a *Bhāgavata*.

The *Bhāgavata-dharma* is the predominant and popular form of Hinduism. Though it is avowedly theistic, it is not, generally speaking, antagonistic or opposed to other forms of religious life. And though each major form of Hindu religious life tries to establish its supremacy over the other we do not

26. *Nārada Bhakti Sūtras*, aphorism 1.

27. *Bhāgavata Purāṇa*, 11.17.1.

find any antagonism between them leading to open conflict. However, in the historical development of Hinduism, attempts are made from time to time to prove the superior validity and meaningfulness of one form of religious life over the other, as well as to subordinate one form of religious life to the other. The conflict between the two major forms of Hindu religious life is due largely to the basic difference in the conception of the divine, and the emphasis placed either on the contemplative (*jñāna*) or on the devotional form of religious life. While the devotional form of religious life tries to play down the importance of human intellect in the religious life of man, the *jñāna* form of religious life tries to subordinate the devotional or emotional life of man to his intellect or to intellectual understanding. However, significant attempts are constantly made to recognise the value and importance of both in the religious life of man, and in knowing or realising the divine. The *Bhagavad Gītā* excels all other attempts in reconciling and harmonising both. The divine can be known by means of both intellect and heart of man, and, therefore, what is known through either of them is the same divine reality. Thus, it is said in the *Bhagavad Gītā* that the higher knowledge (*parā-jñāna*) is the same as higher devotion (*parā-bhakti*).[28] Both *parā-jñāna* and *parā-bhakti* refer to the same state of divine realisation. However, the tension and conflict between intellect and heart of man is real at the level of practical religious life or *sādhanā*, and also at the level of theological beliefs and doctrines. But the real problem is whether the intellectual understanding of man can satisfy and fulfil the demands of human heart, and whether human heart can satisfy the demands of man's intellectual or rational understanding. What is their importance and value in revealing the nature of the divine? Can rational understanding of man which tends to be skeptical about the existence of God, about the possibility of knowing Him, and also about the claims of human heart in knowing the divine can be reconciled and harmonised with the emotional or devotional life of man? Does the emotional life of

---

28. *Bhāgavata Purāṇa*, 3.29.12-14; *Bhagavad Gītā*, 7.16-19;12.20; 18.55.

man, which finds its fulfilment in love and devotion to God, has any cognitive value? Can it satisfy the demands of human intellect, and reveal the nature of the divine objectively? Can we say that the divine known through intellectual or rational understanding of man, and the divine that is revealed in and through love and devotion are one and the same? Or is it the case that each is capable of knowing some aspect of the divine which the other cannot, and, therefore, what is known by means of one cannot be understood and appreciated by the other? How to establish that it is the same divine reality that is known by means of both head and heart of man? Though these are the problems of philosophy of religion they are relevant and significant in understanding religion. The *Bhagavad Gītā* is a highly significant attempt at reconciling and harmonising the claims of both, though it has preference to the *bhakti* form of religious life. It sees the importance and value of both in the religious life of man or in fulfilling the supreme end of his existence. Therefore, instead of trying to reconcile and harmonise both at the conceptual level if we try to understand their importance and value in terms of their positive influence on the religious life of man we may not see any conflict between them. The satisfaction and fulfilment of both head and heart are essential for the fulfilment of human existence, as without the satisfaction and fulfilment of one or the other man cannot realise the fullness of his being; both are integral to the nature of man. Though they may not have the same significance and value from the point of view of ordinary religious life of man, nevertheless they help man in knowing the nature of the divine more fully and integrally as well as in fulfilling his existence when they are divinely inspired.

Parā-bhakti or pure love and devotion to God is the same as *parā-jñāna* or direct and immediate knowledge of the divine, and each is considered an end in itself. In the state of divine realisation the antagonism between *jñāna* and *bhakti* is overcome. Thus, *jñāna* and *bhakti*, which represent two major forms of religious life in Hinduism, find their harmony in the state of divine realisation. Both the forms of religious life are natural to man, and both find their ultimate fulfilment in the realisation of the divine, though before the divine is realised they seem to be opposed to each other, as the language of one is not the same as that of the other. But those who have attained the state of *parā-jñāna* or *parā-bhakti* do not see any conflict between them. However, they express or describe the state of divine realisation in different terms. The divine is experienced in both the states, or the object of their realisation is the same divine reality. However, to the rational understanding of man it remains a mystery as to how both can refer to the same divine reality. It may be pointed out that both can refer to the same divine reality if the divine is both personal and impersonal as the language of *jñāna* in describing the divine is not the same as the language of *bhakti*. But in the state of *parā-jñāna* or *parā-bhakti* the divine is realised as transcending the categories of personal and impersonal though at the level of ordinary *jñāna* and *bhakti* the controversy between the personal or impersonal nature of the divine is meaningful. The divine in itself which transcends both the categories can yet manifest itself in both the forms. While its personal form or aspect is revealed in the human person, nature revels its impersonal nature, but both are integral to the nature of the divine. Though what is revealed in and through nature is distinct from what is revealed within the reality of man they are not opposed to each other. However, those who conceive the nature of the divine in either- or terms may find it difficult to reconcile and harmonise both. This is, however, a problem which remains valid until one is able to transcend both in the state of divine realisation. Thus, what Sāṁkhya could not achieve philosophically, the *Bhāgavata* form of Hinduism could accomplish in terms of its conception of God or *bhagavān* who is the oneness or unity of both *prakṛti* and *puruṣa*. God or *bhagavān* reveals Himself both in nature and in man. While *prakṛti*, which forms the body of God, is the source of nature, the spiritual nature of God manifests itself within man as his self. Just as the human person is the unity of both body and self which though are distinct cannot be separated, the person of God is the unity of both *prakṛti* and *puruṣa* or matter and spirit, and, therefore, both can reveal the nature of God. Both the world and man manifest the nature of God who is one. But then the meaning of religion as *dharma* will be significantly different in both the cases. The meaning of religion as *dharma*, which is based on the impersonal conception of the divine, significantly differs from the meaning of religion as *Bhāgavata dharma* which is based on a personal conception of the divine. However, both these forms of religious life are integral to Hinduism, and Hinduism is a name given to the confluence of the traditions of Śruti and Smṛti. Despite the fact that the traditions of Śruti and Smṛti have not been perfectly reconciled and harmonised in the development of Hinduism, there has been no open conflict and hostility between them which is mainly because of the influence of the Hindu world-view.

5
Man

MAN is a riddle to himself, and his quest to know himself or the nature of his own reality is as ancient as his quest to know the nature of the world around him. Though man has achieved much progress in his understanding of himself yet he realises that there is something about himself which eludes his clear grasp and understanding, as at no stage in the progress of his self-knowledge and understanding man is satisfied with the state of his existence or content with what he is. Man's quest to know his own reality more and more clearly and comprehensively has given rise to several philosophies of man. And his quest to know the world is not unrelated to his quest to know himself. Man's understanding of himself and his understanding of the world are inter-related.

Before we try to understand the nature and meaning of human existence, according to Hinduism, we have to address ourselves to the problem whether man's understanding of himself and his understanding of the world are inter-related so that the understanding of one helps in understanding the other. Is it the case that man's understanding of himself reveals only the nature of human reality, and has no significance and relevance in knowing or understanding the nature of the world? Can we say that man's knowledge and understanding of his own reality helps him in knowing and understanding the nature of the reality outside of himself more significantly and integrally? Or is it the case that man's knowledge of his own reality has no place of significance in knowing the nature of the world? To put it differently, can we say that the reality of one is integral to the reality of the other so that the knowledge of one will help in knowing the other ? Is it meaningful to think that man's knowledge of himself and his knowledge of the world are two distinct modes or ways of knowing the same reality? Can we say that though the method of knowing one is different from the method of knowing the other, yet the ultimate object of both is the same? Or is it the case that the knowledge of one has nothing to do with the knowledge of the other? What is the relationship between man and the world? Are they ontologically independent realities or are they related to each other integrally? However, the problem whether the knowledge or understanding of the reality of one can provide significant insights into the reality of the other has attracted the attention of several thinkers. Although we accept the importance and relevance of our knowledge of the world in understanding human reality as we think that man's existence is dependent on the world, and even the meaning of his life is determined by the world, most of us are not prepared to accept the importance and relevance of man's knowledge or understanding of his own reality in knowing or understanding the nature of the world. While religion and literature help us in knowing or understanding the nature of human reality in a significant and comprehensive manner, the empirical or positive sciences help us in knowing the world. And if we think that the difference between man and the world is ontological then to seek in the knowledge of one any significant insights into the knowledge of the other would be futile. But, on the other hand, if we think that both in their own characteristic ways, but together, help us in knowing the nature of ultimate reality, as they are integral to it, then the value man attaches to his self-knowledge in knowing the nature of ultimate reality will be meaningful. We cannot then understand the nature of ultimate reality either exclusively on the basis of human reality or on the basis of the reality of the physical world. And if we consider that the reality of man and the reality of the world are integral to the nature of ultimate reality then its manifestation and revelation cannot be viewed as limited either to the reality of man or to that of world. Then both man and world manifest and reveal the same reality though in different ways and forms.

If a religious tradition is founded on a vision or world-view that all that is there is a manifestation of the divine then in understanding its nature man's knowledge of himself as well as his knowledge of the world will be equally significant and relevant. If the divine is the ultimate source of existence of both man and the world then the nature of the divine can reveal itself in and through the reality of both man and the world. On the other hand, if according to the world-view of a tradition, man and world are two distinct and independent realities then the knowledge of one will not be of any significance in knowing the other, as the logic and language of one will not be intelligible and meaningful in terms of the other.

According to the world-view of Hinduism, the same divine reality is the ultimate source of existence of both man and the world. Man and the world are different forms of manifestation of the same divine reality, and, therefore, both manifest and reveal the divine though in different ways and forms. It is, therefore, meaningful to think that the knowledge of one is both significant and relevant in knowing or understanding the nature of the other, and more importantly the knowledge of both is essential to comprehend the nature of the divine. Man and nature, as manifestations of the divine, reveal the nature of the divine though in their own characteristic ways. And unless it is presupposed that both man and nature are not integral to the reality of the divine we have no reason to believe that the nature of the divine reveals itself either within the reality of man or in the reality of nature.

However, those who tend to recognise the presence of the divine only within the reality of man, especially in his higher nature, may not be able to recognise its presence either in the physical nature of man or in the natural world. Similarly, those who tend to understand the nature of ultimate reality on the basis of physical world may not see anything significant within the reality of man or in his inward life that will be meaningful in understanding the nature of ultimate reality. Thus, we find different systems of metaphysical thought in which the nature of the divine is defined either predominantly or even exclusively in terms of human reality, especially the higher nature of man, or in terms of the physical world and its structure. And as they find a gulf or gap between the two which, according to them, cannot be bridged, at least at the level of man's empirical experience and rational understanding, divine or religious significance and value are attached more or less exclusively to the reality of man. While the scientific attitude and method prevent science from seeing in the human reality anything that can provide a valuable insight into the nature of ultimate reality, religious or theological understanding and wisdom fail to or rather refuse to recognise the presence of the divine within the realm of physical nature. Thus, the nature of the divine is sought to be understood and defined either on the basis of human reality or on the basis of nature, but not on the basis of both.

Whether the nature of the divine can be known either on the basis of human reality or on the basis of the physical world depends ultimately upon the world-view of a tradition. A world-view is not completely rational. And no empirical evidence is sufficient to prove the meaningfulness and validity of a world-view. It is ultimately a matter of deep faith. And to the extent a religion is more integral and comprehensive its beliefs and doctrines cannot have justification individually or independently of its world-view. They derive their meaning and justification from the world-view, as they are developed on the basis of the world-view or follow from it . Therefore, they remain meaningful as long as the world-view, the real source of their meaning and justification, has not lost its meaningfulness.

According to the Hindu world-view, all is divine or all that is there is permeated by the divine as all that is there is a varied manifestation of the divine. Then what is it to see or realise the divine within all that is there which is not homogeneous? Man and nature are two distinct realities which at the empirical level or in terms of man's rational understanding cannot find their explanation in one another unless we are prepared to go in for reductive analysis. They cannot also find their explanation in the same reality as from the point of view of man's empirical experience it is not possible to reconcile matter with spirit as they are opposed to each other in nature. However, according to the Veda, the divine is present within all the realms of existence, and attempts are made in the Vedic literature to identify the divine within all the realms. According to the Veda, all that is there is classified into three realms of *ādhibhautika* (physical realm), *ādhidaivika* (the realm of deities) and *ādhyātmika* (inward life of man). All that is there is a manifestation of the divine though the forms of its manifestation differ from realm to realm. And being a manifestation of the divine each realm reveals the nature of the divine in its own characteristic way. According to the seers of the Veda, this is a matter of divine inspiration and direct experience. It is revealed to them in the state of divine inspiration. However, attempts are later made to provide a sort of philosophical or metaphysical justification for the same. A seer, who is known variously as *ṛṣi*, *kavi*, *vipra*, *maṇīṣin*, *dhīra*, etc., is one who sees the divine unity of all that is there, or who sees the presence of the divine within all the realms of reality, and the Veda, the final authority for Hinduism, represents the divinely inspired wisdom of the Vedic seers. Thus, according to the revealed wisdom of the Veda the divine is present within all the three realms of reality. We shall discuss in the next chapter what is it to see the divine within all or in all the realms of reality.

Although the Vedic vision cannot be justified on the basis of man's empirical experience we can nevertheless point out to one significant proof or evidence in its favour, and that is the reality of man. In man all that is there is integrated into one whole, and, therefore, he is seen in the Vedic tradition as the best form of divine manifestation. Nature is present in man as his body consists of all the basic elements of nature, and all the deities reside in him in the form of his senses and other faculties. And above all as a self-conscious spiritual being man is a clear and best possible form of manifestation of the divine.[1] While all other things, particularly the living beings, manifest the divine in different degrees of clearness and perfection, the manifestation and revelation of the divine within the reality of man is more and more clear and full or perfect. We quote here in full a passage from the *Aitareya Āraṇyaka* which clearly reflects the Vedic wisdom about the place and significance of human reality in revealing the divine and its nature.

> He who knows *ātman* more and more clearly and comprehensively (*ātmānam vistāram veda*) obtains fuller being. In plants, trees and animals he knows *ātman* more and more clearly. In plants and trees only sap is seen. In animals consciousness. In animals *ātman* becomes more and more clear. While thought is not seen in other living beings, *ātman* is more and more clear in man for he is endowed with intelligence. He says what he has known; he sees what he has known. He knows tomorrow. He knows the world and what is not the world. By the mortal he desires the immortal being thus endowed with (intelligence). As for animals hunger and thirst comprise their power of knowledge. They say not what they have known. They go so far, for their experiences are according to the measure of their intelligence.[2]

Man is superior to all other living beings because he is endowed with intelligence (*prajñā* or *dhī*) which constitutes his glory. In the Vedic tradition intelligence is given supreme importance and value. The Sanskrit word *śreṣṭha*, which means superior or eminent, is derived from *śir* which means head or intelligence. It is the intellect of man that is primarily the seat of divine inspiration. Divinely inspired intellect of man enables him in knowing the divine and its nature. Often intelligence and speech

---

1. *Aitareya Āraṇyaka*, 2.3.3.3; *Atharvaveda* 11.8.32.
2. *Ibid.*, 2.3.2.

or wisdom (*vāk*) are identified in the Veda though intelligence is regarded as more comprehensive than speech, as it is the seat of speech also. However, divinely inspired speech or wisdom is the same as the divinely inspired state of intelligence. Speech or wisdom (*vāk*) is the manifested or expressed form of intelligence. It is speech that defines intelligence or tries to determine its nature. Intelligence is undetermined while speech is determined.[3] It is because of his intelligence man is what he is. His greatness as well as his misery are due to his being endowed with intelligence. Because of his intelligence man is not happy with what he is, and seeks to know what is not given to his senses. He tries to transcend himself not being happy with what he is at every stage of his development. Otherwise he is an animal (*paśu*). "Man is created from Prajāpati's mind or soul. He is an animal but foremost (among them)."[4] Because of his intelligence man is most near to or like Prajāpati, the creator and lord of living beings.

In the *Sāṁkhāyana Āraṇyaka*, it is said that the world would be unintelligible without intelligence. Without intelligence man cannot know the world as it is the intelligence which gives form to the world of objects.[5] The world of objects and intelligence depend upon each other for their knowledge, and reveal each other. Either of them is not known by itself or independently of each other. Each is known in relation to the other, and are inseparable like the rim and spokes. It is further said that the rudiments of intelligence like thinking, knowing, etc., act on nature, and vice versa, and reveal each other. One knows oneself or intelligence comes to know itself while acting on or in apprehending the elements of nature, and due to this process the world is known in the sense that it is given a form by the intelligence. In other words, the conceptual activity of man is due to his intelligence, which is not possible without intelligence

3. *Sāṁkhāyana Āraṇyaka*, 5.5.6.
4. *Śatapatha Brāhmaṇa*, 1.4.4.7.
5. *Sāṁkhāyana Āraṇyaka*, 5.5.

acting on nature. There is no understanding of the world without form, and it is intelligence which gives form to the world. This has been later developed into the theory of *tanmātras*, according to which, the various sense-organs can act upon and know the various elements of nature because the sense-organs are the subtle representation of the basic elements of nature in man. The eyes can act upon and know colour and light because the eyes are the subtle representation of light in man.

> Speech is taken out as one portion of intelligence to correspond with a rudimentary element, and name was placed outside. Likewise smell is a portion of intelligence, and odour is placed outside. For bereft of intelligence speech cannot know any name or concept. My mind has been somewhere else. I have not perceived that name, etc., for bereft of intelligence no thought could be complete nor what is to be known is known.[6]

It is further said that the intelligence of man or *ātman* in him is not touched by what it acts upon and knows.

> It becomes not greater through a good deed, nor less through an evil deed. It causes him (man) to do good deeds whom it desires to lead forth from these worlds or evil deeds whom it wants to plunge down or below. This is the guidance of the world, the lord of the world, the ruler of the world. This is my self. This let a man know.[7]

The supreme importance and value attached to human intelligence and knowledge is clearly reflected in the following passage.

> That which is heart and the mind, perception, injunction, understanding, knowledge, wisdom, vision, firmness, thinking, considering, memory, resolution, etc., are only names of knowledge (*prajñā*). That is *Brahman*, Indra,

6. *Sāṁkhāyana Āraṇyaka*, 5.5.6-7.
7. *Ibid.*, 5.8.

> Prajāpati and all the deities, and all the elements. All that is there is guided by knowledge. It rests on knowledge. The world is guided by knowledge. Knowledge is its foundation. It is *Brahman*. He (Vāmadeva) by knowing his self or by his *prajñā* having left the world and having obtained all the delights in the world and heaven became immortal.[8]

It is because of the importance given to human intelligence or understanding in knowing or comprehending the world greater importance or value is attached to the knowledge of man in knowing the nature of the divine. The reality of man is seen as holding the key to understanding the nature of the divine. "One should not seek to know the speech (the objects of speech) but the speaker. One should not seek to know the knowledge but the knower, etc."[9] Intelligence which is indicated by the words *dhi*, *medha*, *prajñā*, *buddhi*, and even *manas* is seen by the Vedic seers as the supreme faculty in man because of which he is nearer to the divine, and is, therefore, superior to all the created beings. Among all the living beings man is the best (*sukṛta*). He is foremost among all the living beings, and his being is like that of Prajāpati. And because of his intelligence man can be autonomous or self-ruled (*svarāṭ*) which is considered by the Vedic seers as superior to any other thing achieved by man, including royal power.[10]

In a prayer which is highly significant for the purpose of understanding the nature of man it is said that intelligence is the light of the lights (senses), the range of which is far and wide unlike that of the sense-organs.

> It is that which is knowledge or understanding, the immortal light, which creatures have within themselves, and without which men do no single action. May that

8. *Aitareya Āraṇyaka*, 2.6.1.3-8.
9. *Sāṁkhāyana Āraṇyaka*, 5.8.
10. *Ibid.*, 1.7.

my mind be moved by true or right intention.[11]

It is that whereby all is comprehended, the world which is (empirical or phenomenal) and what shall be hereafter. It controls men and guides them like a skillful charioteer drives the horses of the chariot.[12]

The Vedic ideal of man indicated by the terms like *dhīra*, *maṇiṣin*, *vipra*, *kavi* and *ṛṣi* are related to human intelligence or the divinely inspired state of its existence. They refer to the various functions of intelligence through which it manifests and reveals itself.

Ordinary or un-inspired intelligence which can comprehend the world can intuit or apprehend the divine when it is divinely inspired or made divine (*daivya dhiya*).[13] The Vedic seers constantly pray that their intelligence be divinely inspired. The famous Vedic hymn known as Gāyatrī, which is addressed to Savitā, the deity of inspiration (*savitā* or *sāvitrī* or *prasavitrī*) is an invocation to inspire one's intelligence divinely.[14] Divinely inspired intelligence is the source of devotion and prayer, and a prayer is also known as *dhi* or *mati*. In the Veda the divine is known and identified as that which inspires the intelligence of man. And when the intelligence of man is divinely inspired he knows the divine, and at the same time realises the divine nature of his intelligence. When his intelligence is divinely inspired man is divinely transformed, and sees the presence of the divine within all that is there or sees nature as a creative manifestation of the divine. He sees nature as an abode (*dhāma*) of the divine or sees in each and every phenomenon of nature the presence of a deity, a primary and cosmic manifestation of the divine. To see nature as the abode of various deities is to see the presence of the divine in nature or nature as a creative manifestation of

---

11. *Vājasaneya Saṁhitā*, 34.3.4.
12. *Ibid.*, 34.3.6; *Kaṭha Upaniṣad*, 1.3.3.
13. *Ṛgveda*, 10.176.2.
14. *Ibid.*, 3.62.10.

the divine. In other words, what is empirically or ordinarily known as nature is known to a divinely inspired person (*ṛṣi* or *kavi*) as a manifested form of the divine. It is said in a *Brāhmaṇa* text that the supreme fulfilment of human existence consists in seeing or realising the divine as the inner unity or oneness of all that is.[15] To see or realise the world as a creative manifestation of the divine is itself a spiritual experience. While a *kavi* is one who sees nature in its varied forms as a creative self-expression or manifestation of the divine, a *ṛṣi* is one who sees the divine as the unity or oneness underlying all that is there. However, both these are the intuitions of a divinely inspired intelligence by which a *ṛṣi* and *kavi* are known. Unless one is divinely inspired one cannot be a *kavi* or a *ṛṣi*. According to the Veda, the seat of divine inspiration in man is his intelligence, though occasionally human heart is also regarded as a seat of divine inspiration.

The realisation that all that is there is a manifestation of the divine, and is, therefore, permeated by the divine dawns on man when his intelligence is divinely inspired. Divinely inspired intelligence enables man to see the divine as the source as well as the inner unity or oneness of the universe. It is also said that human intelligence attains or regains its pristine or original purity due to divine inspiration. The divinely inspired state of existence is man's supreme fulfilment. Thus, to be a *kavi* or a *ṛṣi* or a *dhīra* or a *maṇiṣin* is the ideal state of human perfection and fulfillment, according to the Śruti tradition. Even the ideal of *stita-prajña* of the *Bhagavad Gītā* means the same as it refers to the one who is firm or stable in his intelligence (wisdom), or one who is not swayed by his emotions and passions.[16]

It is said in the *Ṛgveda* that a mysterious and mist-like power envelopes the intelligence of man, and prevents him from knowing or seeing the divine nature and unity of the world.[17] Though as a matter of ontological fact the divine is the inner

---

15. *Śatapatha Brāhmaṇa*,10.4.2.2.21-22; *Aitareya Āraṇyaka*,3.2.6.
16. *Bhagavad Gītā*, 2.54.
17. *Ṛgveda*, 10.82.7.

unity of all that is there man fails to know it due to the mysterious power that envelopes his vision or intelligence. The Vedic seers express it clearly when they say that the violation of *ṛta* by man is not because he lacks the knowledge of what is right or true, but because of his sinful state of existence.[18] It is, therefore, said that though seeing one does not see, and though hearing one does not hear because of the mist-like ignorance that envelopes his intelligence and prevents him from seeing the divine as the inner unity or oneness of all that is. This dark force is mostly identified in the Veda as sin. And in the post-*Saṁhitā* literature it is mostly identified as *avidyā* or *ajñāna* or *māyā*. The Vedic concern is not so much with *avidyā* or *māyā* as with sin known differently as *pāpa*, *agha*, *enasa* and *durita*. Sin is primarily a moral concept or category with the Vedic seers as it has to do with the conduct of man. The wise or the seers are those who live a righteous life or whose conduct is in accordance with *ṛta*, the divine order, while the sinful (*anṛta*) are those whose life and conduct are not in accordance with *ṛta*.

> I have verily acquired the intelligence (*medha*) of the father or protector of *ṛta* (*pituḥ ṛtasya*). I have become bright as the sun or I have received from the father of *ṛta* deep and comprehensive knowledge of *ṛta* (*pituḥ pari medham ṛtasya jagāma*).[19]

> What thing I truly am I know not clearly, mysteriously fettered in my mind. I wander (without knowing my true nature) when the first born of *ṛta* approached me, and then of this speech I first obtained a portion.[20]

Sin which is related to *ṛta* is a concept which is religious as well as moral. *Ṛta* is divine order as revealed in nature and within man, and, therefore, its violation is sin. Sin is seen as violation of *ṛta* or violation of the laws of Varuṇa, and significantly Varuṇa

18. *Ṛgveda*, 7.86.6; see also 7.89.3.
19. *Ibid.*, 8.6.10.
20. *Ibid.*, 1.164.37.

is often described in the Veda as the form of *ṛta* (*ṛta pesa*).[21] *Ṛta*, which is later identified with *dharma*, is not something that is given to man from outside. It reveals itself to man in nature, and more clearly within his own reality. What is so known is to be followed by man, and its violation, which man is capable of, leads to sin. Sin is, therefore, against the divine as *ṛta* or *dharma* is the revelation of the divine at the level of manifestation. Therefore, one who knows *ṛta* and is filled with it or lives in accordance with it is divine, and the one who violates it is sinful or commits sin. *Ṛta* reveals itself in man as *dharma* or moral order, and, therefore, to be a man of *ṛta* (*ṛtavān*) or to be filled with *ṛta* is to lead a life of *ṛta*. To live in accordance with *ṛta* is to see one's life as a *yajña* or as an offering to the divine, and enjoy it with the sense of an offering (*haviṣmatā manasā*). It is often expressed in the Smṛti literature that the one who enjoys the world as the left over of *yajña* or as sanctified by *yajña* (*yajñāvaśiṣṭa*) is a knower of *dharma*. Everything is to be offered to the divine before it is enjoyed, and what is so enjoyed will be consistent with the spirit of *yajña*. While an act done with the realisation that all is divine attains the significance and value of *yajña*, an act that is done without such a realisation is sinful. As expressed in the *Īśa Upaniṣad* all that is there is divine or is permeated by the divine, and, therefore, one has to enjoy the world with a sense of renunciation or sacrifice.[22] It is often asserted in the *Mahābhārata* that *dharma* consists in enjoying everything as a left-over of *yajña* (*yajñāvaśiṣṭa*) or with a sense of *yajña* (*haviṣmatā manasā*). The same idea is expressed in the *Ṛgveda* when it is said that one who eats alone eats sin.[23]

If the divine order or *ṛta* or *dharma* is inherent in nature and man what makes him to violate it. While all other living beings follow their *dharma* which manifests itself within them in the form of instinct which they do not violate, it is only man

21. *Ṛgveda*, 5.66.l.
22. *Īśāvasya Upaniṣad*, l.1.
23. *Ṛgveda*, 10.117.6; see also *Śatapatha Brāhmaṇa*, 2.4.26.

who can violate *ṛta* or *dharma*.

> Neither the gods, nor the fathers and beasts transgress Prajāpati's ordinance. Some of men alone transgress it. Hence, whenever man grows fat he grows fat in unrighteousness. One who eats righteously speaks truth, and lives full measure because he observes the divine truth, that is *brahmatejas* by keeping the law of Prajāpati. One who knows *Brahman* is not affected or touched by sin as a lotus leaf by water. By knowing *Brahman* one shakes off sin as horse its hair.[24]

Sin is thus basically a violation of divine order or righteousness as revealed within man and in nature. Everyone knows what is *ṛta* or *dharma* though the seers, who are known for the purity of their hearts and intelligence, know it more fully and comprehensively. It is expressed in the *Kaṭha Upaniṣad* that both good and bad (*śreya* and *peya*) or what is desirable and what is pleasurable approach man or are known to him.[25] But when man chooses one over the other or chooses what is sweet or what gives pleasure instead of what is good or desirable it is not because he does not know what is good or what is desirable but because of some mysterious force in him. As beautifully presented in the *Mahābhārata*, Duryodhana says that he knows what is good though he has no inclination or will to do it, and instead tends or wills to do what is unrighteous (*adharma*) knowing full well that it is reprehensible.[26]

To act in the spirit of *yajña*, and to enjoy everything as the left over of *yajña* is possible when one has the realisation that all that is there is divine or is permeated by the divine. Then the sense of ego and its satisfaction will not be the reason for

---

24. *Chāndogya Upaniṣad*, 8.13.
25. *Kaṭha Upaniṣad*, 1.2.1.
26. *Mahābhārata* Sabhā-parva. The same idea is expressed in the *Śiva Purāṇa* (13.4) I know what is virtuous but I am not inclined to follow it. I know what is unrighteous but I am unable to desist from it. 'O' Mahādeva I do everything as prompted by you stationed in my heart.

doing things. Unless one realises that all is divine one cannot realise that one's life is a *yajña*, and is, therefore, a means of fulfiling the divine purpose. In other words, the realisation that one's life and actions are not simply for his satisfaction and fulfilment of his desires but are a means to serve and fulfil the divine purpose frees or releases one from sin. Then every act of man will acquire the significance of divine worship or *yajña*. It is, therefore, said that the knowledge of *ṛta* destroys sin, and anything that is done by man as his *dharma* or in the spirit of *yajña* absolves him from sin.

According to the *Ṛgveda*, man commits sin not by choice but because of his (sinful) condition.[27] It is, therefore, not the case that one who has an ordinary understanding of the Vedic wisdom that all is divine derived from one's study of the Veda is automatically freed from sin. One has to overcome one's sinful state of existence which means living for oneself and doing things for one's own pleasure and satisfaction, or free oneself from ignorance that envelops his vision, and because of which one is not able to see the divine presence within all. To overcome one's sinful state of existence one has to gain spiritual strength. One has to overcome one's sinful state of existence or the state ignorance to realise the divine or see its presence within all.

> I know not I am all this. When the fetters dropped I came to know I am all this.[28]

> Human beings enjoy various fruits in this world but it is only those who know the divine or the Father above who tastes the real sweetness of life.[29]

Our understanding of the nature and destiny of man, according to Hinduism, will not be complete without understanding the nature and destiny of man according to the Smṛti tradition. The

27. *Ṛgveda*, 7.86.6; see also 7.89.3.
28. *Ibid.*, 1.164.37; *Atharvaveda*, 9.10.5.
29. *Ibid.*, 1.164.39.

Smṛti tradition is basically theistic in which the divine is conceived as God (*bhagavān* or Vāsudeva). According to the Smṛti tradition which is more pervasive in its influence on the Hindu religious life, or is the basis of popular form of Hinduism, human destiny is in the hands of God or is completely dependent upon Him. Human existence is dependent upon God as everything else is. Everything belongs to God, and there is nothing which man can claim for himself. Therefore, the feeling of man's independence or the sense of his individuality is the fundamental reason for his suffering and misery. And the ultimate bliss of man or the ultimate fulfilment of his existence is dependent upon his total surrender to God, the ultimate source of his existence. It is by surrendering oneself to God totally and unconditionally, that is, by offering or surrendering one's *dharma*, one's knowledge, one's pride in himself and even his ignorance to God one can overcome his sense of ego which is the same as his sinful state of existence. Any trace of ego in man or the sense of his independence or individuality which separates man from God is to be given up completely to receive the grace of God which is essential for attaining the highest end of his life. One's surrender to God is not complete and total without giving up the sense of his individuality. As expressed in the *Bhāgavata Purāṇa* the sense of 'I' or 'mine' is the root cause of human suffering, and unless one surrenders oneself to God totally one cannot hope to receive the grace of God essential for the supreme fulfilment of his existence.[30] Man has to surrender to God his *dharma* and *adharma* seeking nothing from Him in return. Such disinterested or pure love of God, and total and unconditional surrender to Him is the supreme end of human existence. Love of God is an end in itself, and is the real meaning and end of human existence. Even to surrender oneself to God unconditionally requires the grace of God as other wise man cannot give up his ego-centred existence or individuality.

What distinguishes Smṛti from of Hinduism from that of

30. *Bhāgavata Purāṇa*, 6.16.39-44.

Śruti, as far as the nature and destiny of man is concerned is its insistence on man's dependent existence on God. Though Smṛti accepts the wisdom of Śruti it is not much influenced by Śruti in its theology. It accepts and adapts Śruti to serve its theistic and sectarian needs. Because of its uncompromising theism it has paid little or no attention in understanding the nature and meaning of human existence independently of God. The reality of man is absolutely dependent upon God as everything else is. The Smṛti form of religion known as *Bhāgavata dharma* insists on pure or disinterested and unconditional love and devotion to God as the highest end of human existence, and as pure love and devotion to God are not considered possible without the grace of God man has to depend himself on God for the supreme fulfilment of his existence. Love of God, which is an end in itself, is regarded as the highest end of human existence. It is an independent or the fifth *puruṣārtha*. Love of God is superior to *mokṣa* or liberation as love of God is an end in itself. It is not a means for achieving anything else. A *Bhāgavata* is indifferent to his welfare and happiness, including his liberation, in being devoted to God. To be a *Bhāgavata* which is to love God and be devoted to Him disinterestedly and unconditionally is the ultimate meaning of human existence according to the Smṛti form of Hinduism.

6

Divine

BEFORE we try to understand the Hindu view of the divine we should try to understand the manner or mode of its revelation, according to Hinduism. The nature and meaning of the divine are significantly related to the mode of its revelation. The nature of human experience which reveals the divine and its nature or in the light of which man comes to know the existence and nature of the divine is crucial in understanding the nature of the divine. This problem is raised not for any theoretical purpose, but to have a clear and comprehensive understanding of the nature of the divine according to Hinduism. This is an important problem as the basic character of Hinduism is shaped by its conception of the divine. Do we have enough evidence in the Hindu tradition or in the sacred texts of Hinduism to know the manner of divine revelation to the seers and sages of Hinduism? How is the divine revealed to the Vedic seers, or what is the manner or mode of its revelation to the Vedic seers? What is the nature and meaning of revelation, according to Hinduism? In other words, what is the source of knowledge of the divine according to Hinduism? Is there sufficient evidence in the Veda which can help us in understanding the nature and meaning of divine revelation?

The following discussion is based primarily on the Veda (*Saṁhitās*), particularly the *Ṛgveda*, which consists mainly of prayers and praises addressed to various deities, either individually or collectively. The *Ṛgveda* (*Saṁhitā*) is essentially a Veda of prayer and worship, and most of its hymns are prayers and praises addressed to the deities, either individually or collectively, and express in poetic language, often employing highly significant metaphors, inwardly experienced and soul stirring devotion of the seers to the deities or the divine.

The idea of ultimate reality, the ultimate explanation of all that is there, which may be arrived at on the basis of man's rational understanding is distinct from the divine which is revealed or directly experienced. *Mānameyodaya*, a Pūrva Mīmāṁsā text, makes a highly significant distinction between the God of the philosophers (*īśvara* of *tarka*) and the God of the Veda (*īśvara* of the Veda).[1] While rational understanding of man about the existence and nature of ultimate reality gives rise to metaphysics, direct experience of the divine gives birth to religion or to religious life of devotion and worship. The God of philosophers or of rational understanding is different from the God of religion or God that is directly experienced or revealed. We find in the Veda, particularly the *Ṛgveda*, which is representative of the Vedic thought or vision, a clear description of the divine as directly experienced. This is also the case with the Upaniṣads who speak of *Brahman* that is known or experienced directly and immediately. However, in some of the Upaniṣads significant attempts are made to provide rational justification for the existence of the divine, or rather to confirm the existence of *Brahman* known directly and immediately. Even in the Smṛti literature, particularly in some of the major Purāṇas, like *Viṣṇu* and *Bhāgavata*, which has largely influenced, and even shaped the popular form of Hinduism, we find both the approaches. Besides adducing several arguments to prove the existence of God, they refer to the direct experiences of the devotees, like Prahlāda, in knowing the nature of the divine. Before the emergence of philosophic schools of thought, like both the schools of Mīmāṁsā, Sāṁkhya, etc., in which rational inquiry and understanding played a crucial role in understanding the existence and nature of the divine, both Śruti and Smṛti, the

1. In *Mānameyodaya*, (2.47-48) a distinction is made between *īśvara* (God) of *tarka* and *īśvara* (God) of Śruti.

major sources of Hinduism, entertain reason or admit the importance of man's rational understanding in knowing the existence and nature of the divine. The Veda or Śruti whose authority is equated with that of perception in non-empirical matters describes, mostly in poetic language, the nature of the divine as revealed to or directly experienced by the seers of the Veda.[2] The Veda is not known for its speculative understanding and philosophic inquiry though they are not completely absent in the Veda. The Vedic skepticism about man's ability to know the existence and nature of the divine in itself as well as about the existence of certain abstract deities, like Indra, shows that rational understanding is given due importance in the Veda. However, the Veda is primarily known for its divinely inspired knowledge or wisdom about the nature and meaning of the divine. The term 'divine' is preferred in our discussion to the term 'God' as it is free from certain religious and cultural presuppositions. Though they refer to the same reality yet the concept of divine is relatively free from certain connotations which the idea of God has acquired in relation to some of the major cultural and religious traditions.

Our primary concern in this chapter is to present and discuss the nature and meaning of the divine as revealed to the seers of the Veda or as directly experienced by them due to divine inspiration. Although Śruti and Smṛti differ significantly in their conceptions of the divine, and its nature and meaning, the difference is not, however, radical. The nature of the divine as described in the Śruti texts is not the same, in all respects, as that is described in the Smṛti texts. While the term 'God' is not adequate and appropriate to express the Vedic sense of the divine (*divya*), the term divine is not appropriate to express the Smṛti view of God (*bhagavān*). The term God in the sense of a creator transcending the world, and existing independently of it cannot adequately represent the Vedic view or vision of the divine. But both represent Hinduism or the Hindu view of the divine. We

2. Śaṅkara' commentary on *Vedānta Sūtras*,1.3.28.

do not, therefore, discuss them separately. The difference in the conception of the divine between Śruti and Smṛti instead of generating tension and conflict within Hinduism helped in enriching the Hindu religious tradition, and making it more integral and comprehensive. However, differences in the conception of the divine occasionally gave rise to tension and conflict among certain Hindu sects and schools of theological thought, though significant attempts are constantly made to reconcile and integrate them.

We do not find in the post-*Saṁhitā* literature any significant account or description about the birth of divine in Hindu consciousness, or what is it to experience the divine or God, or how does man come to know its or His existence or presence. But in the post-*Saṁhitā* tradition, which accepts the authority of the Veda and its view of the divine, we find a systematic and more comprehensive discussion and understanding of the concept of the divine, its relation to man and world, and other theological problems. However, it has not developed a conception of the divine of its own, but adopted the Vedic view or vision of the divine, and tried to interpret it according to its theological needs. The Vedic view of the divine is the basis for all theological discussion in Hinduism, or the Veda is the source as well as the authority for the Hindu conception of the divine though it has been developed and articulated more and more clearly in the post-Vedic literature of Hinduism. Therefore, to understand the birth of divine in human consciousness, according to Hinduism, we have to depend on the Vedic *Saṁhitā*s, particularly the *Ṛgveda Saṁhitā*, in which we find a clear description of the nature and meaning of the divine as revealed to or directly experienced by the Vedic seers. Such description is absent in the post-*Saṁhitā* literature of Hinduism. The post-*Saṁhitā* Hinduism accepts the Vedic experience of the divine, and all the theological or metaphysical discussion on the nature and meaning of the divine or God is based primarily on the Vedic experience of the divine. And more significantly the post-*Saṁhitā* discussion and understanding of the nature of the divine or God will not be intelligible and meaningful independently of the Vedic experience or revelation.

As the major concern of this chapter is to understand the nature and meaning of the divine, according to Hinduism, we have to understand the Vedic experience of the Divine which has been the basis and authority for all future discussion on the nature and meaning of the divine in Hinduism. Though the Vedic vision of the divine has been well articulated and presented in the post-*Saṁhitā* tradition, the basic meaning of the divine has not undergone any significant change. Thus, the basic Hindu vision or view of the divine, as well as the character of Hinduism, to a large extent, are shaped and defined in terms of the Vedic experience.

The Veda is not a revelation in the sense of *Bible* or *Korān*, as it does not contain the word or wisdom of God as revealed to someone or some persons as in the case Old Testament. However, the Veda is a revelation in the basic sense that it does not represent the wisdom of certain human beings about the divine. It is not a collection of views or ideas or wisdom of some persons about the divine. The fact that the Veda is regarded as impersonal (*apauruṣeya*) or having no author, either human or divine, points to the fact that the Vedic seers, whose names are associated with the literary composition of the Vedic hymns, are not, however, the authors of the truth which the hymns express. They are not actively involved in knowing the truth expressed through the hymns; the truth of the Veda is not due to their efforts and understanding (*na tasya vidma puruṣatvatā vayam*).[3] It is only when a person is actively involved in knowing the truth or when the truth is known due to human effort and understanding, we can attribute the truth so known to a person or persons as it is in the case of ordinary knowledge and wisdom. The Veda constantly refers to or speaks about divine inspiration as the real source of its wisdom, and, therefore, the persons who receive the inspiration are not important; they are not actively involved in knowing the truth. On the other hand, if the

3. *Ṛgveda*, 5.48.5.

knowledge is due to the effort and understanding of a person then the role and importance of the person in acquiring knowledge will be significant, and the character and ability of the person and his other limitations may have some impact or influence on the nature and validity of the knowledge so attained. The Vedic seers declare that the wisdom of the Veda is not due to their own efforts and understanding. "It is not due to our efforts and understanding (*puruṣatva*) we have come to know the divine."[4] The wisdom of the Veda is not acquired due to human effort, though some effort is involved in preparing oneself to receive divine revelation. However, there is no causal relationship between the two. "I know not if I am this for I go perplexed and bound in mind and thought when the first born of the truth reaches me. Then immediately shall I obtain a portion of that sacred word."[5]

The Veda, as it is later understood and interpreted, is impersonal in the sense that the persons or seers who made or composed the hymns are not actively involved in attaining the knowledge or wisdom that is expressed through the hymns of the Veda. However, it is admitted by the seers of the Veda that the manner of expressing the divinely inspired wisdom or truth in language is in accordance with the mental ability of the seers.[6] The form of the hymn, the beauty of the language and the metaphors employed to express the truth depend on the mental ability of the seers who made or composed the hymns. But the truth that is expressed through the hymns is attributed solely to divine inspiration, and the intention of the Vedic seers in expressing it in language is primarily to express the inwardly experienced devotion, and also to communicate the truth to future generations.[7] The experience of devotion makes one bow down to the divine, and bowing down (*namaḥ*) in reverence is spontaneous when the divine is experienced. And bowing down

4. *Ṛgveda*, 5.48.5; see also 1.145.2.
5. *Ibid.*, 1.164.37; see also 1.145.2.
6. *Ibid.*, 10.111.1.
7. *Ibid.*, 10.72.1.

in reverence is to worship the divine; it is the chief form or mode of Vedic worship.

The hymns are primarily prayers and praises addressed to various deities, either individually or collectively. Prayer is born when the inwardly experienced devotion is expressed in language. And, according to the Veda, the divine reveals itself within the state of devotion or rather as devotion itself. The divine inspires devotion in man, and man comes to know the nature of the divine in the state of devotion or as devotion itself. And a prayer as an expression of devotion in language, is regarded by the seers of the Veda as a debt returned to the divine for the gift of inspiration.[8] The Vedic seers often express that they pray to the divine with the prayer that is inspired by the divine. The divine gift of inspiration is returned to the divine in the form of prayer as a shepherd returns sheep to the master.[9] In this process man comes to know the nature of the divine or the divine is revealed to him, and his life is supremely fulfilled thereby.

The term most frequently employed in the Veda to convey the sense of devotion is Brahma which is also used to mean prayer and hymn. Thus, we find in the *R̥gveda* a clear description of the birth of divine in human consciousness. The birth of divine in human consciousness is the same as to experience devotion, which is due to divine inspiration. And man bows down in reverence to the divine as spontaneously as water seeks declivity when he experiences devotion. The divine is, therefore, known primarily as that which inspires devotion, prayer and worship in man. Devotion (*brahma*) which is ineffable (*acittam brahma*) is an end in itself, and it is what is mostly prayed for by the Vedic seers, as in its birth, man comes to know himself fully, or the hidden riches of his being are revealed to him. In other words, man comes to realise the divine nature of his existence, and sees nature, the immediate source of divine revelation, in its divine aspect or as a creative manifestation of the divine. Because

8. *R̥gveda*, 8.61.12.
9. *Ibid.*, 1.114.9.

of inwardly experienced devotion man's understanding of himself as well as of the world gets completely transformed. Then the world is seen as the creative work of the divine (*devasya kāvyam*).[10] In short, a person becomes a *kavi* or a *ṛṣi*, and his life is supremely fulfilled (*dhanya*).

Most of the hymns of the *Ṛgveda* describe, either directly or with the help of metaphors, the nature of devotion. Devotion is divine (*divya*). It is uncaused. The birth of divine in human consciousness has no explanation as its experience is not due to any effort on the part of man. It is a matter of inspiration, and inspiration is not the same as causation. Divinely inspired devotion which does not involve any human effort cannot be regarded as caused. And as to see or experience the divine is the same as to experience devotion, without experiencing devotion one cannot know the divine. Nevertheless, they are not one and the same as the birth of devotion in man is dependent upon the divine. It is only when one is divinely inspired one experiences devotion, but not otherwise. However, from the human point of view or phenomenologically speaking it is devotion that is directly experienced, and man sees something in it which is not empirical, or has no empirical explanation. It is known or identified as divine.

Before we discuss the nature of devotion we have to understand the nature and meaning of the divine, the source of inspiration of devotion in man. The divine that reveals itself in the state of devotion or as devotion itself is not meant to explain anything. The Vedic seers experience the divine in nature or as it reveals itself in nature. However, it is not nature in its phenomenal aspect, the object of common experience, that is the source of divine inspiration to the Vedic seers, and at the same time the divine is not experienced by the Vedic seers independently of nature. When a creative poet speaks of nature he does not describe nature in its phenomenal aspect or as it is commonly experienced by all. It is something more than what is commonly experienced. The capacity to inspire is inherent in

---

10. *Ṛgveda*, 10.55.5; see also 10.29.6; 8.41.5-6.

nature though all may not be inspired by nature in the same manner. The nature's capacity to inspire devotion in man is similar to its capacity for poetic inspiration. The purpose in referring to poetic inspiration is only to help understand the nature of inspiration, but not to compare it with the inspiration the Vedic seers speak of. Both admit nature's capacity to inspire man. Nature, which is the source of poetic inspiration to a poet, is the source of inspiration of devotion to a Vedic seer. It is not, therefore, nature as nature or in its phenomenal aspect that is seen or experienced as divine by the Vedic seers. The source of devotion in man is the divine that is present in nature, or its 'hidden riches' as the Vedic seers put it. The hidden divine aspect of nature reveals itself to those who are completely free from all kinds of sin, and whose intellect is subtle (*aṇu*) and pure. In other words, the presence of the divine in nature, which is hidden, as it were, to ordinary vision or experience, is revealed to the Vedic seers when devotion is born in them.

The seat of divine inspiration in man is primarily his intellect. Human heart is also regarded as a seat of divine inspiration by the Vedic seers. The Vedic prayer, known commonly as Gāyatrī hymn, is a prayer addressed to Savitā, also known as Sāvitrī or Prasavitrī, the deity of divine inspiration, to inspire human intelligence. The divine Uṣā, the emerging form of divine inspiration, is addressed as the mother or matrix of deities, and the sign of *yajña*, the Vedic form of worship. She is described as the 'brilliant guide of the truthful (*sunrutānām*)'.[11] She opens the doors of man (which can mean either the senses or the faculties of man), and manifests his riches. The senses are often referred to in the Vedic literature as doors. When his intellect is divinely inspired man is able to realise his own divine nature. "This is to-day the divine gift of Savitā, this thought we have when now the deity is furthering us (*deva prasave*)."[12] And when Savitā inspires his intelligence man is able to worship the divine with hymns.

---

11. *Ṛgveda*, 1.113.4.
12. *Ibid.*, 1.159.5.

Nature is seen as a source of revelation of the divine as it can inspire devotion in man which is divine. It is not that the divine has chosen nature as a medium or source of its revelation, which would be meaningful if the divine is not already present in nature. According to the Vedic seers, the divine is immanently present in nature or the capacity to reveal the divine by inspiring devotion in man is inherent in nature. How otherwise could nature be a source of inspiration of devotion in man? Nature acts on man, and influences or inspires him in several ways, and its divine aspect is revealed to the Vedic seers mainly because of their moral purity (*ṛta*). The Vedic seers are known for their moral purity (*ṛta*); they are full of or are filled with *ṛta* (*ṛtavān*). Being a manifestation of the divine, nature is divine, though all are not able to see it. Thus, while the phenomenal aspect of nature is open to all that aspect of nature which can inspire devotion in man is hidden, as it were, to ordinary experience and knowledge.

All are not able to see the divine in nature is no reason to deny the possibility of nature being the source of inspiration of devotion to the Vedic seers. The Vedic seers often pray to the deities to bless them with divine grace (*sumati* or *bhagaḥ*) or for the gift of divine inspiration. Since seeing or experiencing the divine in nature is not due to human effort, as it is not a kind of metaphysical or theological explanation or interpretation of nature in divine terms, we cannot rationally explain the fact of divine inspiration. And no attempt was made in the Veda to explain the nature and meaning of the divine in rational terms. We do not find in the Vedic *Saṁhitā*s any attempt to construct a theory or doctrine of the divine. The divine is described in the Vedic hymns by way of praising the deities in divine terms for the gift of divine inspiration, the source of the Vedic hymns. The Vedic hymns are primarily prayers addressed to various deities, either individually or collectively, in which the deities are praised in divine terms. They are, therefore, the source of our knowledge of the nature and meaning of the divine, according to the Veda, as well as the mode or manner of its revelation to the Vedic seers. On the basis of their direct experience of devotion the Vedic seers are able to see the presence of the divine within all, including themselves. And the Upaniṣads are the first to articulate the nature and meaning of the divine as revealed to the Vedic seers or on the basis of Vedic revelation. Most of the Upaniṣadic statements about the divine or *Brahman* are intelligible and meaningful only in the light of Vedic experience or revelation. However, the Upaniṣads are interested more in describing the nature of the divine as it reveals itself within human reality, or the manifestation of the divine at the *adhyātma* level, while the *Saṁhitā*s describe the nature of the divine as it reveals itself at the level of deities (*ādhidaivika*) who reveal themselves in and through nature, and the *Brāhmaṇa*s are an attempt to understand the nature and meaning of the divine at the *ādhibhautika* level.

The Vedic statements about the divine in itself, which are a few, are mostly speculative in character. The Vedic seers are generally skeptical about the knowledge of the divine in itself which is clearly reflected in all the speculative hymns of the Veda. These hymns cannot help us in knowing the divine that is revealed to or directly experienced by the seers of the Veda. We cannot know the nature of the divine, according to the Veda, on the basis of the speculative hymns of the Veda. They are skeptical about man's ability to know the divine in itself, and do not, therefore, have religious significance and value. It is because of its revealed character the Veda is of foundational value to Hinduism, and the Hindu vision of the divine is fundamentally Vedic. The Hindu view or vision of the divine formulated and expressed, either in the Upaniṣads or in the Smṛti literature, has its experiential basis and justification in the *Saṁhitā*s. The Vedic hymns are an expression, in poetic language, of divinely inspired devotion, often employing rich metaphors in conveying the sense of divine directly experienced by the seers in the state of devotion. A theological or metaphysical construction of the nature of the divine on the basis of direct experience of the seers is attempted mostly in the post-*Saṁhitā* literature, especially in the Upaniṣads.

As nature in its various phenomena is the immediate source of divine inspiration to the Vedic seers they see nature as a manifestation of the divine or as the dwelling place (*dhāma*) of the various deities, the primary and cosmic manifestations of the divine. The view that the divine is immanently present in all creation (*viśveṣu bhuvaneṣu antariti*; *īśāvāsyamidam sarvam*)[13] is what is commonly accepted by all the schools and sects of Hinduism, though in the Smṛti tradition the divine is identified with God or is viewed as a personal being. The Vedic expression that the world is an expression of divine creativity or a creative work of the divine (*devasya kāvyam*) is a most beautiful way of expressing the Vedic vision of the divine. The universe is an expression of divine creativity and wisdom, just as a *kāvya* expresses the creativity of a poet. Nature is divine as it is an expression of divine creativity or a manifested form of the divine. The Vedic deities are also addressed as poets (*kavi*), and nature in its various phenomena is seen as an expression of their creativity. In the language of the Veda, the different deities live in different phenomena of nature or the various phenomena of nature are the abode of the deities, the Vedic (poetic) way of expressing that nature in all its phenomena is a manifestation of the divine. Each phenomenon of nature, being a manifestation of the divine, reveals the nature of the divine in its own characteristic way, and all the phenomena of nature together reveal the splendour and glory of the divine. For instance, Agni in the Veda does not simply mean fire for it is only a form of manifestation of the divine Agni. Agni refers to the principle of heat or warmth in whatever form it manifests itself in nature, including man. And being a form of manifestation of the divine it is divine, and is, therefore, addressed as a deity. In the Veda no one deity is identified with the divine though all the deities are described and addressed in divine terms. All the deities are only different forms of manifestation of the divine. As clearly expressed in the *Puruṣa-sūkta*, which has also been expressed in other hymns though metaphorically, the divine glory that

13. *Īśāvāsya Upaniṣad*, 1.1; *Ṛgveda*,1.113.4.

manifests itself in and through all that is there does not exhaust the divine. The divine is more than (*ati*) or transcends its own glory.[14] The Vedic expressions, like the matrix of the deities (*devānām parame janitri*) or the father or origin of the deities (*devānām janita* or *pitā*) indicate that all the deities addressed to and prayed in the Veda have only derived existence. They have no ontologically independent existence or existence of their own. And this fact has not been lost sight of throughout the development of Hinduism. "One only exists, and those who are moved by the divine (*vipra*) name it or speak of it variously."[15] The Vedic meaning of the term *vipra* (*vepate*) is one who is moved by the divine. The same idea is expressed more significantly when it is said that the divine though is one is conceived or imagined and described or addressed variously by the seers through their praises and prayers (*suparṇam viprāḥ kavayaḥ vacobhiḥ* (*stutirūpa vāk*) *ekam santam bahudhā kalpayanti*).[16] "The spirit or life (*asu*) that permeates and enlivens all the deities is one; who knows it and who can tell us about it. Even the deities cannot as they (being its manifested forms) are posterior to it."[17] The assertions like that there was a time when the deities did not exist (*arvāk devāḥ*), or the time before the deities have come into existence (*devānām pūrve yuge*), show that the deities have no ontologically independent existence or are not ultimately real. From non-reality or non-existence reality has come into existence is interpreted by Sāyaṇa to mean that nothing can be said about ultimate reality as it is formless, and that gave birth to the deities with determinable forms.[18] The various deities, being the self-manifestations of the divine, share the nature of the divine, and reveal it to man. Although the deities differ among themselves in terms of their phenomenal attributes they all share in common the nature of the divine which they manifest

14. *Ṛgveda*, 10.90.1 (*Puruṣa-sūkta*).
15. *Ibid.*, 1.164.46.
16. *Ibid.*, 10.114.5.
17. *Ibid.*, 10.129.6; 10.72.2-3.
18. *Ibid.*, 10.129.1.

and reveal in their own characteristic ways. The divine is their definition (*nāmadha*).

It will be difficult to subscribe to the doctrine of polytheism if we grasp the spirit of the Veda, and comprehend its meaning in the total context of the Hindu tradition. The Vedic deities have no existence of their own. They depend for their existence on the divine, and come into existence in the process of self-manifestation of the divine. Thus, while the deities have their oneness in the divine, their individuality is due to the differences in the forms of manifestation of the divine which they represent. As a manifestation of the divine each deity represents a phenomenon of nature with which it is identified. Such identification gives the deities their individuality as otherwise they are one and indistinguishable. In other words, in terms of their identification with the various forms of manifestation of the divine the deities acquire their individual identity, and in being the manifestations of the divine they point to the divine, their source and oneness. As the deities reveal themselves in and through different phenomena of nature, they are viewed as different, but as manifestations of the divine they have their unity in the divine, and share in common all the attributes of the divine. While the divine attributes are common to all the deities, those attributes which give the deities their individuality differ from deity to deity depending upon the phenomenon of nature with which a deity is identified or in and through which it reveals itself. Therefore, the individual identity of the deities is meaningful and valid only at the level of manifestation or becoming. Each deity not only reveals itself in and through a phenomenon of nature, but also forms the unity of the phenomenon. Thus, while a deity is the unity of a phenomenon of nature, the divine, as the unity of all the deities, is the unity or oneness of all that is. All the deities share the divine nature, and, therefore, all the attributes of the divine are commonly attributed to all the deities. They share the power of the divine to inspire and illumine human intelligence. Each deity or each phenomenon of nature has the capacity to inspire in man devotion which is divine. It is because of divinely inspired devotion the Vedic seers are able to see the divine aspect of nature or nature as a creative manifestation of the divine, as well as its divine unity or oneness. However, the revelation of the divine at the level of deities is one mode of divine revelation (*ādhidaivika*).

Man is also a form of manifestation of the divine, and is an integral part of the manifested world. The revelation of the divine at the human level, or the manner or mode of its manifestation within human reality is known as *ādhyātmika*. Nature in its various elements, and all the deities in their subtle form are present in man. It is said that all the deities have entered into man and dwell within him. For instance, Agni entered into the mouth of man, and forms his speech. And the divine that is the essence and inner unity of nature is present within man as his self or *ātman*, the essence and unity of man. In the *Bṛhadāraṇyaka Upaniṣad* it is said that *Brahman* is the essence (*ātman*) of each and every phenomenon of nature as well as the essence (*ātman*) of man.[19] Thus, while the divine reveals itself within man as his self, it reveals itself in nature as its essence and inner unity. Man is an abode of *Brahman* (*puruṣaḥ brahmaṇo lokaḥ*), and the revelation of the divine within human reality is more full or perfect. It is said in the Upaniṣads that *Brahman* did not prosper fully or come to know himself fully by creating various living beings, and, therefore, he created man in whom he could prosper, and know himself more fully or perfectly.[20] The whole creation, including man, is a manifested form (*vyakta*) of the divine, and it is man who is capable of realising this truth. It is in and through man, a self-conscious being, the divine comes to know or realise itself more and more clearly and fully; and that is the greatness of man. He is the best form of divine manifestation (*sukṛta*).[21]

---

19. *Bṛhadāraṇyaka Upaniṣad*, (*Antaryāmī Brāhmaṇa*),3.7.3.
20. *Aitareya Upaniṣad*,1.1.1-4; *Bṛhadāraṇyaka Upaniṣad*, 1.4.1, 10 and 17; 1.4.10.
21. *Aitareya Āraṇyaka* II,4.2.2; *Aitareya Upaniṣad*, 1.2.3.

The divine which reveals itself within the reality of man (*ādhyāmatika*) reveals itself equally within the realms of *ādhidaivika* and *ādhibhautika*, though the forms of its manifestation differ from realm to realm. While the Vedic *Saṁhitās* describe the divine as it reveals itself in nature, the Upaniṣads express the nature of the divine as it reveals itself at the human level or within the reality of man. Accordingly, attempts are made in the Śruti tradition, particularly in the *Brāhmaṇas*, to establish correspondence among the manifestations of the divine within all the three realms. The Śruti tradition classifies all that is there into three realms of *ādhidaivika*, *ādhibhautika* and *ādhyātmika*, and the divine is seen as the source and unity of all the realms. The various deities, including Prajāpati and Hiraṇyagarbha, come into existence in the process of self-manifestation of the divine. However, the deities, Prajāpati and Hiraṇyagarbha, who are associated with the process of creation, are regarded as the functional names of the divine, while the deities like Indra, Agni, etc., represent the various forms of manifestation of the divine.

The essence of each phenomenon of nature, and hence the nature of the deity that manifests itself within a phenomenon of nature and forms its essence and unity, is different from other deities that reveal themselves as the essence and unity of other phenomena of nature. Each deity is a form of manifestation of the divine, and the divine is what is commonly revealed in and through all the deities. It is their capacity to reveal the divine by inspiring the intelligence of man divinely or to inspire devotion in man. The capacity to inspire devotion in man is commonly attributed to all the deities in the Veda, or the various phenomena of nature are regarded as divine because of their capacity to inspire devotion in man.

The birth of devotion in man because of which he sees the presence of the divine in nature is what is commonly celebrated in all the hymns of the Veda. Devotion reveals the divine in nature which is hidden, as it were, to ordinary experience and understanding. Thus, to see a phenomenon of nature as a manifestation of the divine is to represent it as a deity. And as nature is a manifestation of the divine, the divine is the inner unity and controller of nature. The various phenomena of nature, though differ in their forms, are all equally the manifestations of the divine, and reveal the richness and glory of the divine. As a manifestation of the divine nature reveals the nature of the divine, and, therefore, most of the attributes of the divine as found in the Hindu tradition are meaningful in terms of nature, the source of divine revelation.

While the Upaniṣads describe the nature of the divine predominantly in terms of human reality, as they describe the nature of the divine as it manifests and reveals itself within the reality of man, the Vedic description of the divine is mostly in terms of the attributes of nature as the Vedic hymns describe the divine as it manifests and reveals itself in nature. Therefore, the Upaniṣadic description of the divine is significantly different from its description in the Vedic hymns. According to Hinduism, the divine is within all — within man and in nature — as it is the essence of all that is there, and, therefore, one who sees his self or essence (*ātman*) in all, and all in his self knows or realises the divine. In other words, to realise the divine is to see or realise it as the essence and inner unity or oneness of all that is there. The divine unity or oneness of all that is there is what is commonly asserted in all the texts of Hinduism, both Śruti and Smṛti, and is sought to be realised by all the seers and saints of Hinduism. It is the supreme end or consummation of religious life, according to Hinduism. As the ultimate source of origin of all that is there, the divine is the essence and inner unity of all. It is not only the inner reality or essence of man but also of all that is there. This is almost a dogma with Hinduism, and is accepted by all the schools and sects of Hinduism. It defines the fundamental character and meaning of Hinduism. We cannot, therefore, understand the meaning of Hinduism, whether based on Śruti or on Smṛti, without comprehending its vision of the divine, and the manner of its revelation. Since the Vedic vision of the divine is a matter of direct experience inspired by the divine itself there is no meaning in arguing about its validity.

As it is not a matter of rational understanding it would be superficial to try to provide any rational justification for the Hindu view of the divine.

Despite their sectarian differences all the Hindus, who are aware of their religious tradition, accept the Vedic vision of the divine, according to which, the divine is the essence (*ātmā*) of all that is there, and, therefore, constitutes the unity or oneness of all that is there. Though the divine manifests itself in varied forms yet it transcends all the forms of its manifestation. The world of manifestation reveals the glory and splendour of the divine, and the divine is more than its glory and splendour. Therefore, the nature of the divine cannot be defined and determined in terms of the forms of its manifestation though it is known in and though its manifestations. The divine is all in the sense that there is no reality other than the divine. The divine would have remained a complete mystery to human understanding had it not manifested itself. The divine immanence helps man in knowing the nature of the divine, and without such knowledge of the divine religious life of man would not be possible. Thus, within the Hindu tradition a significant distinction is made between the divine in itself, which is beyond all definition and description, and the divine that is known in and through the forms of its manifestation.[22] And such distinction is the basic reason why Hinduism is not dogmatic in its attitude towards the nature and meaning of the divine.

As we shall soon see even the Smṛti tradition of Hinduism, which is avowedly theistic and identifies the divine with God (*bhagavān* or *īśvara*), has not lost sight of the distinction between the divine in itself and the divine that is known in and through

22. All that we experience is becoming only, and the Being is not an object of human experience. At the empirical level the divine is known in and through its manifestations (becoming), and the divine in itself is beyond all the forms of its manifestation. And all the forms in which the divine is conceived and worshipped belong to the divine though it transcends them all. Therefore, no one form of the divine can be identified with the divine. *Bṛhad-Devatā*, 1.31; *Ṛgveda*, 10.90.1 (*Puruṣa-sūkta*); see also *Bhāgavata Purāṇa*, 6.9.36.

its manifestations and incarnations. Even though the Smṛti tradition identifies the divine with God, God is viewed as transcending His various forms of manifestation and incarnation. The major sects of Hinduism, who differ among themselves in terms of their identification of the divine with their sectarian deities like Viṣṇu and Śiva, and the emphasis they place on some of the attributes of the divine, have not rejected the Vedic vision of the divine as being both immanent and transcendent. However, in the history of Hinduism several significant attempts have been made to reconcile and harmonise the theistic conception of the divine with the Vedic view or vision of the divine.

The saints and thinkers of Hinduism have recognised the foundational value of the Vedic vision of the divine to Hinduism, and, therefore, have tried to interpret it so as to make it more and more meaningful in terms of the changing historical and social circumstances and the ways of human understanding. The free use of metaphors and analogies in elucidating the meaning of the divine, which vary from sect to sect and from thinker to thinker or even from saint to saint, may give rise to the view that their vision of the divine is not basically Vedic. This we shall discuss soon. The various saints and thinkers of Hinduism born in different regions of India and at different periods of time — many of them established different sects or different forms of religious life and worship either by way of interpreting the scriptures or by way of projecting a particular form or attribute of the divine — are basically Vedic in their faith and outlook. In their outlook and thought they do not radically depart from the Vedic vision or wisdom, as it is in the case of the Buddha and Mahāvīra, the founders of Buddhism and Jainism respectively. All of them accept the basic Hindu view of the divine that it is immanently present within all, and, therefore, constitutes the unity of all, even though they disagree among themselves with regard to other aspects of religious life.

The theistic tradition of Hinduism also accepts the immanence of God. The basic reason for the harmony among the various sects of Hinduism is their acceptance or adoption of the Vedic vision of the divine despite differences in their understanding about the nature and meaning of the divine. To accept all that is there is a manifestation of the divine or God is to see its or His presence even in those who are opposed to a particular view of the divine or of God , and a particular form of religious life. Prahlāda, a great devotee of Viṣṇu, and a paradigm of devotional way of religious life, could see in his father, who was opposed to his form of religious life, and even tried to destroy him for his religious faith, the presence of God or Viṣṇu.[23] It is not, therefore, so much religiously important to have a belief in a particular view or conception of the divine or God as to see its or His presence within all, including those who are opposed to such belief. Those whose conception of the divine is different from that of the Veda may oppose the followers of the Veda, but the followers of the Veda have no reason to oppose those who oppose them as according to their vision of the divine it is equally present within them also.

Before we present and discuss the Smṛti conception of the divine, which is the source and authority for the popular form of Hinduism, we have to understand the reasons why a distinction is made and maintained between Śruti and Smṛti. What is the conception of the divine according to Smṛti tradition? Does Smṛti tradition stand for a clear and unambiguous personal conception of the divine? Before we discuss this problem let us understand the nature of the divine as described in the Vedic hymns. The Veda seldom makes any doctrinal statements about the divine and its nature. Everything that is said in the Veda about the divine and its nature is said primarily by way of prayer and praise. However, in some of the hymns, which are a few, and are speculative in character, an attempt was made to understand the nature of the divine in metaphysical or abstract terms. Secondly, all that is said about the divine is said indirectly by way of praising the divine nature of the deities who are

---

23. *Viṣṇu Purāṇa*, 1.19.36-37. (What is there that cannot be predicated of You (Viṣṇu).

unmistakably regarded as different manifestations of the divine. The divine is revealed to the Vedic seers in and through the deities. As manifested forms of the divine the deities have their own identity and individuality. Each deity has an identity of its own in terms of which it is distinguished from other deities. Agni as a deity has his own identity which is different from that of Indra. Each deity representing a form of manifestation of the divine possesses the attributes peculiar to the form of manifestation, and the deity acquires its individuality in terms of those attributes. While Agni represents the phenomenon of heat or warmth in whatever form it is found in nature, Indra represents power in whatever form it manifests itself. Thus, the nature of Agni is not the same as that of Indra, and, therefore, both of them are not addressed in identical terms in the Veda though both of them are divine. But the attributes which all the deities have in common are the attributes essential to the nature of the divine. While the divine acquires certain qualities in terms of its manifested forms, the qualities which are essential to its nature are not lost in the process of its manifestation. Thus, each deity is described or addressed in terms of two kinds of attributes; the attributes that are characteristic of it as a deity, and those that are essential to the nature of the divine which all the deities share in common. Each deity manifests within itself the essential nature of the divine as well as the nature of the phenomenon which it represents. However, the attributes which are peculiar to each deity are also the attributes of the divine, but are meaningful and valid only in relation to the forms of its manifestation.

We discuss here some of the essential qualities of the divine which are distinctive of the Vedic conception of the divine. There are certain other attributes of the divine which are common to every conception of the divine. The divine, according to the Vedic tradition, reveals itself primarily as *ṛta*, the cosmic order which sustains, regulates and governs the world. And *ṛta* reveals itself in man as moral order. In its nature and meaning *ṛta* is the same as *dharma* of the post-Vedic Hinduism. *Ṛta* holds together all, and governs all. As pointed out earlier *dharma* is also ontological for it is seen as the foundation of the whole world. Nevertheless, it is primarily conceived as the moral principle governing the human conduct at all levels.

Ṛta is both identified with and distinguished form the divine. It is the same as the divine but as revealed within the realm of manifestation. *Ṛta* is *satya*, but as revealed at the level of manifestation. All the Vedic attributes of the divine are meaningful in relation to the divine in the state of its manifestation or becoming. *Ṛta* manifests itself within all the realms though the forms of its manifestation are not the same in all the realms. The sun, the moon, earth and heaven, all the deities or the entire universe, including man, manifest it and reveal it in different ways and forms. It reveals itself in man as moral principle or order. It is identified with righteousness in man, and, therefore, to be divine is to follow *ṛta* or to be righteous. The seers of the Veda are known for their *ṛta* (*ṛtavān*). The deities are also described as the followers of *ṛta*. They are also its protectors. To follow *ṛta* or to live in accordance with *ṛta* is to realise that *yajña* is the meaning of one's life. The root meaning of *yajña* is to worship (*yaj*), and to worship the divine is to participate in the divine process involved in creation (divine *yajña*), and to extend it to all the spheres of one's life. *Yajña* is a creative process because of which the divine has become all this, and the deities also in their own characteristic ways extend it at the level of nature. In contrast to the real *yajña*, which is to be extended (*tanoti*), the ritual form of *yajña* is an act that is to be performed. However, all the components of a ritual *yajña* are symbolic representation of the cosmic elements or principles.

As a form of worship of the divine *yajña* consists in the realisation that one's life and actions are an offering to the divine, or to consecrate one's life and actions to the divine. The various kinds of *yajña* ritually performed are only symbolic in character as the various elements employed in their performance are symbolic representation of the cosmic phenomena. When one acts, either at individual or at social level, with a sense of fulfilling the divine purpose his actions acquire the significance of *yajña*. Then they become means of worshipping the divine, and the human life is supremely fulfilled thereby. Even the funeral rites are regarded as *yajña* or the final offering of man in which his body is offered. In the *Mahābhārata*, service (*sevā*), the ordained duty of a śūdra, is regarded as *yajña* (*sevā-yajña*) on the part of a śūdra if it is done in the spirit of *yajña*. It is his form of worship of the divine.[24] Every act of man acquires the significance of *yajña* if it is done as an act of divine worship or in imitation of the divine *yajña* whereby the world has come into existence, or as a continuation and extension of the divine process and purpose involved in creation. When one realises that all is divine his life is divinely transformed, and then every act of his will be an act of worship of the divine. It is said in the *R̥gveda* that when devotion increases and transforms man totally every act of his, including such mundane acts like harvesting, will be an act of worship of the divine, and a means of glorifying the divine.[25] As the divine is all or all is divine the various qualities of both nature and man ultimately belong to the divine. And Tantra is an attempt to see or realise the divine even in the terrible things, such as death.

What is commonly revealed both in nature and man is creativity because of which nature is rich in variety, and man is known for his varied creations. The divine creativity which is the source of variety in the world also sustains the world. Both differences and unity which a wise man discerns both within himself and in nature are a manifestation of the divine. The divine which in its creativity creates all is also the unity of all that is there. These two aspects of the divine are revealed to a *kavi* and a *r̥ṣi* respectively. While a *kavi* is one who sees the divine in all the forms of its creative manifestation, a *r̥ṣi* is one who sees the divine as the inner unity of all that is manifested. A *kavi* is known for his creativity which expresses itself in all his creation, and a *r̥ṣi* is known for his unitive vision, and sees the unity of what is created. The Veda often addresses and

24. *Mahābhārata* Śānti-parva,238.12; Anuśāsana-parva, 141. 57 and 60.

25. *R̥gveda*, 1.30.7; see also 1.100.7; 3.31.13.

describes the deities or the divine as *kavi* and *ṛṣi* which represent the two basic aspects of the divine that are revealed in creation. The spontaneous outburst or expression of divine creativity (*sruj*) results in creation. The divine and its creative power because of which the divine manifests or expresses itself in the form of the world are like the breathing process in a living human being.[26] Though they can be distinguished they are not different. In the Hindu tradition creation is not seen as an act taking place in space and time. Creation is a beginningless process, and as an expression of divine creativity it is spontaneous. Creative power of the divine known as *māyā*, even in the Veda, is inherent within the reality of the divine. Though formless the divine manifests itself in various forms because of *māyā*, the creative power inherent within itself. The manifested world is, therefore, described as the *kāvya* of the divine or as an expression of divine creativity. The creative power of the divine, which is fully informed by the divine wisdom, expresses itself in the form of the world. In this sense all the deities are addressed as *kavi* and *ṛṣi* in the Veda. Because of its creative power the divine manifests itself in the form of the world, or the sole reason for coming into existence of the world is divine creativity. And as a creative self-expression or manifestation of the divine the world reveals the divine and its nature.

The oneness of the divine is meaningful only at the level of manifestation or in relation to the world of differences as otherwise there is no point in asserting the oneness of the divine. The differences as well as the unity or oneness underlying them reveal the divine. They are two ways of expressing the meaning of divine revelation. The Veda as a revelation of the divine reveals both the aspects of the divine. As the divinely inspired wisdom of the Vedic seers (*kavi* or *ṛṣi*) the Veda reveals the creative power of the divine because of which it has become all that is as well the inner divine unity or oneness of all that is there. Therefore, to realise the divine is to see it in all the forms of its manifestation, and at the same time to realise it as the inner

26. *Bṛhadāraṇyaka Upaniṣad*, 2.4.10; 4.5.11.

unity or oneness of all that is manifested. Thus both multiplicity and unity are equally meaningful in knowing the nature of the divine that reveals itself in and through creation. But as the world is only a creative manifestation of the divine all that can be said of the divine on the basis of its manifestations can be true of the divine only indirectly or in relation to its manifestations. And what is revealed in and through the world of manifestation is the glory of the divine (*mahima*).[27]

What holds the world together and sustains it is *ṛta* which is the direct revelation of the divine within the realm of manifestation. *Ṛta* is divine, and is identified with truth (*satyam*) though not in an absolute sense. It is used more meaningfully to distinguish the divine in itself or in its unmanifested state of existence from the divine in its manifested state of existence. *Ṛta* means cosmic order as well as the ground of the inner unity of the world. In the Veda *ṛta* is both identified with and distinguished from the divine. It is the divine but as it reveals itself in and through the forms of its manifestation. Its identification with the divine (*satyam*) is meaningful only at the level of manifestation. Even the concept of truth (*satyam*) is meaningful and valid only at the level of manifestation as the divine is the truth of the manifested world or the empirical reality. *Ṛta* and *satyam* are both meaningful only at the empirical level or in relation to the world of manifestation. All the terms that are used to express or indicate the divine are meaningful and valid only in relation to the divine in its manifested state of existence.[28] And the divine in itself or in its unmanifested state, which is more a matter of logical understanding, is referred to by such indefinite terms like 'That', 'One', etc., in the Veda.

---

27. *Ṛgveda* 10.90.1.

28. What we experience is a manifested form of *Brahman* or *Brahman* is known in and through the forms of its manifestation. The idea of *Brahman* in itself is a logical necessity as it transcend all the forms of its manifestation, and all the categories of human understanding are meaningful and valid only in relation to *Brahman* in its manifested form. Therefore, all that is said about *Brahman* is meaningful only in relation to its manifested state of existence. *Bṛhad-Devatā*, 1.31.

Before we present and discuss the nature of the divine as conceived and developed in the Smṛti tradition, which is as influential as the Śruti tradition in the life of Hinduism, or even more pervasive in its influence than that of Śruti, particularly at the popular level, we have to understand the difference in the conception of the divine between Śruti and Smṛti. Do they differ basically in their conception of the divine? The distinction made in the Upaniṣads between *mūrta* (formed or with form) and *amūrta* (unformed or without form) does not mean the distinction between the personal and impersonal conception of the divine. Śruti and Smṛti differ basically in their conception of the divine. While Śruti though not explicitly opposed to a personal conception of the divine is definitely in favour of an impersonal conception of the divine, the Smṛti tradition is avowedly theistic, and believes in the personal nature of the divine. Though Smṛti is avowedly theistic it is not completely opposed to the Śruti conception of the divine which is more impersonal than personal. And the difference in the conception of the divine distinguishes Śruti from Smṛti. Smṛti is fully aware of the basic difference between its conception of the divine and that of Śruti, and, therefore, in an attempt to integrate itself with Śruti it tried to reconcile and harmonise its theistic conception of the divine with that of Śruti. In a sense the whole of Hindu theological tradition is an attempt to reconcile the Śruti view or vision of the divine with the Smṛti conception of God. But both the conceptions of the divine are integral to Hinduism. Though it is not easy to reconcile and harmonise both the conceptions, the Smṛti tradition has made significant attempts to reconcile and harmonise both.

In this context, we have to understand whether the Śruti conception of the divine can be theistically interpreted. Is it the case that the divine of the Śruti tradition is purely impersonal, and is, therefore, not amenable to theistic interpretation? Is the Smṛti conception of the divine purely personal? We have to consider in this context whether the conception of the divine necessarily involves the idea of its being personal. Is it the case that to be spiritual is to be personal? We have also to consider whether the categories of personal and impersonal are adequate to comprehend and express the nature of the divine? Can we say that what is spiritual is necessarily personal? Is it meaningful to determine the nature of the divine in personal terms or to identify the divine with God? The spiritual and personal need not necessarily go together though there is no contradiction in understanding the spiritual in personal terms. The divine which is essentially spiritual need not necessarily or essentially be personal though spiritual is not opposed to personal. The divine can be both personal and impersonal though in itself the divine transcends both the categories. Therefore, to conceive the nature of the divine either in personal or in impersonal terms will be a matter of one's choice and disposition. However, we have to understand the whole problem in the context of the Hindu tradition. While the Smr̥ti tradition is avowedly theistic, and conceives the divine as a personal being or God, Śruti conception of the divine cannot be characterised in either terms. However, Śruti addresses the divine mostly in impersonal terms, and prefers to use impersonal pronouns to address and describe the divine though occasionally we come across the use of personal pronouns or terms to address the divine. In such Śruti expressions like "He wanted to create, so He created", or "in the beginning *puruṣa* was all this" the divine is seen and described as a personal being.[29] In the *Puruṣa-sūkta* the divine is identified and addressed as *puruṣa*, a personal being. In the Veda the divine is attributed with *kratu* or will or intention, and all the deities are addressed as if they are personal beings. They are prayed and praised for their auspicious deeds. If the deities, the primary and cosmic forms of manifestations of the divine, are viewed as personal, and above all man, the crown of creation or the best form of divine manifestation (*sukr̥ta*), as he represents the divine more fully (*puruṣo brahmaṇo lokaḥ*) is personal, the Vedic conception of the divine need not be opposed to the idea of God, a personal being. However, in the Śruti tradition, though

29. *Br̥hadāraṇyaka Upaniṣad*, 2.3.1; *Maitrī Upaniṣad*, 6.3.

the divine is addressed in personal terms it is not identified with God.

The divine is more often addressed and described in neutral terms, and generally impersonal or indefinite terms like 'that' (*tat*) and 'one' (*ekam*) are used to indicate the divine. The coming into existence of the world out of the divine or the manifestation of the divine in the form of the world is seen as something spontaneous, but not as willed or created by the divine. The world flows from the nature of the divine as spontaneously as a spider weaves a web, or as hairs grow from a living human body, or as sparks emanate from fire.[30] The divine is present not only within human reality but is also immanent in nature. It is within fire, within water, within earth, etc. It is within all and governs all, and the term 'all' is used universally to include all that is. The divine cannot, therefore, be essentially personal as the essence of fire, water, earth etc., is not personal. However, it will be meaningful to think that the divine is personal as it manifests itself in man as a personal being, and man is regarded as the best form of manifestation of the divine, for in him the divine is more fully manifested. Therefore, being personal is not opposed to the nature of the divine, as otherwise we cannot explain the manifestation of the divine in man as a personal being. Since the reality of man reflects more fully the reality of the divine our understanding of the nature of the divine on the analogy of human reality will be more meaningful. Man is both spiritual and personal. But if we admit this position we have to think of another reality to explain the physical world or to think that world is not a manifestation of the divine as we cannot meaningfully explain the material or physical side of the world in terms of the divine which is purely spiritual. To overcome this difficulty the Smr̥ti tradition adopts the position that both matter and spirit or *prakr̥ti* and *puruṣa* constitute the nature of the divine or God. While the physical aspect of the divine (*prakr̥ti*) is the source of manifestation of the physical world, the spiritual

30. *Aitareya Upaniṣad*, 1.1.1-4; *Br̥hadāraṇyaka Upaniṣad*, 1.4.1, 1.4.17; 1.14.10.

aspect of the divine is the source of all that is spiritual. On the other hand, if the divine is essentially spiritual it cannot be immanent in matter, and if the divine is essentially personal it cannot be immanent within all, including the physical world, as the personal nature of the divine is revealed within human reality only. Then the reality of man cannot be related to the divine in the manner of manifestation.

Another vital aspect of the problem is whether the impersonal divine reality can be a fit object of religious life of prayer, devotion and worship. However, this would be more meaningful and valid if the divine is conceived in purely material terms as matter as we know it is insensitive to human feelings, needs and aspirations. On the other hand, if the divine is spiritual but not personal will it be sensitive or responsive to the religious feelings or life of man. Is it meaningful to think of the divine, which is essentially spiritual, in impersonal terms? Can we meaningfully disassociate spiritual from personal or can we at least make a valid distinction between spiritual and personal? Is it the case that what is spiritual is essentially personal? Is spiritual meaningful without being personal? This controversy must have engaged the attention of Hindu thinkers for a long time, and even now it is highly significant. However, the dominant view within the Hindu tradition is that the divine is personal. The other view which is more philosophical, and is consistent with the Śruti tradition is that the nature of the divine cannot be determined in terms of the categories of personal and impersonal as the divine transcends all such categories, though a personal conception of the divine satisfies the demands of man's religious life.

Being personal is unintelligible without being individual. Individuality or individual identity is intrinsic to the concept of person, and individuality is seen as a hindrance to the spiritual growth and perfection of man within the Hindu tradition, particularly the Smṛti tradition. However, Hinduism thinks that an impersonal conception of the divine is more meaningful and valid. The divine can be spiritual without being personal. It all depends on what is it to be spiritual. If spiritual is to be equated with consciousness then the problem whether to be spiritual is to be personal can be approached and understood in one way, and if spirituality is to be equated with the selfhood of man then the problem will have a different dimension. These are, however, fit problems for philosophy of religion. But the real problem before Hinduism is whether a personal being can form the essence of all that is, and be immanent within all without transcending its personal character. But the Śruti tradition of Hinduism does not see any problem in viewing the divine as both spiritual and impersonal. However, this does not mean that the divine cannot be personal. Though the divine in itself transcends all kinds of categories, including personal and impersonal, yet it has within itself all the possibilities, including the possibility of being personal. It can be personal though in itself it is neither personal nor impersonal. On the other hand, to define it in personal terms is to determine its nature in terms of what is meaningful to human needs and aspirations. Therefore, the Śruti does not see any contradiction in viewing the divine as transcending personal-impersonal distinction, and yet manifesting itself as a personal being or God. Thus, there is no problem in not defining the divine nature in personal terms, and yet in accepting the possibility of the divine manifesting itself in a personal form. The emergence of man from the divine shows the possibility of the divine being personal, but it does not mean that the divine is essentially or necessarily personal. Thus, there is no opposition or conflict between the spiritual nature of the divine and its being or not being personal. The divine can become personal though conceptually a personal being cannot be immanent within all, including physical nature. God, a personal being, can only influence or inspire those who are essentially like him or human persons, but cannot form the essence of all that is there, including nature.

Smr̥ti is a literature or tradition which has human origin or authorship. It includes all the works on *dharma*, like Manu-Smr̥ti, all the epics (*itihāsa*) and Purāṇas, and all the works on Hinduism that represent the wisdom of various saints and sages born in different periods of time and in different regions of India. However, for the purpose of understanding Hinduism it means all the Purāṇas, and other sectarian scriptures known as Āgamas. The *Bhagavad Gītā*, as an integral part of *Mahābhārata*, is a Smṛti text though it is regarded by all the Hindus as a basic text on Hinduism, and its influence cuts across the sectarian differences. Its influence is pervasive, and in its authority it is next only to Śruti. While Śruti is revealed, and is, therefore, regarded as impersonal and infallible, Smṛti representing the wisdom of enlightened men is fallible. However, much of its wisdom is attributed to some deity or the other. The Smṛti form of Hinduism consists mainly of the Vaiṣṇava, Śaiva and Śākta traditions with their sectarian theologies and forms of worship. While the followers of these sects of Hinduism are somewhat exclusive in their beliefs, doctrines and forms of worship, the Smārttas, who form the majority of Hindus, are open in their attitudes and forms or worship though they also are the followers of Smṛti tradition (*smārtta*). Though they are distinguished from the followers of sectarian traditions they are not a sect in the strict sense of the term as they are not rigid and exclusive in their beliefs and forms of worship, and do not have scriptures of their own. They are more open and catholic in their approach and attitude to Hindu tradition. However, all those who follow Smṛti tradition also follow Śruti tradition, and all those who follow Śruti tradition also follow Smṛti tradition. There is no strict division between the followers of Śruti and the followers of Smṛti. Nevertheless, those who are entitled to follow only Smṛti tradition are not entitled to follow the Śruti form of religious life.

The Smṛti tradition has an identity of its own though it claims the authority of Śruti to its teaching or wisdom. It accepts the authority of Śruti, and asserts that its teaching or wisdom is based on or inspired by Śruti. It regards itself as an extension or continuation of the Śruti tradition, while some of the thinkers of Smṛti tradition think that it is only an interpretation of Śruti. It is beyond the scope of this work to go into the problem whether

Smṛti is basically an independent tradition developed along side Śruti tradition. However, both the traditions have developed together influencing each other, and enriching thereby the Hindu tradition. The attempts on the part of Smṛti tradition to maintain its basic theistic position or character, and at the same time to reconcile itself with the Śruti tradition, without compromising its basic theistic character, shows its distinctive identity and independence. It is a different problem whether the attempts on the part of Smṛti to reconcile itself with Śruti have really helped Smṛti in any significant and substantial manner. Another major reason for the emergence and development of Smṛti tradition, which the Smṛti itself endorses, is that it is a serious attempt to adjust and adapt classical Hinduism based on Śruti to the changing historical and social circumstances. It is an on-going process in any living religious tradition. Since the basic vision of Hinduism or its world-view, which is shaped by Śruti, has not lost its meaningfulness and validity to Smṛti thinkers and authors, they have tried to show its meaningfulness and validity to successive generations by way of interpreting it.

There is not much textual evidence to show that Smṛti represents a different religious tradition though in certain important aspects the Smṛti form of Hinduism is quite distinct from the Hinduism of Śruti. The fact that a particular religious tradition or a school of religious thought is born in a region is no reason to suppose that it is native to that region. All the sects of Hinduism, which the Smṛti tradition represents, are Hindu in the sense that all of them have accepted, and are positively influenced or inspired by the basic vision or world-view of Hinduism. We cannot also say that a personal conception of the divine, and disinterested love and devotion to God, as the meaning and end of religious life, are exclusively true of Smṛti form of Hinduism. The Ṛgvedic hymns or prayers are an expression of soul stirring love and devotion to the deities or the divine.[31] And as pointed out earlier Śruti is not against or opposed to a personal conception of the divine, and the Smṛti, generally

31. *Muṇḍaka Upaniṣad* 1.1.7; *Bṛhadāraṇyaka Upaniṣad*, 2.1.20.

speaking, is not opposed to *jñāna* form of religious life. It is not dogmatic in its emphasis on devotion or *bhakti*. In some of the major Smṛti texts like the *Mahābhārata*, Viṣṇu and *Bhāgavata* Purāṇas, intellectual or rational understanding of spiritual problems leading to *jñāna* is encouraged. And though the divine is identified with God in the Smṛti tradition, it is fully aware of the transcendental dimension of God. Otherwise, Smṛti should not have accepted the authority and validity of Śruti, and tried to reconcile and harmonise its position on the nature of the divine with that of Śruti.

The Smṛti tradition, which is more pervasive in its influence on the religious life of the Hindus, and is continuous in its development, represents the popular form of Hinduism. It is an earnest attempt to make the wisdom of Śruti more and more intelligible and meaningful to the popular Hindu mind, and to make it available to all the sections of Hindu society irrespective of their social and cultural status. In this the impact or rather the challenge posed by the rise and spread of Buddhism must have played a significant role. Smṛti form of Hinduism also tried to overcome some of the prejudices and restrictions which are basically social and cultural, but are somehow mixed up with Hinduism as they are not to be found in the Śruti literature, and tried to make Hinduism open to all. Towards achieving this end Smṛti interprets the Śruti form of Hinduism without, however, giving up or altering the basic character of the Śruti world-view.

The Hinduism of Śruti tradition is not open to all. It is limited, at least in practice, to certain sections Hindu society though its vision or its world-view is really universal. The Indian social structure and its divisions and prejudices were somehow mixed up with the timeless and universal wisdom of Śruti, and attempts are, therefore, made in the Smṛti tradition to separate or disassociate religion from social order. In other words, the Smṛti tradition recognises that social and cultural distinctions and prejudices should not affect and determine the religious life of a person. The religious life of a person should not be linked or related to his social and cultural status. The *Brāhmaṇa* form of religious life, which consists mainly in performing various rituals developed in the *Brāhmaṇas*, is limited to the twice-born of the Indian society. Vedic learning, and the performance of rituals developed in the *Brāhmaṇas* are not open to all the sections of Indian society. Thus, a larger section of society consisting of śūdras and others are excluded from the fold of Śruti form of Hinduism, though we do not find in the Veda (*Saṁhitās*) any sanction and authority for such restriction. It is only in the *Brāhmaṇas*, and in some of the early Smṛti texts dealing with the rules of conduct of various castes, like the *Manu-saṁhitā*, such restrictions are explicitly imposed. The *Brāhmaṇa* texts are an attempt, based on their interpretation of the Vedic *Saṁhitās*, to adapt the Vedic revelation to the religious needs of man. The *Brāhmaṇas* are regarded by the early Smṛti texts as an integral part of the Veda, though they do not enjoy the same status and authority of the *Saṁhitās* and the Upaniṣads. However, the fact that the *Brāhmaṇas* try to interpret and adapt the Vedic revelation or wisdom to the ritual or practical religious needs of man shows that they are not revelatory in character. The *Brāhmaṇas* are basically liturgical texts, and describe elaborately the procedure involved in performing various rituals with justification, and their performance is restricted to the twice-born of the Hindu society. The brāhmaṇa form of religious life is based on a literal interpretation of the Vedic *Saṁhitās*.

Smṛti also claims that its teaching is based on the Veda as the various Smṛti texts proclaim the Vedic authority for their teaching. Smṛti form of Hinduism may, therefore, appear to be based on Vedic authority or a kind of interpretation of the Veda. While the Smṛti texts refer to some of the Upaniṣadic passages when they talk of Vedic authority, the *Brāhmaṇas* refer to the *Saṁhitās* when they talk of the Veda. And the Smṛti is not strictly speaking an interpretation of the Veda as the Smṛti texts while enunciating their beliefs and doctrines seldom refer to any Vedic authority, including that of the Upaniṣads. They simply assert or avow that their teaching is based on the Veda though as a matter of fact we do not find any Vedic authority or basis for most of their beliefs and doctrines. *Mahābhārata* very often asserts that its teachings or wisdom is in accordance with the Veda though we do not find any Vedic authority or justification for what it teaches. Furthermore, the Veda is not concerned with the problems with which *Mahābhārata* is concerned. Therefore, such assertions are made in the Smṛti texts simply to derive the sanctity and authority of the Veda for their various beliefs, views and doctrines.

The Smṛti form of Hinduism, whether it is really based on the Veda or not, is open to all the sections of Hindu society without any kind of discrimination. And as a religious tradition Smṛti must have been as ancient as the Śruti tradition, for we find mention of Smṛti in some of the Śruti texts.[32] However, most of the Smṛti texts were composed or compiled much later. The Purāṇa texts, which are also known as collections or compilations (*Saṁhitā*), are not the source of origin of the Smṛti religious tradition. They are compiled or composed to present and justify an already existing tradition. In other words, Smṛti tradition does not start with Smṛti literature as the latter is only a literary representation of an already existing religious tradition. The theistic form of Hinduism must have been in vogue long before the Smṛti as a literary tradition came into existence for the chief object of the Purāṇa texts is to present and justify the theistic form of religious life in contrast to the ritualistic form of religious life of the Brāhmaṇas. The way the Purāṇa texts try to reconcile and harmonise their religious claims with the ontological vision or world-view of Śruti with a view to providing the sanctity and authority of Śruti for their theistic beliefs and doctrines is interesting. For instance, the *Devī Bhāgavata* asserts that the various village deities are different forms of manifestation of Śakti mentioned in the Gāyatrī hymn of the *Ṛgveda*.[33] Similarly, an attempt is made in all the Purāṇa texts and *Mahābhārata* to show that the various sectarian Gods or deities are different forms of manifestation of *Brahman*, and

32. *Chāndogya Upaniṣad*, 3.4.1-2.

33. *Devī Bhāgavata* Book 9 chapter l.

are, therefore, not different from *Brahman*. Furthermore, as Veda-Vyāsa, who is supposed to have classified the Veda, is also credited with the compilation or composition the Purāṇas and *Mahābhārata*, we may be right in thinking that he was the first person who initiated the process of reconciliation and harmonisation of the popular form of Hinduism represented by the Smṛti tradition with that of Śruti. A need must have been felt to base the popular form of Hinduism on the authority of the Veda or to provide Vedic basis and justification for the popular form of Hinduism so that it can gain the authority and sanctity of the Veda. While the Vedic form of religious life and worship is not open to all, the Smṛti form of Hinduism is open to all. The Smṛti cannot claim to itself the authority and sanctity of revelation as it represents human wisdom, and, therefore, it must have tried to derive for itself the authority of the Veda by claiming that its theological beliefs and doctrines are based on the Veda or are an extension of the Vedic wisdom.

The Smṛti form of Hinduism is essentially theistic, and is centred around a personal conception of the divine (*bhagavān*), identified and worshipped as either Viṣṇu or Śiva or even as Śakti. It regards love and devotion to God as the meaning and end of man's religious life. *Bhakti* or devotional form of religious life is open to all, and is easy to follow. According to Smṛti tradition, disinterested or pure and passionate love of God, which is an end in itself, is the meaning and end of religion. It is even regarded as an independent end of life (*puruṣārtha*). In one of the Smṛti texts God is identified with love itself (*parama prema svarūpa*).[34] However, the sectarian forms of religious life and worship are not really universal as, according to the Hindu concept of *iṣṭa-devatā*, an individual can choose the deity of his worship, as all the sectarian deities are only different forms of manifestation of the divine. While the Vaiṣṇavism identifies the divine with Viṣṇu, the Śaivism identifies it with Śiva, and the Śāktism with Śakti. The Śāktas try to identify Śakti with the divine on the logic that there is no difference between the divine

34. *Nārada Bhakti Sūtra, sūtra* 2.

and its creative power or Śakti. Thus, every sect tried to provide an elaborate justification for identifying its own deity of worship with the divine. However, while identifying its deity of worship with the divine each sect regards the deities of other sects as only different forms of manifestation of its own deity.

While Vaiṣṇavism regards Viṣṇu as the supreme reality, and considers all other deities, including Śiva, as manifestations of Viṣṇu, Śaivism identifies Śiva with the divine and regards Viṣṇu as only a manifestation of Śiva. And Śāktism identifies Śakti with the divine and regards Viṣṇu and Śiva as only manifestations of Śakti. The tendency on the part of each sect to identify its deity of worship with the divine, and to regard other sectarian deities as only different forms of manifestation of the divine, reflects a healthy trend. It helped the process of reconciliation of the various sects at the transcendental level, and harmony and good will at the level of devotion and worship. However, in certain extreme cases this process is defied. All the sects accept the transcendental dimension or aspect of their deities, and, therefore, admit that at the transcendental level the sectarian differences, which are due to identification of the divine with each sectarian deity, are no longer valid and meaningful. The identification of the divine by the various sects with the deities of their worship, in howsoever glorious and all comprehensive terms the sectarian deities are addressed and worshipped, is valid and meaningful only at the level of religious worship and devotion, but not at the transcendental level. The sectarian differences have no ontological validity and justification. Therefore, the various sects do not find any philosophical problem in identifying the divine with the deities of their worship as they admit that the divine transcends all the deities. The divine can assume or manifest itself in various forms, and all the forms in which the divine is conceived, prayed and worshipped belong to the Divine, though in itself it is more than or transcends all forms. This is largely because of the acceptance of the ontology of Vedānta by all the sects of Hinduism.

All the forms are the forms of the divine though in itself it has no form, and, therefore, it cannot be identified with any one form. The divine is formless yet it manifests itself in various forms. On the other hand, any attempt to determine what is and what is not possible for the divine in terms of human understanding and its limitations, which most of the theologians commit in their zeal to justify their respective theological positions, is to set limits to divine creativity, power and wisdom. What is not intelligible to human understanding may not be meaningful to man's religious life, but such an understanding should have no problem in seeing the divine as transcending all types of determination. What is not meaningful to some may not be so for all, and what is religiously satisfying and fulfilling to some may not be so for others. However, determination of the nature of the divine in terms of its manifestations is valid and meaningful for the practical purpose of religious devotion and worship. However, the transcendence of the divine is a basic requirement for man's religious or spiritual life as at every stage in his spiritual development man sees clearly the possibility of attaining further growth and perfection, the consummation of which is not something that can be clearly defined and expressed. If the divine is pure possibility, and its creativity has no bounds, as otherwise it cannot be divine, trying to define its nature in terms of what is meaningful to human understanding, and significant to religious life of man will be un-divine. The acceptance of the transcendental character of the divine in the sense that the divine is what all it has become, and yet it transcends all that it has become is basic to Hindu religious thought and understanding. This openness in approach to understanding the divine and its nature is characteristic of Hinduism. The sense of divine transcendence is expressed by the concepts of *māyā* and *līlā* which basically convey the sense of mystery involved in our attempts to understand the nature of the divine. What is sought to be conveyed with the help of these concepts is to show the inadequacy of human understanding in relation to the divine, and its creativity. On the other hand, to identify the divine with what one understands it to be and worships though religiously satisfying and fulfilling may not be ontologically true and valid.

As expressed clearly in the *Puruṣa-sūkta*, the divine is all that is there, which is a manifestation of the divine glory, and the divine transcends its own glory.[35] This idea is present throughout the Śruti tradition, and is the essence of the Upaniṣadic thought and wisdom.

The Smr̥ti form of Hinduism, though is not really exclusive in its theological beliefs and doctrines, is, however, sectarian in terms of religious devotion and worship. It is aware of the divine transcendence which is expressed by the concept of *līlā*, and, therefore, it admits that the sectarian deities in their identification with the divine are really beyond the sectarian theological categories and description. Though the divine is identified with the sectarian deities like, Viṣṇu or Śiva, it is nevertheless seen as transcending them, and, therefore, the categories in terms of which the deities are addressed and described are considered inadequate to comprehend and express the nature of the divine. The major Smr̥ti texts accept the authority of Śruti, by which they invariably mean the Upaniṣads, and are, therefore, clearly aware of the problems involved in identifying *Brahman* or the divine with the sectarian deities. One major problem with which the Smr̥ti tradition of Hinduism tried to grapple with is how to reconcile and harmonise the Vedāntic ontology with its theism without denying meaningfulness and validity to either.

The divine is all that is there, and yet transcends all that is there is meaningful if we accept the Vedāntic world-view, but the crucial problem is how to reconcile it with the theistic position of Smr̥ti. In other words, how to maintain the ultimacy and personal character of the sectarian deities, like Viṣṇu or Śiva, and yet identify them with Vedāntic *Brahman*. How to make intelligible the claim that the sectarian deities like Viṣṇu and Śiva, who are personal and have an identity of their own, are at the same time immanent within all, including the non-spiritual and non-personal aspects of nature. It is meaningful to think

35. *R̥gveda*, 10.90.1.

that God is the indwelling spirit of all the human beings who are both spiritual and personal. God can be the self of all the selves, but how to understand Him as constituting the essence of non-spiritual and non-personal nature, or manifesting Himself as nature. The Smṛti tradition tries to understand and solve this problem with the help of Sāṁkhya philosophy without accepting its dualistic ontology. Accordingly, the person of Viṣṇu or Śiva is conceived as having two essential aspects of spirit and matter or *prakṛti* and *puruṣa*. While the physical aspect of nature forms the body of God, the self of God is the source of all that is spiritual. While the world is the body of God, His self is the self of all the selves. God is, therefore, the unity of both matter and spirit or *prakṛti* and *puruṣa* as they constitute His person. Thus, the divine is personal, and yet is the reality of all that is. By conceiving the divine as the unity of both spirit and matter the Smṛti tried to reconcile its avowedly theistic position with the ontology of Vedānta. God is one without a second, and yet is the unity of both matter and spirit. Thus, according to Smṛti tradition there is no problem in conceiving the divine as a personal being or in identifying it with God, and yet in accepting its immanence.

One more important feature that can be discerned in the development of Smṛti form of Hinduism is its endeavour to adjust and adapt Hinduism to the changing historical and social circumstances without compromising the basic vision or world-view of Hinduism based on Śruti. Viewed from this perspective some of the problems which Śruti tradition has given rise to, and are really vital for the development of Hinduism are sought to be resolved by the Smṛti tradition. One of the major concerns of the Smṛti tradition in developing Hinduism is to meet the challenges posed by certain historical factors, like the rise and rapid spread of Buddhism, and the internal contradictions within the Hindu thought and society. The glaring disharmony between the Hindu social order, which gave rise to certain cultural and social prejudices and even aberrations, and its world-view, which is truly universal and all-inclusive, and, therefore, cannot be the justification of the social order attracted the attention of many Smṛti thinkers and saints. They in their own characteristic ways tried to understand and resolve the tension and conflict between the Hindu world-view and its social order and cultural values. These come to view prominently during the periods of internal crisis and external challenge.

Most of the social and cultural prejudices and certain unspiritual beliefs and practices that crept into Hinduism have no Vedic authority and justification. They are, therefore, to be corrected, and even rejected if the situation so demands to restore and maintain the meaningfulness of the basic vision of Hinduism. And unless Hinduism is alive to the changing circumstances and challenges it cannot remain meaningful and valid. While the validity of Śruti transcends space and time, the validity and meaningfulness of Smṛti, at least in theory if not in practice, are bound by time and space. Therefore, there is nothing un-Hindu in correcting or even in rejecting certain religious beliefs and practices when they are not compatible with and go against the world-view of Hinduism. This is a continuous process in which the major concern of Smṛti is to maintain the meaningfulness and validity of the Hindu world-view, and to adjust and adapt it to changing circumstances and challenges, both internal and external. The Brāhmaṇic ritualism from which majority of Hindu society is excluded, and the subtle and abstruse truth of Vedānta which all cannot understand and appreciate and, therefore, follow it when compared to Buddhism and Jainism, which are open to all as they do not exclude anyone from the bliss of spiritual life on the basis of birth and other social factors, must have been the guiding force of the Smṛti tradition in correcting or even in rejecting some of the ideas and practices introduced into Hinduism in course of time. Most of the prejudices and aberrations introduced into Hinduism in the course of its development have no Vedic sanction and authority.

The Smṛti form of religious life is more universal in the sense that it is open to all, irrespective of their social and cultural status, and is easy to follow as it does not involve elaborate and intricate ritual practices and subtle intellectual understanding.

With its emphasis on love and devotion to God the Smṛti form of religious life is open to all the sections of Hindu society, including those who are outside the fold of Hinduism or Hindu social system, like the various tribes. Love of God is an end in itself, and is regarded as the supreme end of human life (*parama puruṣārtha*). All those who are excluded from the study of the Veda, and the brāhmaṇa form of religious life can follow the *bhakti* form of religious life in which the initiative really comes from God. The traditional means of attaining *mokṣa* like *jñāna* and *karma* are not really open to all as they involve in one form or other one's direct acquaintance with the Śruti texts which is denied to all. As a result most of the Hindus are denied participation in the Vedic form of religious life. This serious weakness of Śruti form of Hinduism as developed in the *Brāhmaṇa*s, which has no real theoretical or scriptural justification, is sought to be overcome by several Smṛti thinkers and saints by means of developing fully the theistic form of Hinduism, which must have been as ancient as the Śruti form of Hinduism, without openly opposing or challenging the Śruti form of religious life and worship.

The validity of Śruti, as divinely inspired truth or wisdom, is not conditioned by any cultural or social factors or by space and time, whereas the Smṛti is a continuously developing tradition, and in its development it is influenced by the changing historical and social circumstances as well as the limitations of human understanding. Smṛti is a developing tradition. It is not a closed tradition as it represents the wisdom of several creative and enlightened Hindu thinkers and saints. Theoretically speaking, the world-view of Hinduism allows scope for developing newer forms of religious life and worship as it does not insist upon any one form of religious life to reach the goal of religious life or to attain spiritual perfection. As long as the world-view remains meaningful it can find newer form of expression. The forms of its expression can change. At the empirical level or at the level of manifestation truth is dynamic as the creative process of divine manifestation does not come to an end at any given point of time. And human creativity, which is an extension of divine creativity at the level of manifestation, is equally a continuous and endless process. Therefore, in trying to see or realise the divine in all the forms of its manifestation, especially in all the forms of human creativity, Hinduism does not limit its vision of the divine to any one form. This is expressed clearly and wonderfully in the *Vibhūti-yoga* of the *Bhagavad Gītā* which is a major text of the Smṛti form of Hinduism.[36] Smṛti also represents various significant attempts to adapt the vision or world-view of Śruti to specific historical and social situations which do not always remain the same. In other words, Smṛti tries to find out the meaning of the Hindu world-view in relation to concrete situation of human life. How to make the basic vision or world-view of Hinduism, which is timeless, meaningful and relevant to newer circumstances and challenges is one of the major concerns of Smṛti tradition. And, therefore, the Smṛti form of Hinduism can have no fixed form. Its form changes as it tries to adjust and adapt itself to newer circumstances and challenges. As maintained by the Hindu tradition while the validity of Śruti is timeless, the validity to Smṛti is bound by space (*deśa*), time (*kāla*) and other circumstances.[37] Thus, there is a continuous growth and development in the Smṛti form of Hinduism, which in modern times is well pronounced. The contributions of all the modern creative thinkers and saints of Hinduism add to the development and enrichment of the Smṛti tradition. What is basically common to all the modern Hindu thinkers and saints is their acceptance of Śruti and its validity though many of them have their reservations about the validity of Smṛti, and some even have rejected it either directly or indirectly.[38] And many of them have tried to interpret Śruti in their own characteristic ways in which they are influenced positively by the modern

---

36. *Vibhūti Yoga* (chapter 10) of *Bhagavad Gītā*.
37. The validity of Smṛti is bound by time (*kāla*) space (*deśa*) and other circumstances (*paristhiti*).
38. Generally speaking, the modern movements within the Hindu tradition do not recognise the authority and relevance of the Smṛti tradition in understanding the nature and meaning of Hinduism, and the Ārya Samāj is open in its rejection of it.

thought, and other religious traditions. Therefore, to plead for a well-defined form of Hinduism, and for a fixed or single method of Śruti interpretation is something basically un-Hindu. All the methods of Śruti interpretation, all the forms of religious life and worship or all the forms of *sādhanā* developed over the centuries are Hindu, and have their justification in the changing social and historical circumstances, and changing forms of human understanding. And, therefore, when any one or more of them lose their validity and meaningfulness Hinduism does not suffer any loss. It can find its expression in newer forms. On the other hand, when Hinduism is identified with any one form of it as developed in the Smṛti tradition or when its nature and meaning are defined or determined in terms of any one form of religious life, which is against the world-view of Hinduism, it suffered stagnation and decay.

As traditionally maintained the Smṛti as a tradition can grow and develop meaningfully as long as it does not give up its faith in the validity of the wisdom or world-view of Śruti. On the other hand, if the basic vision or world-view of Śruti is rejected by a person or a movement they cannot remain Hindu though their contributions may otherwise be important and rich. The Smṛti tradition with its preference for or emphasis on a personal conception of the divine, and *bhakti* as the meaning and end of religious life, has not, however, rejected the world-view of Śruti. According to the *bhakti* form of religious life also to love God is to love all, especially those who are in need of help and service. One who loves God and is devoted to Him cannot be indifferent to the suffering and misery of others as he sees God within them.[39] To love God is to love all, and serve them without any motive or reason is the supreme meaning of *Bhāgavata-dharma* or the *Bhāgavata* form of Hinduism as developed in the Smṛti tradition. In a deeper sense, the Śruti ideal of *brahma-jñānī* and the Smṛti ideal of *Bhāgavata* really mean the realisation of the divine within all (*vāsudeva sarvamiti*). It is to love all or to

---

39. *Bhāgavata Purāṇa*, 11.2.6; 6.10.91; 8.7.43; 11.1.12.

see oneself in all and all in oneself. Such vision of the divine, whether conceived in personal or impersonal terms, is common to all the forms of Hinduism, whether based on or inspired by the Śruti or Smṛti. It constitutes the essence of Hinduism, and is the basic source of its unity despite differences which are otherwise real and significant.

7

Destiny

IN this chapter we try to understand the nature and meaning of human destiny according to Hinduism. We exclude from our discussion all the theories or doctrines of *mokṣa*, the ultimate meaning of human existence as conceived and developed by various philosophical schools of India, and devote our attention to the basic texts of Hinduism to understand the ultimate goal of man's religious life. We find several views about the meaning and end of human existence as conceived by Hindu theologians and thinkers, and though they are avowedly based on or inspired by the sacred texts of Hinduism, yet being sectarian in their outlook and approach they paid little or no attention to those texts and passages of the Hindu scriptures that are not considered significant from their sectarian points of view or theological perspectives. I do not deny such a bias in the present discussion, but as has been attempted throughout this work I try to view Hinduism in its growth and development, and as far as possible without overlooking anything that is basic and important to Hinduism. Every attempt to construct a theory or doctrine will be insensitive or indifferent to certain facts which cannot meaningfully be explained in terms of a theory or doctrine.

What man thinks about the state of his possible perfection and fulfilment is not unrelated to what he thinks is the real nature and meaning of the world around him, and the way he relates himself to the reality of the world. If man thinks that his being is not essentially related to the world, but is somehow caught within it, his attitude to the world and his understanding of his own possible perfection will be different from the view in which man thinks of himself as essentially related to the world, and his reality is integral to the reality of the world.

Much of what goes under the name of Hinduism looks strange from the Vedic point of view. And at the same time it is difficult to discern what is Vedic and what is non-Vedic in Hinduism. In discussing the Vedic view or vision of human destiny or the meaning and end of human existence, according to the Veda, I limit myself to the *Saṁhitā* part of the Veda as it reflects fully the basic vision or wisdom of the Veda. The primary object of the *Brāhmaṇa* texts is to develop a ritual form of religious life and worship supposedly on the basis of Vedic revelation, and deal with the elaborate procedure of performing various rituals, their justification and their possible results. They do not have anything significant to say about the meaning and end of human existence.

We find within the Hindu religious tradition several forms of religious life with their distinctive conceptions of human destiny. We choose from among them three major forms of religious life, which are representative of Hinduism, and try to present and discuss the nature and meaning of human destiny according to them. They represent both Śruti and Smṛti forms of Hinduism. They are *ṛṣi(tva)* or *ārṣa*, *dharma* and *bhakti* forms of religious life which represent three significant phases in the development of Hinduism. *Ṛṣi* as an ideal state of human existence and fulfilment represents the Vedic form of Hinduism, and with some modification the ideal of the Upaniṣads as well. While the *dharma* form of religion represents that phase of Hinduism which is not completely Vedic nor completely Smṛti based (*smārtta*), the *bhakti* form of religion clearly represents the Smṛti form of Hinduism.

Veda does not speak of *mokṣa*, and the Upaniṣads are not explicit in their concern for it. We do not come across the concept of *mokṣa* in the Upaniṣads as it has been developed later by different schools of Vedānta, may be under the influence of

Buddhism.[1] It is Buddhism which for the first time in India clearly conceives and sets before man the idea of his destiny in the form of *nirvāṇa*. Buddhism identifies suffering as the problem of human existence, and, therefore, provides a solution to it in the form of *nirvāṇa*. And Buddhism has shown more concern for demolishing the Vedic ontology than in developing an alternative one. The Veda has an ontology of its own which finds its clear articulation and expression in the Upaniṣads. The Smṛti tradition of Hinduism has developed an ontology or rather a theology of its own, not so much in opposition to the Vedic ontology, but to a large extent independently of the Vedic tradition. It is appropriate to talk of Smṛti theology rather than of its ontology. The theistic tradition, which the Smṛti tradition represents, must have been in existence long before it is articulated and expressed in the texts of Smṛti. Though there is tension between the theism of Smṛti and the ontology of the Śruti attempts are constantly made to reconcile and harmonise both at a philosophical level. However, Smṛti considers itself as an interpretation or rather as an extension of Vedic truth or wisdom with a view to making it intelligible and meaningful to the popular Hindu mind, and to make it available to those who are denied direct access to the Śruti tradition. The post-Vedic Hinduism is a result of the process of reconciliation and integration between the Śruti and Smṛti traditions, and the Hinduism that emerged as a result is, therefore, neither completely Vedic nor completely based on and developed by Smṛti. There has been continuous interaction between Śruti and Smṛti in which each has tried to influence the other, though occasionally attempts are made to sharply distinguish them and their influence in the development of Hinduism, and even to purify Hinduism of Smṛti influence. Therefore, when we discuss the Vedic view or vision of human destiny it is with a view to understanding the meaning and end of human existence,

---

1. In the Indian religious tradition it is Buddhism that has introduced the concept of liberation or salvation in the form of *nirvāṇa*. Earlier to Buddhism we do not find the concept of liberation (*mokṣa*) in Hinduism as later developed in the different schools of Vedānta.

according to the Veda, that has not lost its meaningfulness and validity in the life of Hinduism. Our main concern in understanding the nature and meaning of human destiny, according to the Veda, is to the extent it has influenced Hinduism in its successive phases of development. We do not discuss separately the Upaniṣadic view as there is no basic difference between the vision of the Vedic *Saṁhitās* and that of the Upaniṣads. The Upaniṣads are more or less a philosophical representation or re-statement of the truth revealed in the Vedic *Saṁhitās*. In comparison to the Vedic *Saṁhitās*, the hymns of which are a poetic expression of inwardly experienced devotion, the Upaniṣads are more philosophical in their outlook and approach.

We have to reconstruct the concept of human destiny, according to the Veda, as we do not find any explicit statement about it in the Veda. The Vedic hymns, which are primarily prayers and praises addressed to various deities, either individually or collectively, are an expression in poetic form of language of the divinely inspired devotion of the Vedic seers. Besides expressing grateful thanks to the deities for their various gifts, especially the gift of divine inspiration, the hymns express the inwardly experienced devotion which the seers of the Veda consider as a divine gift or is due to divine inspiration. What is cherished most by the Vedic seers is the divine gift of inspiration. They often pray for the gift of inspiration, the source of Vedic wisdom. What is popularly known as *Gāyatrī*-hymn, addressed to Savitā, the deity of inspiration, is a prayer for divine inspiration. "May Savitā inspire our intelligence (divinely), or may our intelligence be inspired (divinely)."[2]

The Vedic seers see in the experience of devotion, which is divinely inspired or is a divine gift, the supreme fulfilment (*dhanya*) of their existence. We do not find in the Veda the concept of *mokṣa* in any form. However, the Vedic seers often speak of the sinful state of human existence which they want to overcome by experiencing the divine or the divinely inspired

2. *Ṛgveda*, 3.62.10.

devotion. Sin envelopes man's vision, like mist, and prevents him from seeing the divine.

Divinely inspired intellect of man enables him to see or realise the divine as the reality as well as the unity or oneness of the empirical world of differences. When one is divinely inspired one's vision of nature as well as of himself is totally transformed, and he then sees nature as the abode of the deities, or as a form of manifestation of the divine. The representation of nature as the abode of various deities or the divine is not intelligible and meaningful in terms of man's ordinary or uninspired wisdom and understanding. It is only when the intellect of man is divinely inspired nature is seen as an abode of the divine or as a manifestation of the divine or as expressing the glory and splendour of the divine. The divine nature of the world, which is hidden, as it were, to ordinary knowledge and understanding, reveals itself to divinely inspired intellect. Then nature becomes an object of reverence and worship, and is seen as an expression of divine wisdom (*kāvya*). According to the Vedic seers, the supreme fulfilment of human existence consists in being divinely inspired or in experiencing devotion. It is a state of light and immortality. One who has inwardly experienced devotion, which is due to divine inspiration, is known as a *ṛṣi* or a *kavi*, the divine state of human existence.

Besides the sense or meaning of divine, the divine unity or oneness of all that is there is revealed to man in the state of divinely inspired devotion. The divine reveals itself to an inspired person as the reality as well as the inner unity of all that is there. In the poetic language of the Veda, which is mostly metaphorical, the vision that all that is there is divine is represented by describing nature as the abode of the deities. As the essence or reality of a phenomenon of nature a deity constitutes its unity, and the divine as the source of all the deities constitutes the unity of all that is there. For instance, to see Agni as a phenomenon of nature, and to describe it in its phenomenal aspect does not require any inspiration or the wisdom of a *ṛṣi*. But to worship Agni as a deity is to see it as a form of manifestation of the divine, and that is possible only when the intellect of man is divinely inspired. Nature reveals its divine nature as well as its inner divine unity or oneness to a divinely inspired person who is known as a *ṛṣi* or a *kavi* in the Veda. All the phenomena of nature or all the deities that dwell within them are capable of inspiring devotion in man, the source of revelation of the divine. Nature is divine or is seen as the abode of the deities because of its capacity to inspire devotion in man. Man comes to know the nature and meaning of divine in the state of devotion or as devotion itself.

A deity which constitutes the essence of a phenomenon of nature or dwells within it will have the attributes of the phenomenon in terms of which it is distinguished from other deities. And at the same time as different forms of manifestation of the divine, the deities reveal the nature of the divine, and share commonly the divine power to inspire devotion in man, which is divine.

While a *ṛṣi* is one who sees the divine in its unitive aspect or as constituting the inner unity of all that is there, a *kavi* is one who experiences the divine in its creative aspect because of which the divine manifests itself in varied forms. In other words, while to see the divine as the oneness of all that is there requires the wisdom of a *ṛṣi*, to see the divine in its creative aspect requires the wisdom of a *kavi*. Though the wisdom of both *ṛṣi* and *kavi* is due to divine inspiration it is distinguished in terms of its significance. While a *kavi* is one who sees in nature the expression of divine creativity or a manifestation of the splendour and glory of the divine, a *ṛṣi* is one who sees the divine as constituting the inner unity or oneness of all that is manifested. As expressed in one of the *Brāhmaṇa* texts, the divine has lost itself, as it were, in becoming the world of multiplicity, and the object of the Veda is to reveal the oneness of the divine in and through all that it has become.[3] Thus, the Vedic revelation is

3. *Śatapatha Brāhmaṇa* 10.4.2.2 and 21; see also *Aitareya Āraṇyaka* 3.2.6.

two-fold in its meaning. The Veda reveals both the creative and unitive aspects of the divine. It reveals the creative aspect of the divine because of which it manifests itself in the form of the world, as well as the divine unity or oneness of all that is manifested. And nature as a manifestation of the divine or as an abode of the divine is divine and sacred, and is, therefore, an object of reverence and worship. As the Veda expresses through its hymns the knowledge or wisdom that is divinely inspired, it is also divine and sacred. To a divinely transformed vision of man everything is divine, and is, therefore, sacred. Truth is self-revealing provided man is pure enough to apprehend it, and the purity of man primarily consists in his moral perfection or in his being righteous (*r̥tavān*). The seers of the Veda are known for the subtlety (*aṇu*) of their intellect, and for their moral purity or righteousness. Because of moral purity the intellect of man becomes divine. The Vedic seers are known for their moral purity. They are knowers of *r̥ta* (*r̥tacit*), or are full of *r̥ta* (*r̥tavān* or *r̥tavantaḥ*), or have realised *r̥ta* (*r̥tabodhi*). Moral perfection or being full of *r̥ta* is essential to know the divine as the divine reveals itself as *r̥ta* within the realm of manifestation. One cannot, therefore, realise the divine without being righteous. *R̥ta* is not different from the divine. It reveals the divine within the realm of manifestation or the divine reveals itself as *r̥ta* within the realm of manifestation. *R̥ta* is identified with the divine at the level of manifestation. Therefore, to see nature as a manifestation of the divine is to realise that nature as well as the laws that govern it are a manifestation of the divine. And in the form of its manifestation within man *r̥ta* is known as *dharma*. *Dharma* is based on the realisation that one's own reality as well as the reality outside him are two different forms of manifestation of the divine, and are, therefore, guided and governed by the same principle or *r̥ta*.

Yajña, which is the primary form of Vedic worship, is closely related to *r̥ta*. *Yajña* is the process whereby man realises the divine meaning of his life. It is by means of *yajña* the divine has become all that is, and, therefore, all that is, including man, depends for its existence on the divine. All the deities come into existence because of divine *yajña*. The process of divine *yajña*, the reason for the existence of all that is there, including man, culminates in the self-realisation of the divine in and through all that it has become. It is like a seed realising itself in and through its growth as a tree. It is by self-sacrifice the divine has become all that is; and when man realises that all that is, including himself, depends on the divine *yajña* for existence, he comes to realise that the meaning and fulfilment of his life consist in participating in the process of divine *yajña* or in extending it to his own life.

Yajña, in the Vedic context, means a process in which man has to participate or to extend it to his own life in contrast to various kinds of *yajña* that are ritually performed. Even in a *yajña* that is ritually performed the various elements employed in its performance are symbolic representations of the various cosmic elements. When man realises the meaning of divine *yajña* he realises that his own life is a *yajña* meant to serve and fulfil the divine purpose in becoming the world, that is, to realise itself in and through all that it has become. Therefore, if man acts in imitation of the divine *yajña* all his actions will acquire the significance of *yajña* or divine worship. On the other hand, when man sees in his actions the means of satisfying his desires and purposes he lives a life of sin. Divine *yajña*, which is being extended by the deities at the cosmic level, is to be extended by man at the human level. What is, thus, basic to *yajña* is the realisation that the world, including man, depends for its existence on the divine *yajña*, and is, therefore, meant to serve and fulfil the divine purpose of self-realisation. As expressed in the Veda every act, including the ordinary and mundane acts like harvesting, if done with the realisation that the divine is all that is will have the significance of *yajña*, or will be an act of divine worship.[4] *Yajña* which is to be extended by means of *yajña* is seen by the Vedic seers as an act of repaying the debt to the divine or the deities for the gift of divine inspiration, and in so

4. *Ṛgveda*, 1.30.7.

doing one's life is supremely fulfilled.

To realise that the divine is all is to act in the spirit of *yajña*. Then every act of man will acquire the significance of divine worship. In the *Mahābhārata* service to others, the duty of a śūdra, is regarded as his form of *yajña* (*sevā-yajña*) or the form of his worship of the divine, just as study and teaching constitute the *yajña* of a brāhmaṇa (*brahma-yajña*). Without such realisation anything that is offered into fire will be as meaningless and futile as throwing the offerings into ash.[5] *Yajña* sanctifies the life of man, and fulfills his existence. As expressed in the *Bhagavad Gītā*, the offering, the oblation, the fire into which it is offered and what is thereby attained are all *Brahman*.[6] Thus, the whole life of a person acquires the significance of *yajña* when it is lived with the realisation that all that is there is divine. It is often expressed in the *Mahābhārata* that one who enjoys life after its consecration to the divine or after offering it to the divine, as if it is the left-over of *yajña* (*yajña-avaśiṣṭa*), knows the meaning of *dharma*.[7] Such a person is freed from sin. On the other hand, one who eats alone, that is without the sense of *yajña*, eats sin.[8]

As pointed out earlier *yajña* is the Vedic form of religious life, and is based on the realisation that the divine has become all that is there through self-sacrifice. Therefore, one who enjoys life in the spirit of *yajña* lives the life of sacrifice (*tyāga*). *Yajña* is meaningless without self-sacrifice. Even the offering of one's body into the funeral fire is regarded as the final *yajña* (*antya-iṣṭi*).

The Upaniṣadic vision of human destiny is not basically different from that of the Veda. It is more a philosophical representation or re-statement of the Vedic vision. Both the Vedic

---

5. *Chāndogya Upaniṣad*, 4.24.1.
6. *Bhagavad Gītā*, 4.26.
7. *Mahābhārata*, Śānti-parva,11.24; *Bhagavad Gītā*, 4.31; 3.13. The same idea is expressed in the *Ṛgveda* as *Havismata-manasa* 7.67.1.
8. *Ṛgveda*, 10.117.6; see also *Śatapatha Brāhmaṇa*, 2.4.2.6.

Saṁhitās and the Upaniṣads insist that seeing the divine involves transcending the ordinary or empirical human understanding and vision because of which man sees differences. The ordinary or uninspired vision or understanding of man fails to see the divine unity underlying all the empirical differences. When man realises more and more the divine unity or oneness of all that is he grows spiritually which culminates in the realisation that all that is there is divine. The vision of the divine unity or oneness of all that is there has been expressed in several ways and forms in the Upaniṣads. One who sees oneself in all, and all in oneself sees truly or knows the truth; all that is there is permeated by the divine; the creation is not different from the divine (I am the creation); there are no differences anywhere, and one who sees differences goes from death to death.[9] However, we do not find in the Upaniṣads any significant attempt to define or determine the nature and meaning of human destiny. The idea of *mokṣa*, which is not explicitly expressed in the Upaniṣads, is basically negative in its import as it means getting rid of or being freed from something. It does not state in positive terms the meaning of divine life. On the other hand, seeing the divine is an end in itself, and the one who sees the divine will have no desires left unfulfilled.

Smṛti form of Hinduism is more open and universal when compared to Śruti form of Hinduism. And the Hinduism that is commonly or popularly known and practised is largely based on and shaped by the Smṛti tradition. Smṛti is not a closed tradition, and has no fixed form and canon. It is a tradition which has been continuously developing. However, it represents mainly the sectarian forms of Hindu religious life and worship. Therefore, no one Smṛti text is authority for all the Hindus, and at all times. Nevertheless, what is common to all the sects of Hinduism, which are based on or inspired by the Smṛti tradition, is the theistic form of religious life which in its pure form is more or less alien to Śruti form of Hinduism. The different sects

9. *Bṛhadāraṇyaka Upaniṣad*, 4.4.19; *Kaṭha Upaniṣad*, 2.1.10-11.

of Hinduism basically differ from one another in terms of their identification of the divine with their sectarian deities. But all of them believe in the personal nature of the divine. They identify the divine with God, and worship Him in several forms. Theistic form of religious life, and love of God as the meaning and end of religion are the major contribution of Smṛti tradition to Hinduism. And if we think that religious life is more meaningful and fulfilling if it is centred round God, a personal being, then Hinduism as a religion is largely based on and developed by the Smṛti tradition. The traditions of Śruti and Smṛti must have developed independently of each other till the need was felt to reconcile them and integrate them. The process of reconciliation between Śruti and Smṛti is continuous as newer sects and sub-sects come into existence, and seek reconciliation with the Śruti tradition. One of the major concerns of the Smṛti tradition is to reconcile, and integrate itself with the Śruti tradition, and has been attempted by almost all the Hindu saints and thinkers in their own characteristic ways. Towards achieving this end they find in the Sāṁkhya philosophy, particularly in its metaphysics, a significant means. How to reconcile and integrate the Smṛti concept of the divine, which is theistic, with the Śruti vision of the divine, which is not viewed in clear personal or theistic terms, has exercised the minds of several saints and thinkers of Smṛti tradition. How can God, a personal being, be the essence of all that is, including the physical or material aspect of creation, or how can God be immanent in all is a crucial problem that engaged the attention of the thinkers of Smṛti tradition, while the problem faced by the interpreters of Śruti tradition is how to understand and explain the existence of material or physical world on the basis of the divine which is purely spiritual. Most of the Smṛti thinkers have tried to understand and resolve the problem with the help of Sāṁkhya metaphysics without, however, accepting its dualism. While Sāṁkhya conceives *puruṣa* and *prakṛti* as two ontologically independent realities, the Smṛti tries to integrate them in the person of God. The Sāṁkhya philosophy, and its founder Kapila are highly esteemed in the Smṛti tradition. Even Kapila is regarded as an incarnation of Viṣṇu.[10] While Sāṁkhya finds it logically difficult to relate and integrate the realities of *puruṣa* and *prakṛti*, the Smṛti tradition tries to integrate *puruṣa* and *prakṛti* in the person of God with a view to reconciling its theism with the Vedāntic ontology. God is one, and yet in terms of His two-fold nature He is immanently present within the entire creation. While *prakṛti*, which is conceived as forming the body of God, is the source of the material world, *puruṣa* conceived as forming the spirit or self of God is the source of all that is spiritual And both *puruṣa* and *prakṛti* forming the two-fold nature of God are integral to His person. They constitute His being who is one without a second. In terms of His two-fold nature God is immanently present with all, including physical nature. We are not interested in discussing the adequacy of such an attempt as the main object of Smṛti in integrating *puruṣa* and *prakṛti* in the person of God is not metaphysical. It is mainly to reconcile and integrate the theism of the Smṛti tradition with the ontology of Śruti, so as to achieve harmony between the two streams or traditions of Hinduism represented by Śruti and Smṛti. Though occasionally the philosophical problems involved in such an attempt troubled the Smṛti thinkers they did not try to discuss them in any significant manner. Therefore, we are not interested in discussing the philosophical justification and validity of the Smṛti conception of God which is not completely theistic nor completely Vedāntic.

Another important contribution of Smṛti tradition to the development of Hinduism is its attempt to integrate within the fold of Hinduism all the sections of Indian society, irrespective of their social and cultural status, by circumventing the existing restrictions and prohibitions. In contrast to the Śruti form of Hinduism, which is limited to the twice-born of the Hindu society, Smṛti form of Hinduism is open to all the sections of society or to people belonging to all the castes of Indian society, and even to those who are not included within the Indian or Hindu social

10. *Bhāgavata Purāṇa*, 1.3.10; *Śiva Purāṇa*, *Rudra Saṁhitā*, 2.52; *Bhagavad Gītā*, (chapter 10) *Vibhūti-yoga*.

system, like the various tribes or those living on the periphery of Hindu society like the Niṣādhas and the Kirātas. It is also open to those who live outside India, or those who live in other continents, as it has disassociated religion from social system or order. All are competent to read the Smṛti literature, and follow or practice the Smṛti form of religious life without any discrimination. It has also made significant attempts to make available the wisdom of Śruti, though indirectly, to all the sections of Hindu society. And Smṛti considers that it represents the basic teaching of Śruti which in a sense is true as it wholly accepts the world-view of Śruti, and tries to adapt it to suit its theological and popular requirements.

Another major concern of the Smṛti tradition is to meet successfully the various challenges, either from within the Hindu tradition or from without, especially the challenge of Buddhism. Hinduism and its various rituals and practices as developed in the *Brāhmaṇa*s or the brāhmaṇa form of Hinduism is not open to all. And Smṛti made a very significant attempt to free or disassociate Hindu religion and spirituality from the social organisation, or to distinguish and separate social form of life from the religious way of life. Because of such an open attitude to religious or spiritual problems, the Smṛti form of Hinduism could not only integrate within its fold all the sections of Indian society, but could go out of India and spread itself.

We discuss one more major reason for the appeal and popularity of the Smṛti form of Hinduism. It is expressed in the *Bhāgavata Purāṇa* that a rational or analytical approach to the problems of human existence, particularly related to man's religious or spiritual life, is not really meaningful and satisfying. Though a man of rational understanding and analytical ability is superior to ordinary people, he can still be unhappy as far as the emotional aspect of his life is concerned. Emotional life of man expresses itself in love, devotion, faith, compassion, etc., and unless they find their fulfilment man cannot realise the meaning of his life. Though love is more an emotional state yet in its influence it is more pervasive and total. It is deep and profound in its influence, and fulfills human existence supremely as in the state of love man overcomes or transcends his ego-centred existence which is the reason for human suffering and misery. Veda-vyāsa, the author of both *Mahābhārata* and *Bhāgavata Purāṇa*, states that he composed *Bhāgavata Purāṇa*, a religious classic, after *Mahābhārata*, known for its rational and analytical approach to various problems, as the *Mahābhārata* could not satisfy or fulfil his religious or spiritual quest.[11] Though *jñāna* is also a means of overcoming or transcending the sense of ego, and the differences it creates still it cannot satisfy and fulfil the emotional life or heart of man. Furthermore, the life of *jñāna* is not within the easy reach of all. The path of *jñāna* is difficult to follow as it requires the capacity to understand subtle things, and is not open to all the sections of Hindu society as it involves the study of Śruti texts. *Bhakti* form of religious life is open to all, and is easy to follow as it does not insist on the study and understanding of religious texts and subtle and abstract theological doctrines. And, according to Smṛti tradition, *bhakti* form of religious life is in no way inferior to *jñāna* form of life. *Bhakti* form of religious life is even regarded as superior to *jñāna* form of religious life. It is an independent path of God realisation, or as love of God it is an end in itself. It is the supreme end of human existence or the *parama puruṣārtha*. While, according to Vedānta, direct realisation of the divine is possible by means of *jñāna*, God can be realised directly by *bhakti*, according to *Bhāgavata* tradition. While *jñāna* (scriptural knowledge) is a means to realise the divine which is pure knowledge, *bhakti* as passionate love and devotion to God is an end in itself. As pure love of God *bhakti* is an end in itself or is self-fulfilling. God is pure love, and one who has experienced it will have no concern for anything else, including his own salvation, as there is nothing higher than the love of God. In the state of *bhakti* one transcends one's ego-centred existence, and its concerns. And as a *jñānī* realises the divine oneness of all that is, as he sees the divine in all, a *bhakta*

11. *Bhāgavata Purāṇa*, 1.5.3.5 and 12.

or a *bhāgavata* sees God in all and all in God as God is all *vāsudeva sarvamiti.*[12]

Bhakti form of Hinduism is known as *Bhāgavata-dharma* or religion of love and devotion to God. *Parā-bhakti* (higher *bhakti*) or pure or disinterested love of God, which is an end in itself or is the supreme end of human existence, is distinguished from ordinary *bhakti* which is a means of God realisation. *Parā-bhakti* or love of God is an independent end of human existence as it does not subserve any other human purpose or end. It is, therefore, not really meaningful to think whether the divine is personal or impersonal or whether the divine is identical with God or not. In other words, the problem whether the *Bhāgavata dharma* or the theistic form of Hinduism is akin to the classical form of Hinduism, mostly identified with Vedānta, or is significantly different from Vedānta will be of no significance to a religious person as in the actual religious life of a person or in terms of religious experience both have the same meaning and value though conceptually they are distinct and appear to be irreconcilable. The *Bhagavad Gītā* identifies *parā-bhakti* with *parā-jñāna*. Nevertheless, the distinction is valid at the level of ordinary *bhakti* and ordinary or scriptural knowledge which are not ends in themselves. They are only means to God realisation, and, therefore, from the point of view of an aspirant they are distinct.

The monism of the Śruti tradition in which the divine is not identified with God or clearly conceived as a personal being is distinct from the theism of the Smṛti tradition. However, in the *Śvetāśvatara Upaniṣad*, which is regarded as the gateway to theism, the divine is identified with God.[13] And, therefore, theism is not completely alien to the thinking of the Upaniṣads or the Vedic form of Hinduism. However, it is not the dominant position of the Upaniṣads. *Śvetāśvara Upaniṣad* is regarded as the

12. *Viṣṇu Purāṇa*, 2.15.35; 6.5.80-82.

13. Among the major Upaniṣads, *Śvetāśvatara Upaniṣad* is openly and clearly theistic. It speaks of God (Deva) and regards Him as the sole arbiter of human destiny, and He is even identified as Śiva or Rudra.

gateway to theism as it marks the transition from an impersonal conception of the divine to a personal conception of the divine.[14] The occasional Śruti use of the personal term *puruṣa* in relation to the divine shows that the divine or *Brahman* of the Upaniṣads is not totally incompatible or inconsistent with the idea of God. But because of the philosophical attitude and approach of the Upaniṣads in which a free inquiry and understanding into the nature of the divine is positively encouraged, the divine is viewed as transcending all the categories of human understanding, including religious categories. What transcends all the categories of human understanding, including the knowledge or wisdom of Śruti, is pure spirit or consciousness. The reality of consciousness cannot be negated as all negation presupposes consciousness, or it is the pre-condition for all negation. As what is presupposed in all negation the reality of consciousness cannot be negated at any level. And by being the ground or presupposition of all the notions and categories consciousness is not really affected and conditioned by them. All the ideas and categories are given as objects to consciousness, and, therefore, they cannot be attributed to it, or its nature cannot be determined in terms of them. More and more the human mind, whether ignorant or illumined, tries to grasp the nature of the divine and define it in terms of its categories, it realises that its categories, without which it cannot function or operate, can only point to it instead of making it their object. The divine is more than or transcends what the concepts and categories can reveal about it. As the ground of all notions and definitions *Brahman* transcends them all. The various conceptions of the divine reveal the nature of the divine, but the divine is infinitely more than what the concepts and categories can reveal. This is the philosophical significance of the distinction made in the Vedānta tradition between *nirguṇa-brahman* (*Brahman* without form) and *saguṇa-brahman* (*Brahman* with form).[15] Such realisation,

14. *Essays on the Religion of the Hindus*, H.H. Wilson, Vol.II, lecture 2.

15. The significance of the distinction between *Saguṇa Brahman* and *Nirguṇa Brahman* is that the divine or *Brahman* cannot be identified

→

which the human understanding is capable of, will help it in recognising the futility of all its attempts to determine the nature of the divine in terms of certain categories howsoever meaningful they may be otherwise. Personal and impersonal are two such categories. Though human mind cannot grasp and appreciate the nature of the divine without conceiving it in terms of certain categories or without imposing its categories on it which are meaningful to it, yet when it realises the limitations involved in the process, it can admit on its own the transcendental nature of the divine. Such realisation will not, however, hamper one's religious life of devotion and worship in which the divine is identified with a view or conception of it or is worshipped in a particular form. This kind of impersonal approach tries to overcome the limitation of human understanding in knowing the divine, and its nature. Otherwise, the Upaniṣads are as passionate and devout in their attitude to the divine as the devotional literature of Smṛti, and are as sanctifying as any religious text.

The theistic tradition of Hinduism finds its literary representation in the epics and Purāṇas, which are not, however, the source of origin of the theistic form of Hinduism. They are only its literary sources. The Purāṇas, the major source of the Smṛti tradition, are also compilations (*Saṁhitā*), compiled with the purpose of systematically presenting and justifying an already existing religious tradition. The Upaniṣads speak of *itihāsa* and Purāṇa.[16] Historically, a need must have been felt to project the theistic tradition more clearly and systematically so as to counter the challenge of Buddhism. While in compiling the Smṛti tradition, and in giving it a definite literary form, the Purāṇas and the epics tried to provide a kind of philosophical foundation, mostly in terms of Vedānta and Sāṁkhya, to the theism of Smṛti. And as the Śruti tradition is not opposed to theism, the theism

---

→ with any form of concept of *Brahman* as it transcends all the forms and concepts. The Smṛti tradition of Hinduism also accepts the transcendental nature of God identified as either Viṣṇu or Śiva.

16. *Chāndogya Upaniṣad*, 3.4.1-2.

of Smṛti is not opposed to Vedānta. Each has tried to influence the other, and in the process both are benefited and enriched.

Śruti and Smṛti represent two basic approaches of man to know the nature of the divine. And instead of developing themselves in isolation, and in antagonism to each other they more often interacted with each other, and tried to reconcile and integrate one with the other. Towards achieving this end the Śruti texts are interpreted theistically, and the Smṛti tradition tries to reconcile and harmonise its theism with the ontology of Vedānta. And because of such process Smṛti could to a large extent overcome its sectarian attitude to the divine. And while Vedānta has acquired a religious significance and has become the foundation of popular Hinduism, the sectarian religious traditions of Smṛti have become more open and less dogmatic. Thus, Hinduism is not monolithic in its structure, as it is a harmonious blend and integration of two major streams or traditions, though at times each tradition tried to project itself as the most meaningful form of religious life, or as the real meaning of Hinduism. Attempts are also made by each tradition to establish its superior validity and meaningfulness over the other, and to belittle the significance of the other. We witness this trend more in the history of modern Hinduism. However, the tension between the two traditions has not led to open conflict and hostility between them, as no tradition or no form of religious life has tried to suppress the other tradition or the other forms of religious life. The healthy growth and development of both the traditions or both the major forms of religious life within the Hindu tradition helped Hinduism to become less dogmatic and more inclusive and integral. However, the Smṛti tradition by adopting the world-view of Śruti, which has shaped the basic character of Hinduism, has become an integral part of Hinduism. Therefore, Hinduism is one in its spirit and basic outlook or world-view, which otherwise is a conglomeration of different streams of religious thought and forms of religious life and worship.

The Śruti vision of the divine is not antagonistic to or

incompatible with the personal nature of the divine. If by definition the divine is all that is, it includes within the range of its possibilities the personal form of manifestation. The nature of the divine cannot be defined or determined exclusively in terms of any one idea or concept because nothing can be excluded from the divine. The divine does not exclude anything from itself as it is all, or the ultimate source of all that is there, and there is no second reality or a reality other than the divine that can be the explanation of what is not divine. Either we admit the oneness of the divine or accept a second reality to explain certain phenomena whose divine significance and value the ordinary understanding or vision of man cannot grasp and appreciate. The concept of the divine can comprehend the idea of God though the latter cannot comprehend the former. If conceptually God can contain or comprehend the divine, which is neither personal nor impersonal, then the idea of God ceases to be religiously meaningful. Though for the purpose of religious devotion and worship God is conceived in absolute terms, as otherwise total devotion and surrender are not possible, yet when the concept of God is analysed and understood, God is seen as transcending all possible conceptions, including the personal conception of God. The divine can be both personal and impersonal but is not either exclusively. Ultimately it is a matter of human understanding and preference. Therefore, theoretically speaking, Hinduism is not exclusively theistic nor exclusively non-theistic. It is both, and yet it transcends both. One can be a Hindu, in a practical sense, by accepting any one form of divine manifestation for the purpose of devotion and worship, but in a basic sense one can be a Hindu only when he sees the divine transcendence, and, hence, the non-exclusive nature of the divine. The divine is all that is, including all that is possible, and, therefore, it cannot be identified with any one form or idea, though for the practical religious purpose people may identity the divine with a particular form or idea. And the basic vision or world-view of Hinduism asserts itself as and when any sectarian form of religious life and worship tries to dominate the Hindu religious life or Hinduism.

Glossary

Ādhibhautika : According to the Veda, all that is there is classified into three realms of *ādhibhautika*, *ādhidaivika* and *ādhyātmika*. *Ādhibautika* is related to the realm of physical reality.

Ādhidaivika : Related to the realm of deities.

Ādhyātmika : Related to the inner reality of man.

Āgama : Sectarian scriptures of Hinduism, like Śaiva Āgamas.

Apauruṣeya : The Veda is regarded as *apauruṣeya* as its truth of wisdom is not due to any human agency. It has no human origin. It is devinely inspired.

Āraṇyakas : They constitute the Veda, like the Upaniṣads.

Ārya Samāj : A modern Hindu religious movement.

Brahmā : In the Vedic literature it is used primarily to mean divinely inspired devotion, and by extension to prayer and Vedic hymns, the means of its expression.

Brahman : Literally means that which is great or that which grows. The Upaniṣadic term of ultimate reality.

Brāhmaṇas : Liturgical texts. Regarded traditionally as constituting Śruti tradition.

Brahmo Samāj : A modern religious movement within Hinduism.

Iṣṭa-devatā : Chosen deity of worship.

Kavi : A Vedic poet who is divinely inspired. He sees the divine in all the forms of its manifestation.

Kāvya : The creative work of a poet. In the Veda creation is seen as the *kāvya* of God or as an expression of His creativity.

Kirāta : An ancient Indian tribe.

Līlā : Smṛti concept which in its meaning is similar to the Śruti concept of *māyā*.

Māyā : It expresses the sense of mystery involved in our understanding the nature and meaning of the divine and its relation to creation. In the Veda it is used to mean the creative power of the divine.

Mokṣa : Liberation or emancipation.

Nirvāṇa : Buddhist concept of liberation. It means blowing out.

Niṣāda : An ancient Indian tribe.

Nivṛtti : Turning away from the life of attachment and desires.

Prajāpati : Lord of creation; a functional name of the divine.

Pravṛtti : Ordinary life of desires and attachment to which one is ordinarily inclined.

Purāṇas : They constitute the Smṛti tradition, and are a major source of our knowledge of the Smṛti form of Hinduism.

Ṛṣi : A Vedic seer who is divinely inspired. He is known for his unitive vision.

Saṁhitā : Collection of Vedic hymns. There are four such collections of *Ṛg*, *Yajur*, *Sāma* and *Atharva*.

Sāyaṇa : A Vedic commentator of high repute belonging to mediaeval period.

Smṛti : A major tradition of Hinduism next only to Śruti in its importance and authority. It is the major source of inspiration for the popular form of Hinduism, and consists of all the Purāṇas, epics and the various works on the *dharma*.

Śruti : The entire Vedic literature. It is orally transmitted or communicated. The ultimate source and authority for Hinduism.

Upaniṣads : The basic texts of Vedānta philosophy, and part of Śruti literature.

Vāk : Speech. In its meaning it is similar to the Greek concept of Logos.

Viniyoga : That which has an application in any Vedic ritual.

Bibliography

Aitareya Āraṇyaka, tr. Max Müller F., *The Upaniṣads*, Vol. I, Sacred Books of the East, Motilal Banarsidass, Delhi, 1981.

Aitareya Upaniṣad, tr. Swami Gambhirananda, *Eight Upaniṣads with commentary of Śaṅkarācārya*, 2 vols., Advaita Ashrama, Calcutta, 1958.

Atharvaveda, tr. Ralph, T.H. Griffith, 2 vols., The Chowkhamba Sanskrit Series, Varanasi, 1968.

Bhagavad Gītā, tr. Franklin Edgerton, Motilal Banarsidass, Delhi, 1996.

Bhāgavata Purāṇa, tr. G.V. Tagare, 5 vols., Ancient Indian Tradition and Mythology Series, Motilal Banarsidass, Delhi, 1987.

Bṛhadāraṇyaka Upaniṣad, tr. Swami Madhavananda, Advaita Ashrama, Mayavati, Almora, 1950.

Bṛhad-devatā, tr. A.A. Macdonell, 2 vols., Motilal Banarsidass, Delhi, 1994.

Chāndogya Upaniṣad, tr. Swami Gambhirananda, Advaita Ashrama, Calcutta, 1983.

Devī Bhāgavata, tr. Swamy Virajananda, Oriental Books, New Delhi, 1977.

Īśāvāsya Upaniṣad, tr. Swami Gambhirananda, Advaita Ashrama, Calcutta, 1958.

Kaṭha Upaniṣad, tr. Swami Gambhirananda, Advaita Ashrama, Calcutta, 1957.

Life Divine, Śrī Aurobindo, Sri Aurobindo Ashram, Pondicherry, 1960.

Mahābhārata, tr. Kishori Mohan Ganguli, 12 vols., Munshiram Manoharlal, Delhi, 1976.

Mahānārāyaṇa Upaniṣad, tr. Swami Vimalananda, Sri Ramakrishna Math, Madras, 1957.

Mānameyodaya, tr. Kunhan Raja and Suryanarayana Sastry, S.S., Adyar Library and Research Centre, Madras, 1975.

Manu-smṛti, tr. Burnel, A.C. (Ordinances of Manu), Oriental Books, Delhi, 1971.

Muṇḍaka Upaniṣad, tr. Swami Gambhirananda, Advaita Ashrama, Calcutta, 1957.

Nārada Bhakti Sūtras, tr. Nandlal Sinha, Oriental Publishers, Delhi.

Rāmāyaṇa, tr. Makhanlal Sen, Munshiram Manoharlal, Delhi, 1978.

Ṛgveda, tr. Ralph T.H. Griffith, Motilal Banarsidass, Delhi, 1973.

Sānkhāyana Āraṇyaka, tr. A.B. Keith, Oriental Books, New Delhi, 1975.

Śatapatha Brāhmaṇa, G.J. Eggeling, 5 vols., Sacred Books of the East, Motilal Banarsidass, Delhi, 1976.

Satyārtha Prakāśa (Light of Truth), tr. Durga Prasad, Jangyan Prakashan, New Delhi, 1972.

Śiva Purāṇa, tr. J.L. Shastri, 4 vols., Ancient Indian Tradition and Mythology Series, Motilal Banarsidass, 1987.

Śvetāśvatara Upaniṣad, Gita Press, Gorakhpur.

Vāyu Purāṇa, tr. G.V. Tagare, Ancient Indian Tradition and Mythology Series, Motilal Banarsidass, Delhi, 1987.

Viṣṇu Purāṇa, tr. H.H. Wilson, Punthi Pustak, Calcutta, 1972.

Other books on Hinduism

Basham, A.L., *The Origins and Development of Classical Hinduism*, Oxford University Press, 1990.

Bloomfield, Maurice, *The Religion of the Veda*, Indological Book House, Delhi, 1972.

Coomaraswamy, Ananda K., *Hinduism and Buddhism*, Munshiram Manoharlal, Delhi, 1996.

———, *A New Approach to the Veda*, Munshiram Manoharlal, Delhi, 1996.

Chaudhuri, Nirad C., *Hinduism*, Oxford University Press, London, 1979.

Williams, Monier, *Religious Thought and Life in India*, Oriental Books Reprint Corporation, New Delhi, 1974.

Wilson, H.H., *Religion of the Hindus*, Cosmos Publications, New Delhi, 1978.

Younger, Paul, *The Indian Religious Tradition*, Bharatiya Vidya Prakashan, Varanasi, 1970.

Index